Centre for Baptist History ;
Volume

CW01627132

For The Sake of the Church

Essays in Honour of Paul S. Fiddes

Centre for Baptist History and Heritage Studies
Volume 3

For the Sake of the Church

Essays in Honour of Paul S. Fiddes

Anthony Clarke (editor)

Foreword by
Rex Mason

Regent's Park College, Oxford

Regent's Park College is a Permanent Private Hall of The University of Oxford.

First published 2014

Centre for Baptist History and Heritage,
Regent's Park College,
Pusey Street,
Oxford,
OX1 2LB
(Regent's Park College is a Permanent Private Hall of
the University of Oxford.)
www.rpc.ox.ac.uk

19 18 17 16 15 14 13 7 6 5 4 3 2 1

British Library Cataloguing in Publication Data
A catalogue record for this book is available from the British Library

ISBN 978-1-907600-20-3

Cover Illustration: Matisse, Henri. *Still Life with the Dance*.
Oil on canvas, 89.5x117.5 cm. France 1909, GE-9042
© The State Hermitage Museum, St. Petersburg. Photograph
© The State Hermitage Museum/photo by Vladimir Terebenin,
Leonard Kheifets, Yuri Molodkovets.

Typeset by Larry J. Kreitzer
Printed and bound in Great Britain
by Alphagraphics Nottingham
www.alphagraphics.co.uk/uk007

For the Sake of the Church

Essays in Honour of Paul S. Fiddes

Edited by
Anthony Clarke

Acknowledgements

As always a number of people have been involved in this project and have played their parts to bring it to fruition. I am grateful to all those willing to write a contribution to the volume and so give it the content it has. My thanks also go, again, to Fiona Floate, PA to the Principal here at Regent's Park College for help in securing the cover image and general advice in the project; to my Father, Jim Clarke, for proof reading and correcting the whole manuscript; and to Larry Kreitzer, one of the general editors for the publications of the Centre for Baptist History and Heritage for all his work in producing the final copy for printing. In all of this, of course, we acknowledge our gratitude and debt to Paul himself for his scholarship, insight and friendship.

Anthony Clarke
Michaelmas Term 2014

Contents:

Contributors

Myra Blyth is Fellow in Pastoral Studies and Chaplain, Regent's Park College

Timothy Bradshaw is Fellow in Christian Doctrine and Senior Tutor, Regent's Park College

John Briggs is former Professor of History at Keele University and former Chair of Governing Body, Regent's Park College

Oti Bunaciu is Rector of the Baptist College, University of Bucharest and President of the Baptist Union of Romania

Anthony Clarke is Fellow in Pastoral Studies and Community Learning, Regent's Park College

Robert Ellis is Principal, Regent's Park College

Stephen Finamore is Principal, Bristol Baptist College

Ruth Gouldbourne is minister of Bloomsbury Central Baptist Church, London and former Tutor, Bristol Baptist College

Brian Haymes is former Principal, Bristol Baptist College

Richard Kidd is former co-Principal, Northern Baptist Learning Community, Manchester

Larry Kreitzer is Fellow in New Testament and Tutor for Graduates, Regent's Park College

Rex Mason is former Fellow in Old Testament, Regent's Park College

Deborah Rooke is Associate Lecturer in Old Testament Hermeneutics, Regent's Park College

John Weaver is former Principal, South Wales Baptist College, Cardiff

Nigel Wright is former Principal, Spurgeon's College

Nicholas Wood is Fellow in Religion and Culture and Dean, Regent's Park College

Portrait of Professor Paul Stuart Fiddes by Anthony Morris (2009)
Collection of Regent's Park College, Oxford
Photo by Deborah W. Rooke

Paul Fiddes: A Personal Tribute

Rex Mason

It is a great honour and, certainly, an equally great pleasure to have been invited to contribute a personal tribute to this volume honouring the life and work of Paul Fiddes. Other writers are far more qualified than I to speak of the quality of his contribution to the Christian Church by his academic writings and devotional writings in the field of doctrine and theology. But perhaps I may claim, without undue immodesty, two qualifications of my own. The first is that I think I may have known Paul longer than many of his friends and colleagues. His family were members of the Baptist Church in Upminster where, in the mid 1950's, I was Minister. His grandfather was an Elder of that church, and all the family members were deeply and actively committed to its life and service. Sometimes this young grandson of theirs would come with his mother and stay over the weekend. I noticed that when, in the course of my addresses to the children (still a feature of Baptist worship in those days!), I asked a question, one hand would go up in immediate, and always correct, response! I cannot claim that those amateur efforts of mine to instruct the young in the Faith had any part to play in his theological development, other perhaps than to say that, apparently, no ineradicable seeds of heresy were sown. But it did mean that I always followed his outstanding academic career with real interest, long before I was privileged to become a colleague of his in Oxford.

The 'Upminster influence', if I may so term it, did manifest itself many times, however, in later life in another way. His family were not only active members of the church, but great encouragers. Their support and constant encouragement were invaluable to a still young Minister feeling his way into the job. That is a family trait which has most certainly found root in Paul. Both as colleague, and later as Principal, he had the gift for encouraging those working with him, a gift for making them feel better about themselves and giving them greater confidence for their tasks. My second qualification for writing a tribute to him is that this has certainly been true in my own experience of him as friend and colleague again and again. His belief in one, and gift of bringing out the best, make for an atmosphere in which those about him can flourish and produce their best and it is the first quality of his to which I would like to pay tribute.

Such a gift is the mark of a generosity of spirit which is shown only by those whose attention is not centred exclusively on themselves. It is the essence of a genuine humility, and I always thought how fitting it was that Paul was invited to preach the University Sermon on 'The Grace of Humility' back in 2002. Among many instances of it he has shown towards me perhaps I may cite just one. When he was Principal of Regent's Park College the University generously awarded me an honour after my retirement, and Paul arranged and chaired a lunch for me, my family, and some friends. He saw to it that I was exclusively the centre of attention, and it was only by chance that I discovered that he had just been told that the University had awarded him the degree of Doctor of Divinity. He had not mentioned a word of this on what was 'my' occasion, and so it fell to me to announce the good news!

This generosity of spirit has, however, been manifest in far larger and more significant ways. Paul's outstanding intellectual and academic gifts have rightly brought him honour after honour and critics have reviewed his published work in superlatives. So, for example, Oxford appointed him Professor in Systematic Theology in 2002, and there have not been many Baptist Professors in Theology in a Theology Faculty which has been traditionally dominated by Anglicans, although things have been much more notably ecumenical in later years. In 2005 he was invited to deliver the Oxford Bampton Lectures, later published as *Seeing the World and Knowing God: Hebrew Wisdom and Christian Doctrine in a Late Modern Context,* an invitation which over the years has attracted the most distinguished of theologians of world fame. Indeed, to mention all the honours he has been awarded would be to try the patience of the editors of this volume beyond reason.

Yet, all these gifts and this scholarship have been grounded in the service of the Christian Church. It is entirely fitting that the title of this book begins 'For the sake of the Church'. His discussions of the major of doctrines of the atonement, the Trinity and even eschatology have all centred on showing the relevance and efficacy of these themes in the life of believers. Titles like *The Creative Suffering of God*, *Past Event and Present Salvation*, and *The Promised End: Eschatology in Theology and Literature* show something of the range of Paul's interests and concerns. And, broadly ecumenical as his interests have been and are, they are based on firm roots in the Baptist tradition in which he was nurtured, so that he has addressed such issues as the movement for Charismatic Renewal which has had such an influence on the denomination, and leadership in the local church, a topic which the charismatic movement brought again to the fore. In fact it can safely be said that all his theology is 'incarnation theology' for it is all based on and directed towards the faith and practice of the ordinary church member.

Finally, I must pay tribute to another feature of his academic accomplishments, and that is the amazing range of his interests and expertise. In all his writings it is manifest that his first research was in the joint fields of theology and literature, and this literary element is apparent both in his lucid and expressive style of writing and in the subject matter of his publications. It is explicit in the title of his 2000 volume *The Promised End: Eschatology in Theology and Literature*, but implicit in almost all his writings. Nor can I forget his expertise in an area of study in which I am supposed to be an expert! His original doctoral thesis at Oxford was entitled 'The hiddenness of Wisdom in the Old Testament and Later', and this interest in and knowledge of the Old Testament Wisdom literature is apparent in much of his writing. Nor can I forget that he was teaching Old Testament at Regent's perfectly competently before I came! I have never taught doctrine and theology to anyone, much to my relief and theirs I am sure!

I am greatly in debt to Paul for his friendship over the years, for his encouragement in my work which I have already mentioned, for the privilege of teaching in Regent's under his Principalship, and for his example in the faith as his life has always been a living embodiment of the theology he teaches others. He has for so many years found wonderful companionship and support from his wife, Marion, and together, both in times of great joy and personal sadness, they have been a blessing to those who know them.

Introduction

Anthony Clarke

A brief glance at the bibliography of Paul Fiddes' published work, included at the end of this book reveals a number of things. First, one is struck by the sheer volume of all that Paul has been able to write over the years, in the midst of many other commitments and calls on his time. This is testament to Paul's sheer productivity. Students at College have often commented that Paul's study light was invariably on well into the night. Secondly, one notices the wide ranging variety of subjects with which Paul has engaged, written about and taught, from the Old Testament through to contemporary continental philosophy by way of Baptist history, English literature, and films. It is the experience of more than just one contributor to this volume that when one thinks one has read something new and exciting enabling a new line of thought one discovers in conversation that Paul has been there first.

But thirdly, one of the common themes across Paul's writing from his first publication for the Baptist Union in 1980 through to the most recent books and essays is a concern for the church, in its catholicity and apostolicity. While a Baptist both by upbringing and conviction Paul has a deep concern and love for the whole universal church and his writings embrace that catholicity across the centuries, across denominations and across continents. And while, somewhat uniquely among Baptists, ordained to an academic role at Regent's Park College in 1972 Paul's work has always shown a deep pastoral concern for the on-going life and witness of particularly, but by no means exclusively, local Baptist congregations.

As a flavour of his commitment to the universal church, Paul was an active member of the former Oxford and East Gloucester Baptist Association, has been a long-standing member of the Baptist Union Council, Worship and Doctrine Committee and its Faith and Unity Executive. More widely within the United Kingdom Paul has been a significant member of the two phases of Anglican-Baptist Conversations from 1992 to 2005 and from 2012-14, and is currently the Baptist Union representative on General Synod. Equally active within the Baptist World Alliance, Paul has been co-chair of the conversations between the BWA and both the Anglican Communion and the Roman Catholic Church.

And thus the title of this book, *For the Sake of the Church*, which seeks to express this fundamental commitment that runs through his work. It would of course be more accurate to Paul's theological vision to say 'for the sake of the church as it participates in the trinitarian life of God', but that becomes more cumbersome as a title! Paul himself has been deeply involved in the wider life of the University of Oxford for over forty years, in teaching, examining, as chairman of the Theology Faculty, all of which was recognised and honoured in 2002 when Paul was given a personal chair as Professor of Systematic Theology. Yet for Paul there has never been a separation between Academy and Church. In his academic work he was outworking his call to pastoral ministry, and in all his service of the Baptist church he brought the very best of academic scholarship. So this volume of essays published by the College as a *Festschrift* in honour of Paul and all that he has offered to the College, the denomination and the universal church, specifically develops ecclesiological themes in dialogue with Paul's own thinking.

The book, as the list of contributors suggests, is unashamedly Baptist in its make up. The contributors are those who over the years have sat in meetings and councils, collaborated in projects and generally worked with Paul, for the sake of the Church. Yet these contributors, many of whom have been either students of and / or colleagues with Paul over the years, share this same wide vision and so what is offered here is never in the spirit of narrow-denominationalism but as that which is offered to the wider church. The book ends with some reflections again from a long-standing colleague of Paul's, from beyond the Baptist church who continues the conversation. And we hope the conversation does not stop there, for we are convinced that Paul's work will be discussed, drawn on and celebrated in the decades to come.

1.

On Realizing 'The Dance'

Richard Kidd

One of the many delights that we associate with the British edition of Paul Fiddes' *Participating in God: a Pastoral Doctrine of the Trinity* is the picture on its cover – Henri Matisse's *The Dance (first version)* painted in Paris in March 1909.[1] The text of *Participating in God*, however, offers its creative contribution to both trinitarian and pastoral theology without making explicit reference at all to the picture that graces its outer cover. Fiddes wisely leaves Matisse's image to generate its own dialogue with the book's inner content. My intention in this chapter – I hope not too unwisely – is to try and make explicit some of the possible connections between Matisse's image and the book's content. To help us in building these connections, another Matisse has been chosen for the cover of this *Festchrift* – Henri Matisse's *Still Life with 'The Dance'* also of 1909.[2] This will remind us of *The Dance*, and provide a further resource to generate dialogue and to stimulate reflection.

My intention is to explore two possible streams of connections. The first, the most obvious, concerns the image of 'dance' itself. In a tightly argued section entitled 'Perichoresis and Participation'[3], we are introduced in detail to 'dance' as a significant motif in the book, a motif that resurfaces in almost all of the chapters that follow, as a crucial metaphor for exploring its diverse themes. Whether it is intercessory prayer, the problems of suffering and death, forgiveness, or spiritual gifts and sacraments, ripples originating from this seminal section are key to the way in which Fiddes illuminates his contribution to pastoral doctrine.

The second stream of connections concerns the revolutionary 'style' that Matisse was exploring around the time that he painted *The Dance*. Using seemingly simple stylised forms Matisse learnt to evoke complex imaginative responses in his viewers, opening windows of reflection and

---

[1] Paul S. Fiddes, *Participating in God: a Pastoral Doctrine of the Trinity* (London: DLT, 2000).

[2] Henri Matisse, *Still Life with 'The Dance'* (1909), oil on canvas, 89.5cm x 117.5cm (The Hermitage, St Petersburg, Russia).

[3] Fiddes, *Participating in God*, pp. 71-81.

insight that had remained closed for those who were still tied to the inherited, more literal, representational approach to painting. A focus for connection to the 'style' of Fiddes' literary presentation of 'a pastoral doctrine of the Trinity' in *Participating in God* is clearly visible in what I have identified as a seminal section. Through its pages Fiddes is arguing that, in order to do full justice to both Eastern and Western theological traditions concerning the Trinity, it is necessary simultaneously to hold in tension two seemingly irreconcilable metaphors suggested by the image of dance. One, most reminiscent of a 'circle dance', has an implicit danger that it might encourage us to think about God and God's relationship with the world in overly static categories; the other, reminiscent of a 'progressive dance', whilst more effective in capturing a sense of dynamic movement, easily loses something else of no less importance, the idea of God as a secure centre and guarantor of an overall directional movement. A key sentence, one to which we shall return later, reads:

> Though the dance is a complex one, it does not strain the imagination to conceive of a greater mutuality than in a purely 'progressive' movement, integrated with a greater directionality than a purely circular movement.[4]

There is something worth noting here about the way that both artists and theologians need to stretch (even if they want to avoid straining) our imaginations to achieve their purposes. This stretching of the imagination is key to the impact of Matisse's image on his viewers, and it is also key to the way that Paul Fiddes breaches a potential *impasse* at the intersection of Eastern and Western theological traditions.

These two streams of connections will now be explored through the remainder of this essay; but first we need to look in more depth at Matisse and his work as a painter. A series of pictures dating from the early years of the twentieth-century formed an important landmark in the emergence of Matisse's distinctive painterly style. There were two finished oils of *The Dance (I and II, dating from 1909 and 1910 respectively)* and a delicate watercolour sketch *Composition No 1 (dated precisely 11th March 1909).* In addition there were several pictures in which the canvas of *The Dance* forms part of a larger composition, often seen in a corner of Matisse's studio – a motif increasingly employed by the artist from 1910 onwards. There were two versions of *Nasturtiums and 'The Dance' (I and II, both dated 1912)* and *Still Life and 'The Dance' (1909)*, an early experiment and the main focus of this chapter. This motif of repeatedly invoking a core image and

---

[4] Fiddes, *Participating in God*, p. 79.

newly positioning it in relationship to further emergent images and ideas is not peculiar to Matisse and his art; it is often possible to identify a similar pattern of continuity and development in the work of theologians too. It would not be inappropriate, for example, to note here the way that core images and ideas in Fiddes' early work, *The Creative Suffering of God*, have remained lasting points of reference throughout much of his later writing, securely located as it were in a corner of his study.[5]

Matisse was not alone in struggling to forge an artistic identity in the early years of the twentieth century. In terms of his own personal story, these struggles dated back to formative years at Bohain, a small town in the flatlands of Flanders, where his father's expectation that the young Henri's education would lead him into a conventional middle-class profession, left him drained and exhausted, frequently bed-ridden by ill-health. A turning point came in 1890 when, at the age of twenty, we see the first signs of release for what he himself called 'the painter within'. Using a paint-box bought for him by his mother during yet another spell of illness, Henri, sitting with a canvas propped against his knees, made a copy of a picture of a watermill that came with the box. Later, he wrote concerning that time:

> Before I had no interest in anything. I felt a great indifference to everything they tried to make me do. From the moment I held the box of colours in my hand, I knew this was my life. Like an animal that plunges headlong towards what it loves, I dived in, to the understandable despair of my father, who had made me study such different subjects. It was a tremendous attraction, a sort of Paradise Found in which I was completely free, alone, at peace.[6]

Soon after he bought a copy of Frédéric Goupil's *General and Complete Manual of Painting in Oils* (a late nineteenth century DIY manual) and began a disciplined period of artistic study and experiment. His earliest paintings, including the second (which later he always referred to as 'my first painting'), *Still Life with Books (June, 1890)*, were intriguingly signed 'Essitam', his family name spelled backwards. This inversion, as if seen reflected in a mirror, has fuelled the thought that, in these first paintings, Matisse was seeing for the first time a clear reflection of his own inner-self, passionate about painting and, most especially, about colour.[7]

---

[5] Paul S. Fiddes, *The Creative Suffering of God* (Oxford: Clarendon, 1988).

[6] Pierre Courthion, 'Conversations avec Henri Matisse', unpublished texts, Getty Centre for the History of art, Santa Monica, California, p. 8; quoted in Hilary Spurling, *The Unknown Matisse* (London: Penguin Books, 2000), p. 46.

[7] For more detail, see Spurling, *The Unknown Matisse,* pp. 46f.

The struggle was not, however, simply a matter of his own personal development. The period from the mid-1880s through into the second decade of the twentieth century saw some of the most tumultuous developments in the history of Western art for many centuries – and Henri Matisse was at the eye of the storm. The story is now well documented and essentially concerns a decisive break with representational art that had held court in Europe for many hundreds of years – certainly since the late fifteenth and early sixteenth centuries, now famously associated with names like Da Vinci, Michelangelo and Raphael. By the late nineteenth century in northern Europe, this style had been refined into the most extraordinary feats of technical representation, an almost photographic precision that would also become its downfall. Once the camera was able to do to perfection in a matter of minutes, what a skilled artist could only partially achieve over long periods of dedicated time, Western art was on the search for a new identity.

Amongst the pioneers of this new territory, Cézanne soon became a major and lasting point of reference. His vision and method was quickly developed by many of the now famous Impressionists: Van Gogh, Monet, Gauguin, Degas and Renoir amongst them. It then received further impetus in the works of Manet, Picasso, Matisse, Kandinsky and others who later would come to be known as Post-Impressionists. For a time this 'second wave' of Impressionism barely came to the attention British audiences at all, only reaching these shores with significant impact as a result of an exhibition entitled 'Manet and the Post-Impressionists' (1910) at the Grafton Galleries in London, organised by Roger Fry – now credited with the first use of the term 'Post-Impressionist'. In the daring forms of Fauvism, Cubism and so on, the first sketches of an art beyond representation had been drawn, but a storm would rage for many decades to follow.

Of special interest for this chapter, in addition to the efforts of art critic Roger Fry, is the writing of Fry's close friend, Clive Bell. Bell's landmark book, simply entitled *Art*, published in 1913[8], provided an historical commentary to accompany Fry's ground-breaking exhibition. Bell argued in detail for the necessity and rightness of the transition from representation, through Cézanne and Impressionism, to Post-Impressionism, choosing the term 'significant form' to describe what he understood to be a rediscovery in the twentieth century of artistic styles that had been dormant for the better part of a millennium.

For Clive Bell, 'significant form' described the combinations of lines and colours through which 'good' artists are able to express an emotion, an emotion that they themselves have first felt in the presence of what Bell (rather daringly) called 'ultimate reality'. Breaking with common usage at

---

[8] Clive Bell, *Art* (New York: Fredrick A Stokes Company, 1913).

the time, Bell used the term 'form' to include both line *and* colour. These, he argued, deserve to be treated together as the two most significant resources available to visual artists by which they enable us to become aware of a deeper meaning. He wrote:

> Instead of recognising its [*significant form's*] accidental and conditioned importance, we become aware of its essential reality, of God in everything, of the universal in the particular, of the all-pervading rhythm. Call it what name you will, the thing I am talking about is that which lies behind the appearance of all things – that which gives to all things their individual significance, the thing in itself, the ultimate reality.[9]

This talk of ultimate reality, with its intimation of something akin to religion, was unlikely to be any more popular amongst many of Bell's contemporaries than it would be today in these days of a new atheism, which is why it might be identified as unusually daring. In fact, Bell went on to make the link with religion fully explicit:

> Religion, as I understand it, is an expression of the individual's sense of the emotional significance of the universe; I should not be surprised to find that art was an expression of the same thing. Anyway, both seem to express emotions different from and transcending the emotions of life. Certainly both have the power of transporting men (*sic*) to superhuman ecstasies; both are means to unearthly states of mind. Art and religion belong to the same world.[10]

> Art and Religion are, then, two roads by which men (*sic*) escape from circumstance to ecstasy. Between aesthetic and religious rapture there is a family alliance. Art and Religion are means to similar states of mind. And if we are licensed to lay aside the science of aesthetics and, going behind our emotion to its object, consider what is in the mind of the artist, we may say, loosely enough, that art is a manifestation of the religious sense.[11]

These passages are quoted here, not because Bell intended to advocate the cause of religion as such, in the kind of way that many of the authors in

---

[9] This extract from Bell *Art* was accessed as an eBook, under the terms of the Gutenberg Project License, released 2005, location 649.

[10] Bell, *Art*, location 761.

[11] Bell, *Art*, location 850.

this *Festchrift* might hope to achieve, but because some of Bell's insights point in a direction that many, including myself, have sought to express in different ways for a later age; namely, significant parallels between what we experience in the presence of 'good' art and what we experience in the practice of and reflection on 'good' religion.

Bell's language is at times helpfully provocative, and at other times it is notably irritating. His invitation to focus on 'the particular' is striking. Rather than attending to generalisations, he invites us to give our concentrated attention to particular instances – as the most hopeful locus of the real depth in human experience. In 'the particular' he finds an all-pervading rhythm in the universe to which art and religion both enable access. The phrase 'God in everything' continues to be evocative for readers a century later, although we now read it through different lenses in the light of developments in twentieth century philosophy and theology. That century saw many theologians, Paul Fiddes significant amongst them, gradually teasing out ways to reach beyond a crude choice between theism and pantheism. Fiddes alludes to this in my chosen section, when he speaks of 'the dynamic image of God that I am commending for a pastoral theology.'[12] It has attracted a variety of labels, 'panentheism' and 'di-polar theism' amongst them. What it achieves is a much richer and more subtle way to express the relationship between everything and God.

More irritating than provocative is Bell's appeal to the 'unearthly', to 'escape' and to 'going behind', all of which suggest dualisms that now register alarms for many theologians a century later. Bell, however, might still usefully challenge us to dialogue with the concept of 'significant form' and to see if it can help us build our own bridges between Matisse and the theological world we now inhabit.

Much of Bell's effort to define 'significant form' is focused around the work of Cézanne, whose own defining category would have been 'pure form' rather than 'significant form'. Bell wrote:

> Cézanne came to understand it [*pure form*], not as a mode of light, nor yet as a player in the game of human life, but as an end in itself and an object of intense emotion. Every great artist has seen landscape as an end in itself – as pure form, that is to say; Cézanne has made a generation of artists feel that compared with its significance as an end in itself all else about landscape is negligible. From that time forward Cézanne set himself to create forms that would express emotion that he felt for what he had learnt to see. Science became as irrelevant as subject. Everything can be seen as pure form, and behind pure form

[12] Fiddes, *Participating in God,* p. 74.

> lurks the mysterious significance that thrills to ecstasy. The rest of Cézanne's life is a continuous effort to capture and express the significance of form.[13]

This is not an entirely satisfying exposition of Cézanne. It does not, for example, do full justice to Cézanne's own explanation of the place that 'nature' and 'the natural' played in his work. Bell went to great lengths to distance the concept of 'significant form' from every analysable 'natural' human predisposition, which sits very uncomfortably with Cézanne's much cited conviction that 'natural' forms continued to provide the primary inspiration for his art.

It is true, as Bell says, that Cézanne's work did not relate to nature simply in the imitative ways that had been bread and butter for his predecessors. In his conversations with Joachim Gasquet, Cézanne is recorded as saying: 'Painting from nature is not copying the object, it is realizing sensations.'[14] But he also said:

> Art has a harmony which parallels that of nature. The people who tell you that the artist is always inferior to nature are idiots! He (*sic*) is parallel to it. Unless, of course, he deliberately intervenes. His whole aim must be silence. He must silence all the voices of prejudice within him, he must forget … And then the entire landscape will engrave itself on the sensitive plate of his being.[15]

'Parallel' suggests a closer relationship between significant form and nature than Bell seems to allow. The purpose of Cézanne's silence is to allow nature itself to do a work within him, on the 'sensitive plate of his being'.

Bell was insistent that we disconnect the 'significant' in 'significant form' entirely from any echo of what we might call 'natural' form. In context, Bell might well have felt the need to do this in order to distance himself from the representational traditions he was trying so hard to leave behind; but the complete rejection of nature at this point is at odds, not only with Cézanne, but also with the well-documented testimony of many of the Post-Impressionists that Cézanne inspired. Matisse himself – and other

---

[13] Bell, *Art*, location 1796.

[14] Joachim Gasquet, 'What I know or have seen of his life', as quoted in *Joachim Gasquet's Cézanne, - a Memoir with Conversations* (London: Thames and Hudson, 1991), p. 46.

[15] Joachim Gasquet, 'What he told me – the motif', as quoted in *Joachim Gasquet's Cézanne*, p. 150.

pioneers of radical abstraction like Kandinsky and Klee – all of whom make a point of expressing their deep solidarity with Cézanne, and his claim that nature is the starting point (as also the end point) of all significant art.

Perhaps there is a distinction to be made here, which it is easier to make with hindsight now that the crisis of 'the modern' is past; namely, between studying nature for the purpose of representation (as in botanical diagrams and classical *tableaux* of leafy glades) and discovering those significantly abstracted intimations in line and colour, that ignite something much deeper (and profoundly to do with nature) in us humans, whose very DNA roots us in the natural world that has been our biological cradle. I suspect, *contra* Bell, that what the (often minimal) signs and signals in great art actually awaken in us is a deep sense of belonging in this universe, profoundly at one with the entirety of the natural world. My own instinct is to think that the building blocks of significant form are connected with human rootedness in nature, our original belonging in the physical universe, many-layered with genetic, psychological and spiritual dimensions.

Where we might more gladly reconnect with Bell is in his emphasis that 'significant form' connects us with 'reality', reality as the deepest level of truth about the actual world we inhabit, in all its particularity. We are enabled to connect with an 'inner depth' in the world through the work of artists who have already been deeply touched by this reality themselves. Their genius, their extraordinary gift, is their ability to express what they have experienced in line and colour so that others, like us, can engage in turn.

This strong focus on 'reality' is what also enables Bell to make his connection between artistic and religious affections – because (at their best) both deal with the real, and not with illusion or deception. The deceiving nature of representative art has had a long history, the intrinsic untruth, for example, of a two dimensional illusion providing the sense of a three dimensional world. This is a view that can be traced at least back to Plato, and the more that artists have worked to develop their deceiving skills, striving to achieve the *trompe d'oeuil*, the worse the problem has become. (Religion is, of course, frequently accused of deception too – although for different reasons.) Only, argued Bell, in the stylised forms of pre-mediaeval art and again in the post-Cézanne era does art become more true to itself, not pretending that areas of colour and patterns of lines are other than they are, simply marks in what artists call the picture plane. In an interview with Marius de Zayas in 1923, Picasso famously put it like this:

> We all know that Art is not truth. Art is a lie that makes us realize truth, at least the truth that is given us to understand. The artist must

know the manner whereby to convince others of the truthfulness of his (*sic*) lies.[16]

Clive Bell's argument is that the true (or the real), if present at all, is accessed through significant forms and not through anything they appear to represent.

There are many potential parallels to the ways in which theologians alert us to spiritual insight. It might be suggested, for example, that religion's metaphorical and mythical forms function not unlike lines and areas of colour in Bell's understanding of the communicating power of art – both communicating the emotional potential of an encounter, much more than the intellectual content of a proposition. Religion's significant forms, we might argue, are also no more disconnected from nature than those of the artist; there are actual histories that have prompted our metaphors and myths.

There is also common ground here that could be explored by attention to the concept of 'beauty'. After a long period of relegation to the shadows, certainly in the West, talk about beauty has gained new momentum in recent years both in art and in theology. Bell would almost certainly have warmed to that new emphasis on the 'third transcendental' now most obviously associated with the writings of Hans Urs von Balthasar – 'beauty' as the essential companion of 'truth' and 'goodness'.[17] Balthasar appealed with new urgency to the importance of an aesthetic dimension to divine disclosure – not a sentimental beauty but something that has much in common with what Bell associated with 'significant form'. Because 'beauty' and 'significant form' are both about the real, their use need not be restricted merely to the comforting, warm and homely images that so often became the focus of beauty in representational art – a radiant sunset, a peaceful stream, the pastoral idyll. Beauty properly conceived, and significant form according to Bell, also offer the artful theologian resources to engage with the darker and more threatening environs of the real world. We might reflect, for example, on the beauty in Munch's portrayal of his dying sister in *The Sick Child*, or in Grünewald's portrayal of the crucified Christ at the centre of the Isenheim Triptych – in fact, potentially, beauty might be accessible almost anywhere in the complex mess of pleasure and pain that are the real fabric of the real world.

---

[16] The full statement, originally made in Spanish to Marius de Zayas, was translated and published under the title, 'Picasso Speaks,' in *The Arts* (New York, May 1923), pp. 315-26; this quotation is reprinted in Alfred Barr, *Picasso: Fifty Year of his Art* (New York, Martin Secker & Warburg, 1946), p. 270.

[17] Hans Urs von Balthasar, *The Glory of the Lord: a Theological Aesthetics Vol I* (Seeing the Form) (Edinburgh: T & T Clark, 1982).

Bell has given us, then, a fresh handle on why it is that seeing a great picture and reading a great narrative (a Gospel, for example) have so much in common, and why one can easily inform the other. He has shown us why it might be important to allow our own texts to dialogue with pictures, as happens so creatively between the cover and the content of Fiddes' book. Bell's insights, however, might have other ways in which to help us make connections between Matisse's paintings and Paul Fiddes' writings, especially around the focus of dance.

Dance is without doubt written deep into our human story; it is, you might say, an obvious candidate as a certain kind of significant form. Dance has long been recognised as a vital component of the ritual activity that binds communities together, confirming and consolidating their identity. It engages our emotional as well as intellectual intelligence much as Bell identifies in the visual impact of Post-Impressionist paintings. Sadly, however, dance has not featured as strongly in recent British culture as it has in many other parts of the world – except perhaps in limited ways, in Morris and other forms of regional country dancing. In Britain there has been a long-standing fear of dance; today the fear for many men is largely associated with protecting a 'macho' image, but historically the fear can be linked to a subversive power in dance itself. It is possible to catch a glimpse of this, here in my own rural Derbyshire, where today a group of Morris dancers called the 'Powderkegs' still style themselves on just such a subversive tradition. The Powderkegs black their faces and wear reversible jackets that can quickly be turned to display fiery tassels in reds and yellows. This 'disguise', gladly nothing to do with racial stereotyping, is believed to date back to a time when 'tied workers' (those with housing tied to their job) would dance at fairs to make money to support their families when times were hard. Blacked faces and reversed jackets (coal dust and rags) guarded them from potential reprisals if discovered by the local squire who could threaten them with eviction.[18]

All over the world strongly defined communities have their distinctive unifying dance traditions. This was (and still is) true in Matisse's France. We might say, then, that in Matisse's circle of dancers there is an evocation of a significant form, a form that reminds us of powerful forces gathering us and binding us in community. In *Still Life with 'The Dance'*, one way to read the small but symbolically significant break in the circle might be to see it as threatening the bonds of community, as we feel the dancers straining to re-connect and to re-complete the ring.

Colour, the 'disguise' of the Powderkegs, is also highly significant for Matisse's portrayal of dance. What might have been no more than two dull

---

[18] For more information, go to http://www.powderkegs.co.uk.

swatches, a background roughly divided between greens and blues, becomes the evocation of a whole new world. Without the need to construct leafy glades and cotton-cloud skies, there is just sufficient of significance in Matisse's forms to evoke universal pleasures – reminiscent of dancing barefoot on lush-grassed hilltops, backed by the blue brightness of a Mediterranean sky (ever and ambiguously associated with an experience of heaven). Matisse's dance, then, communicates an abundance of energy and joy, its simple forms bridging earth and heaven. There is a deep affirmation of human connectedness, both with each other, and with all the stuff of the created world.

In the section from *Participating in God* that has triggered this chapter, Paul Fiddes also affirms the energetic and subversive power of dance. Before he can develop his own argument, however, there is badly cluttered ground that he needs to clear. As Fiddes explains, the term *perichoresis*, often casually assumed to provide a direct link to the theme of dance, is not actually derived from the root that gives us our familiar word 'choreography' at all.[19] It was the root *perichoreo (*not *perichoreuo*) that first caught the imagination of Christian theologians, both East and West, a root that variously signals ideas of movements of permeation and interpenetration. In fact the image of dance is not based on etymology at all, but is actually an accidental play on words between *perichoresis* and *choreia*, meaning 'dance'. This is, however, a most fortuitous accident. The same vitality of dance that Matisse captures so creatively in his paintings has become a legitimate fertile resource for the continuing development of Fiddes' pastoral theology of the Trinity.

As Fiddes uses this linguistic accident to move his own argument forward, he does so using the creative tension between the two potentially circular forms of dance named earlier in the chapter, the 'circle dance' and the 'progressive dance'. The circle dance correlates most readily with the Western theological tradition, with its defining emphasis on a secure centre and an overall direction of movement. Circle dances maintain the essential integrity of their circular form, the dancers following the circumference, their order largely unchanged. A metaphor based on this kind of dance encourages the idea that breaking the circle, as in Matisse's picture, endangers the coherence of the dance and focuses the urgency of re-connecting. In the progressive dance, however, breaking the circle is actually necessary to enable the complex weaving and exchanging that makes the dance progress. This kind of dance invites a much more dynamic metaphor and opens the possibility of conceiving a very different understanding of God's relationship with the world and its creatures. No longer confined to

[19] Fiddes, *Participating in God*, p. 72.

the still centre, God can be thought to move out, penetrating the circle of dancers, providing their energy and drawing them back into unity of God's own life. On such a model, there is a relational movement enabling our own dynamic participation in God's trinitarian life. This has found most obvious resonance with the Eastern theological tradition.

There is, then, in Fiddes' decision to run with these dual metaphors of dance an important leap of imagination. It takes us back to the quotation near the beginning of this chapter in which we heard an invitation to take the risk of living with the tension of more than one metaphor associated with the concept of dance in order to engage the complexity of a theological challenge. This challenge has more than one dimension: there is a continuing challenge to continue wrestling with the sheer complexity of trinitarian thought – something that Paul Fiddes has helped us do so well; but there is also a timely challenge further to bridge and unify apparently competing emphases between the theological traditions of East and West – a challenge that has surfaced with unprecedented energy in our time. If we are able to imagine these two patterns of dance, the circle and the progressive, as not fundamentally separate from each other but as related forms of one and the same dance, perhaps we will also be able to imagine a new convergence in the long-divided histories of trinitarian thought.

Dance, of course, is no more a literal description of a movement in God, than Matisse's stylised figures are actual dancers. The effectiveness of Matisse's forms and the force of Fiddes' theological discourse both rely on imaginative and complex metaphorical leaps. What they achieve through their liberated and liberating engagements with the image and metaphor of dance is immensely significant for the development both of art and of theology. They have deepened our appreciation of a bigger reality in human life and spiritual experience, firmly rooted in the connectedness of all things; both have provided us with new resources through which truth and beauty can be freshly encountered.

The choice, then, of Matisse's *The Dance* as a cover picture for *Participating in God* is, it turns out, hugely significant. Both the image of dance and very style of painting contribute to a network of connections that further illuminate a vibrant Post-Impressionist painting and a highly creative contribution to global theology.

2.

'Walking in Covenant': The Scriptural Basis for an Early Baptist Principle

Larry Kreitzer and Deborah Rooke

> The Lord's Free People, join themselves by Covenant into a Church-State, to walk in all his Ways, made known, or to be made known to them, according to their best Endeavours, whatsoever it cost them.[1]

With these words William Bradford (1590-1657), the second governor of the Plymouth colony in New England, recalled the lofty ideals of the Separatists in the border regions of Nottinghamshire, Lincolnshire and Yorkshire who sought to reconstitute the Church of God. Early Baptists, including those under the leadership of John Smyth in Gainsborough in 1606, used the metaphor of 'walking' to describe their Christian life, both as individuals and as covenanted communities of believers.[2] Distinctive though it is, this use of the 'walking; metaphor was not something that was invented by the Separatists. This is a metaphor that is present in both Old and New Testaments in different ways, and the early Separatists, including the Baptists, undoubtedly drew the image from the biblical text. In this study we will consider the biblical evidence for the metaphor, and compare the biblical usage with that of Baptists in the seventeenth century.

A. 'Walking' and Covenant in the Old Testament

The metaphor of travelling or journeying to refer to a way of life is common in the Old Testament. The metaphor is expressed using the Hebrew verb

---

[1] William Bradford as cited in Thomas Prince, *A Chronological History of New-England in the Form of Annals* (1736), p. 4.

[2] See, Walter H. Burgess, *John Smith the Se-Baptist, Thomas Helwys, and the First Baptist Church in England* (London: James Clarke & Co., 1911), pp. 81-88. Smyth says that the true form of the church is 'the covenant to walke in al Gods wayes' (*Paralleles, Censures, Observations* (1609), p. 142).

hālak, which is an extremely common verb, occurring over 1500 times in the Hebrew Bible. It is the standard verb of motion, roughly equivalent to the English 'go', and like its English equivalent it can be used both literally and metaphorically. Where *hālak* is used of a way of life, the KJV usually translates it as 'walk'.[3] This metaphorical usage occurs in both individualized and communal contexts, some of which also have covenantal associations. We shall discuss the different uses of the metaphor, followed by their covenantal associations in turn.

Individualized usage of the metaphor: A number of godly characters in the Old Testament are described as 'walking with God', an idiom that appears particularly in Genesis. The first such description is applied to Enoch, who is mentioned in Gen 5:21-24 as the father of Methuselah. As Methuselah is the longest-lived individual in the genealogy of Gen 5, so Enoch his father is the one with the shortest lifespan. But this is not to be seen as a strike against Enoch; rather, his time on earth is short because according to the Hebrew 'Enoch walked with God' (Gen 5:22). Indeed, 'Enoch walked with God: and he was not; for God took him' (5:24). The Hebrew verb *hālak* is used here in the hithpael form to give a sense of continued or habitual action, thus expressing Enoch's continuous commitment to his God.

Noah too is a man who walks with God according to the biblical text, and he is singled out from his entire generation for it. He and his immediate family are the only humans on earth who are saved from eradication via the flood, since he is the one called upon to build and sail the ark on account of his moral character. That character is described by saying that he 'was a just man, and perfect in his generations, and Noah walked with God' (Gen 6:9).[4]

---

[3] Most early Baptists would have accessed the biblical text through its English translation rather than the Hebrew original, and the Geneva Bible of 1560 and the KJV of 1611 were two of the translations which would have been available to them (both translations used the language of 'walking' to render the Hebrew *hālak*). Here the passages under discussion will be cited from the KJV, since it seems that the early Baptists were more reliant upon the KJV for their use of the metaphor.

[4] On the suggestion that there is a deliberate link between Enoch's walk with God and Noah's walk with God, see Jack M. Sasson, 'Word-Play in Gen 6:8-9', *Catholic Biblical Quarterly* 37 (1975), pp. 165-66. John Day, *From Creation to Babel: Studies in Genesis 1-11* (London: Bloomsbury Publishing, 2013), p. 70, notes that the phrase 'walked with God' is applied only to Enoch and Noah in Genesis, and suggests that the writer 'P saw a resemblance between the two.' Day further suggests that flood heroes were presented as immortal in all surviving versions of the Mesopotamian flood story and that the P writer probably transferred this idea from Noah to Enoch in Gen 5:24 (page 112).

Once again the Hebrew verb *hālak* is used in the hithpael, denoting repeated or habitual usage.

A third significant character who is said to walk with God is Abraham. In Gen 17.1 God commands Abram (as he is called at that point) to 'walk before me and be thou perfect'. Later on in Genesis, Abraham's servant quotes Abraham's description of God as 'the LORD, before whom I walk' (Gen 24:40). A third expression of Abraham's walking before God comes from the lips of Jacob as he blesses Joseph in Gen 48:15, speaking of 'God, before whom my fathers Abraham and Isaac did walk'. All of these instances express Abraham's 'walking' by using *hālak* in the hithpael.

One other specific character who is said to walk with God is King Hezekiah, who is remembered for his religious reforms (2 Kgs 18:1-6). He subsequently falls ill, and in his distress prays to God to remember 'how I have walked before thee in truth and with a perfect heart, and have done that which is good in thy sight' (2 Kgs 20:3).

This metaphor of walking with or before God, then, applies to some of the great heroes of the faith whose entire lives are seen as being characterized by their close relationship with God. In addition to such iconic characters being said to walk with or before God, the metaphor of walking to denote a way of life, whether good or bad, is used of individuals more generally, particularly in the Psalms. Ps 1:1 famously opens with the declaration, 'Blessed is the man that walketh not in the counsel of the ungodly'. Ps 15:2 defines the one who is allowed to enter the sanctuary as 'He that walketh uprightly, and worketh righteousness, and speaketh the truth in his heart.'

Communal usage of the metaphor: It is clear from this that the metaphor of 'walking' can denote individuals' adoption of a particular mode of life, whether good or bad, and is also used specifically of obedience to divine commands, or of a life lived in commitment to the LORD. However, in addition to denoting individuals' lifestyles, the metaphor is also used of the lifestyle of the people of God as a whole. This is a usage that appears particularly (though not exclusively) in Deuteronomy. Thus, in Deut 5:33 Moses instructs the Israelites, 'Ye shall walk in all the ways which the Lord your God hath commanded you, that ye may live, and that it may be well with you'. A similar exhortation appears in Deut 13:4 (Heb. 13:5). : 'Ye shall walk after the Lord your God, and fear him, and keep his commandments, and obey his voice, and ye shall serve him, and cleave unto him.' Deut 11:22-23 presents the effect of such walking: 'If ye shall diligently keep all these commandments which I command you, ... to walk in all his ways, and to cleave unto him; then will the Lord drive out all these nations from before you...' Similar exhortations to those in Deut 5 and 13 appear in Josh 22:5 and 22:5. These examples all have plural verbs in the

Hebrew, as indicated in the KJV by the use of 'ye' and 'you' rather than 'thou' and 'thee' for second-person forms, so they are clearly communal. They also all use *hālak* in the qal.

Similar usage appears several times in Leviticus. In chapter 18:3-4 YHWH forbids the people to follow the customs of the Egyptians and Canaanites, telling the Israelites via Moses to keep his ordinances and walk in them. The point is reinforced in Lev 20:23. Moreover, correct walking will produce reciprocal walking on the part of the deity: in Lev 26:3, 12 YHWH tells the people, 'If ye walk in my statutes, and keep my commandments, and do them, ... I will walk among you, and will be your God, and ye shall be my people.'[5] Here, Lev 18:3, 18:4, 20:23 and 26:3 use *hālak* in the qal, but Lev 26:12 uses it in the hithpael, indicating this time a literal walking up and down rather than a metaphorical way of life. The same idiom is used in Gen 3:8 of the LORD God walking in the garden. The point is that the Israelites' metaphorical walking, that is, their adherence to the laws laid down by YHWH, will result in YHWH's actual walking among them, that is, his close presence with them.

A number of the Psalms too use communal language of Israel walking in God's ways. In a diatribe against Israel's disobedience, Ps 78:10 declares, 'They kept not the covenant of God, and refused to walk in his law.' A similarly disapproving verdict is given in Ps 81:12-13 (Heb. 81:13-14), where God declares, 'I gave them up unto their own hearts' lust, and they walked in their own counsels. Oh that my people had hearkened unto me, and that Israel had walked in my ways!' The 'walking' verb is plural in both verses. A somewhat more positive picture comes in Ps 89:15 (Heb. 89:16): 'Blessed is the people that know the joyful sound: they shall walk, O Lord, in the light of thy countenance.'

Some of the instances of the idiom that occur in Deuteronomy are framed in the singular, but they refer to Israel as a people, so they too have collective and thus also communal force. Deut 10:12 is a good example: 'And now, Israel, what doth the LORD thy God require of thee, but to fear the LORD thy God, to walk in all his ways, and to love him, and to serve the LORD thy God with all thy heart and with all thy soul...?' Another good example is Deut 28:9: 'The LORD shall establish thee an holy people unto himself, ... if thou shalt keep the commandments of the LORD thy God, and walk in his ways.' These all use *hālak* in the qal.

All these examples, then, show the 'walking' metaphor being applied to a community rather than simply to individuals.

---

[5] If, however, the people walk contrary to God, God will walk contrary to them (Lev 26:21, 23, 24, 27, 28, 40, 41).

Covenant associations: An additional aspect that is present in many of the references to walking with or before or in the ways of God, whether individually or communally, is that of covenant. Noah and Abraham both have covenants promised to and made with them that are linked to their walking with God. For Noah it is the promise of salvation from the flood (Gen 6:18) and then freedom from the fear of another such flood (Gen 9:9, 11); for Abraham it is the promise of a multitude of descendants (Gen 17:2, 4, 7), a promise to which he must respond by undergoing circumcision himself and implementing it on all future male descendants (Gen 17:9-11). Any covenantal aspects are implicit at best in the material from the Psalms on individuals' walking, but the communally-focused Ps 78 complains that Israel failed to keep the covenant and walk in God's law, which indicates that for them to walk in God's law would have been to keep the covenant. In Deuteronomy, by contrast, the 'walking' metaphor has more obvious covenantal associations. The whole book is structured as a covenant, in which the people are exhorted to commit to following the LORD and to keeping the laws contained in Deuteronomy as a response to God's action in saving them from slavery in Egypt. In fact, one instance of the walking metaphor in Deuteronomy has explicit covenant significance. In Deut 26:17-19, both God and people are said to have agreed to enter into a formal relationship of faithfulness and holiness: 'Thou hast avouched the LORD this day to be thy God, and to walk in his ways, and to keep his statutes, and his commandments, and his judgments, and to hearken unto his voice: And the LORD hath avouched thee this day to be his peculiar people, as he hath promised thee, and that thou shouldest keep all his commandments ... that thou mayest be an holy people unto the LORD thy God, as he hath spoken.' The same covenantal context applies to Leviticus, since the book is set at Mount Sinai and supposedly gives details of the laws that were imparted to Moses as a part of the covenant by which Israel was constituted as the people of God. Indeed, the statement in Lev 26:12 that 'I will walk among you, and will be your God, and ye shall be my people' is nothing more or less than a declaration of covenant.

None of these covenantal overtones have any sense of mutuality between the human parties to the covenant; they are all about vertically directed covenants between humans and God. However, two examples of covenants that include a human, horizontal dimension alongside the vertical, deity-focused dimension appear in the second book of Kings. In the first, Jehoiada the chief priest of the Jerusalem Temple organizes a coup to unseat Queen Athaliah who herself seized the throne via a coup. Having ousted the queen and put on the throne the seven-year-old Davidic heir Joash, Jehoiada makes a covenant between the LORD and the people and the king, that the people will be the LORD's people, and also a covenant between the king and the people which is defined no further (2 Kgs 11:17). There is no distinctive 'walking' language here, but the concept of a covenant between the king and the people gives an added communal dimension to the proceedings. Presumably the point of the covenant between king and people is to invoke the people's loyalty to the young king as their rightful ruler, especially since he has just been put on the throne by a coup and is only seven years old; but against the background of a covenant between the LORD and the king and people, an agreement by the people to recognize this king as their legitimate monarch appears as part of their commitment to be the people of God. They are arguably covenanting together to pursue what is right in the eyes of the LORD. The fact that this covenant is followed immediately by them going and destroying the temple of Baal (2 Kgs 11:18) shows the people acting on their newly-made covenant to be the people of the LORD rather than of Baal.

Another interesting account comes in the narrative of 2 Kgs 23. Here, King Josiah has found the book of the Law in the Temple, and has realized that reforms are necessary, so he has summoned the elders of the people in order to take appropriate action. He reads them the lawbook, and then covenants to keep all of the statutes in the lawbook, and the people join in with this covenant (literally, 'stood in the covenant') (2 Kgs 2:23). As was the case with the Jehoiada/Joash covenant, this covenant is followed by religious reforms: Josiah gives the orders, and the priests bring out all of the idolatrous items from the Jerusalem Temple for destruction. Josiah then goes on to destroy all the outlying shrines in Judah, and even gets as far as defiling the shrine at Bethel, which is beyond the boundaries of his own kingdom. The two aspects to note here are first, that there is a sense of the people covenanting *together* to be the LORD's people, and second, that a covenant to be the LORD's people or to keep the Law of the LORD results in religious reforms. This is in many ways a perfect model for the early seventeenth-century Baptist communities: covenanting with each other to be the LORD's people, they instituted a way of Christian life that in its beliefs and outward expression was significantly different from that which had prevailed to that point.

B. 'Walking' and Covenant in the New Testament

The verb *peripatein* is used 95 times in the New Testament, and is generally rendered as either 'to walk' or 'to live'. At times the verb refers to a literal walking (as in Matthew 4:18 where Jesus 'walks by the Sea of Galilee'). However, the verb is frequently used in a figurative sense, particularly within the Pauline corpus, where it occurs 32 times and appears in all of the

Pauline letters except Philemon and the Pastoral epistles.[6] Here the meaning is more along the lines of 'to live' or 'to behave' or 'to conduct oneself', and an ethical or moral sense of the verb comes to the fore. The background of Paul's metaphorical language has been the subject of some scholarly investigation, particularly as it is by no means immediately clear from whence Paul drew the idea.[7] Frequently the verb *peripatein* occurs with a clarifying prepositional phrase or a dative noun, or with an accompanying adverbial expression which could be used to stress either positive or negative conduct. The exhortation is thus 'to walk *in* (*en*) something'[8] or 'to walk *according to* (*kata*) something',[9] or 'to walk *by* (*dia*) something'.[10] Moreover, the adverbial exhortation is variously expressed, both positively, as in 'to walk *worthily* (*axiōs*)',[11] and 'to walk *properly* (*euschēmonōs*)',[12] or negatively, such as 'to walk lazily (*ataktōs*)'.[13] Throughout there is the contrast between life as it is 'walked' in the realm of Christ and the Spirit, and life as it is 'walked' in the realm of human sinfulness and self-reliance. Most commentators recognize that Paul is here reflecting his Jewish roots and is dependent at some level upon the use of *hālak* in the Old Testament. Indeed, it has been argued that this idea of 'to walk (*peripatein*)' as a

---

[6] Rom 6:4; 8;4; 13:13; 14:15; 1 Cor 3:3; 7:17; 2 Cor 4:2; 5:7; 10:2, 3; 12:18; Gal 5:16; Eph 2:2, 10; 4:1, 17 (*bis*); 5:2, 8, 15; Phil 3:17, 18; Col 1:10; 2:6; 3:7; 4:5; 1 Thess 2:12; 4:1 (*bis*), 12; 2 Thess 3:6, 11. The related verb *emperipatēsō* occurs only once in 2 Cor 6:16, where Lev 26:12 is cited and the reference is to God walking amongst his people.

[7] On this see, Robert Banks, '"Walking" as a Metaphor of the Christian Life: The Origin of a Significant Pauline Usage', in E.W. Conrad and E.G. Newing (eds.) *Perspectives on Language and Text: Essays and Poems in Honour of Francis I. Andersen's Sixtieth Birthday* (Winona Lake, Michigan: Eisenbrauns, 1987), pp. 303-313. Banks suggests that Paul's literal experience of walking around the Mediterranean world in the exercise of his apostolic calling, is partly responsible for his adoption of the metaphor.

[8] Rom 6:4; 2 Cor 4:2; 2 Cor 10:3; 12:18; Eph 2:10; 4:17; 5:2; Col 2:6; 3:7; 4:5. Gal 5:16 – 'walk *in* the spirit' is a similar use of the dative noun *pneumati* although the preposition *en* does not occur.

[9] Rom 8:4; 14:15; 1 Cor 3:3; 2 Cor 10:2; and Eph 2:2.

[10] 2 Cor 5:7.

[11] Eph 4:1; Col 1:10; and 1 Thess 2:12.

[12] Rom 13:13; 1 Thess 4:12.

[13] 2 Thess 3:6, 11.

metaphor for moral conduct is decidedly Jewish and is not known in the Greek world prior to its use in the LXX.[14]

One of the most striking features of Paul's use of *peripatein* is that he almost always uses plural forms of the verb. This is a feature of Paul's language which has not been given much attention by commentators, and is often overlooked completely. In fact, of the 32 occurrences of *peripatein* in the Pauline letters only four are singular forms (Rom 14:15; 1 Cor 7:17; Eph 4:17; 2 Thess 3:6), and even these have what might be described as communal contexts. Thus, the use of the singular *peripatei* in Eph 4:17 is grammatically determined by the subject of the verb, the neuter plural *ta ethne*. The use of *peripateis* in Rom 14:15 is addressed to a believer who no longer walks in love when he causes a brother to be hurt over the issue of eating food offered to idols. The use of the imperative *peritateitō* in 1 Cor 7:17 is an exhortation for a member of the church to walk in accordance with the social positions bestowed upon him or her by God. However, the wider ecclesiological context is stressed by the phrase with which the verse ends: 'and so I instruct in all the churches'. The use of the participle *peripatountos* in 2 Thess 3:6 refers to a brother in the church who is walking unworthily and is therefore to be avoided by the rest of the congregation. The other 28 occurrences of *peripatein* in Paul's letters are all plural forms of the verb. This strikes at the heart of what Paul wants to emphasize about 'walking'. He declares that 'walking' is not something that is done primarily by people as individuals, but that it is done with or alongside others. As a Christian believer one does not 'walk' alone, but always with others.[15] 'Walking' is thus a corporate activity, and for Paul this means that it is also an ecclesiastical activity which is done within the bounds of the covenant in Christ that God makes with his people. 'Walking', in other words, always takes place within the context of a church community. It assumes that an atmosphere of mutual support and responsibility exists between the church members and evaluates ethical conduct accordingly.

---

[14] Heinrich Seeseman, 'πατέω', *Theological Dictionary of the New Testament* 5 (Grand Rapids, MI: Eerdmans, 1967), p. 944, argued that the influence of the LXX on Paul is decisive: '[I]t is impossible that Paul should have taken it from any other source. There are no parallels in classical Greek'. Gerhard Ebel, 'περιπατέω', *New International Dictionary of New Testament Theology* 3 (Grand Rapids, MI: Zondervan, 1978), pp. 943-54, challenges this suggestion, and notes a few examples from Greek writers.

[15] As J. Paul Sampley, *Walking Between the Times: Paul's Moral Reasoning* (Minneapolis: Fortress Press, 1991), p. 37, puts it: 'We have no evidence that Paul ever conceived of a solitary, isolated believer. In his letters … he thinks of believers as called together in Christ.'

Interestingly, at times Paul seems to link walking in this covenantal life with the act of baptism. We see this most clearly in Rom 6:4, where the union of the believers with Christ's death through baptism is the basis upon which 'we are able to walk in newness of life' with the risen Christ. In other words, baptism is the trigger event which validates and confirms one's entry into the covenant. Yet, Paul also stresses this is something that believers share with others, as the plural verbs 'we were buried' and 'let us walk' confirm. The communal or ecclesiological context of this verse is often overlooked or underplayed. Even G.R. Beasley-Murray's magisterial treatment of baptism fails to give due stress to the importance of 'walking' as a communal activity arising out of the shared experience of baptism.[16]

More importantly for our considerations here, some explanation is required as to why Paul uses *peripatein* to refer to behaviour or conduct when it is not so used in the LXX very often (2 Kgs 20:3 and Ecc 11:9 are notable exceptions). The answer seems to be that Paul builds upon the connection that there is between the character of Abraham and establishment of a covenant with God as the basis for a life-style, and the fact that in Gen 17 the Hebrew verb *hālak* is used to describe Abraham's 'walk' with God.

It is surely no accident that John Smyth, the so-called 'Se-Baptist' whose life and ministry was so instrumental for Baptist origins, turned to covenantal ideas when justifying the establishment of separatist churches. As noted above, in 1606 Smyth helped to forge a separatist congregation in Gainsborough, with the members of the church by covenanting together 'to walk in all his Ways, made known, or to be made known to them, according to their best Endeavours, whatsoever it cost them.' The idea of church members agreeing to enter into a covenant with God, and with one another, was foundational within Baptist ecclesiology during the seventeenth century, and it readily became linked in Baptist thinking to the image of 'walking' together, as we shall now seek to demonstrate.

C. 'Walking' in the Thought of Seventeenth-Century Baptists

The idea of 'walking' as a description of Christian life and conduct was a very important feature of early Baptist thought. Its use in surviving sources can be arranged under five distinct but overlapping headings, which we shall handle in turn. We shall here note approximately forty different sources relating to Baptists, all dated between 1609 and 1698, which use the 'walking' metaphor. A number of these are drawn from manuscripts found

---

[16] *Baptism in the New Testament* (Grand Rapids, Michigan: Eerdmans Publishing Company, 1962), pp. 143-146.

within the Angus Library at Regent's Park College, Oxford (ALRPCO) and the Guildhall Library in London (GLL). These sources are by no means exhaustive, but merely serve to illustrate how prevalent the 'walking' motif was within the life of Baptist churches during the seventeenth century.

1. Confessions of Faith - One of the earliest ways that Baptists sought to define and identify themselves in the seventeenth century was through the publication of so-called 'Confessions of Faith'. The language of 'walking' as a description of their corporate Christian life together appears frequently within these Confessions. For example, in *The Confession of Faith* (1644), one of the most influential early declarations of Baptist faith, the idea of 'walking' as an expression of Christian life is used a number of times. The first instance is within the Foreword to the document itself, where the seven issuing London churches explain their reasons for publishing their *Confession*. They stress that this is not the action of just one congregation, but is the collective effort of all seven congregations working together under Christ:

> And because it may be conceived, that what is here published, may be but the Judgement of some one particular Congregation, more refined then the rest; Wee doe therefore here subscribe it, some of each body in the name, and by the appointment of seven Congregations, who though wee be distinct in respect of our particular bodies, for conveniency sake, being as many as can well meete together in one place, yet are all one in Communion, holding Jesus Christ to be our head and Lord; under whose government wee desire alone to walke

Another important example of 'walking' as an expression of Christian life is found within Article 47 of the Confession. Here the independence of each of the congregations is affirmed, as is their collective responsibility towards one another in offering help and mutual support when needed:

> And although the particular Congregations be distinct and severall Bodies, every one as a compact and knit Citie in it selfe; yet are they all to walk by one and the same Rule, and by all meanes convenient to have the counsell and help one of another in all needfull affaires of the Church, as members of one body in the common faith under Christ their onely head.

The description of each congregation as 'a compact and knit Citie in it selfe' is quite striking and is dependent upon the imagery found in Ps 122:3.[17] The idea of the seven London congregations agreeing 'to walk by one and the same Rule' is supported by a marginal note to Col 2:6 ('As you therefore have received Christ Jesus the Lord, *so* walk in Him').

Benjamin Cox published his *An Appendix to A Confession of Faith* in November of 1646, attempting to give a fuller explanation of Baptist beliefs and practices which were set forth in the 1646 *Confession*. Cox presents his discussion using 22 numbered sections, and language of 'walking' appears five times in three of them (No 8, No 9, No 10). For example, No 8 cites Eph 2:10 and affirms the need for Christians to bring forth good works in keeping with their participating in the life of Christ:

> we beleeve and know that being made partakers of Jesus Christ, we do, and shal, and must, through him, and walking in him, bring forth the fruit of good works, serving God (in true obedience, and love, and thankfulness unto him) in holiness and righteousness, being *his workmanship, created in Christ Iesus unto good works, which he hath before ordained that we should walk in them* (pages 6-7).

In #10 the idea of 'walking' as a faithful and obedient Christian is explicitly linked to the Old Testament stories of the people of Israel obeying their Covenant with God as commanded by Moses:

> Christ in his Gospel teacheth and commandeth us to walk in the same way of righteousness and holyness that God by *Moses* did command the Israelites to walk in (page 7).

General Baptists in London published *A Brief Confession or Declaration of Faith* (15 March 1660). Article XVII was given over to the matter of church discipline and asserted that the true church was to reject all heretics and 'to withdraw from all such, as profess the way of the Lord, but walks disorderly in their conversations, 2 *Thes*. 3.6' (page 8).

The *Confession* of 1677 makes several references to the idea of 'walking' together within the discussion headed 'Chapter XXVI – Of the Church'.[18]

---

[17] Although the marginal textual references associated with this Article do not include a mention of Ps 122:3, the passage does appear in the marginal notes of the 1646 and 1652 *Confessions*.

[18] This *Confession* is heavily dependent on *A Declaration of the Faith and Order Owned and Practised in the Congregational Churches in England* (1658), pp. 55-57, for its language and phrasing at this point.

First of all, it affirms that Christ has called out of the world unto himself those whom the Father has given him and that they are 'to walk before him in all the ways of obedience.' It then declares

> Those thus called he commandeth to walk together in particular societies, or Churches, for their mutual edification; and the due performance of that publick worship, which he requireth of them in the World (page 87).

The responsibilities of church membership within the Baptist churches is further explained by appeal to the idea of 'walking together':

> The members of these churches are saints by calling, visibly manifesting and evidencing (in and by their profession and walking) their obedience unto that call of Christ; and do willingly consent to walk together, according to the appointment of Christ; giving up themselves to the Lord, and one to another, by the will of God, in professed subjection to the ordinances of the Gospel (page 88).[19]

The Confession of Faith (1677) was very influential, but it was not without its critics. A good example was Thomas Collier who published *A Confession of Faith Published on Special Occasion* (1678). This was written as a response to *A Confession of Faith* (1677), and offered a theological critique of it, particularly for its Calvinistic views on election and general redemption. At the conclusion of his *Confession* Collier specifically says, 'The Church with whom I walk, is united in the substance of this Faith, before declared' (page 41). Other congregations also composed their own confessions which employed the 'walking' metaphor. For example, on 9 February 1694 the members of Maze Pond Baptist Church in Southwark signed a 'Confession of Faith' which was drawn up by the church and set out their own rather idiosyncratic beliefs in 22 Articles (including one against hymn singing). The 'Confession' then concluded with the affirmation:

> We doe Covenant and agree to give up our selves to the Lord and to each other According to the Will of God to walk together in all the Ordinances and wayes of the Lord as a Church of Jesus Christ.[20]

Similarly, in 1697 Benjamin Keach published *A Confession of Faith Containing the Substance of All the Fundamental Articles in the Larger*

---

[19] This *Confession* was re-issued in 1688.

[20] ALRPCO, Maze Pond Church Book (1691-1708), page 4.

Confession. This *Confession* was issued on behalf of Keach's congregation which met in Horsley-down in Southwark. Keach declares in 'The Epistle Dedicatory' that one of the reasons why the *Confession* was being published was because the larger *Confession* of 1677/1688 was no longer in print, and in any event the previous *Confession* was too expensive for many to purchase (it originally cost 12d). Keach's *Confession* reworks the 32 Articles of the 1677/88 *Confession* into 39 Articles. The imagery of 'walking' appears only one time within this work: this is contained within Article 21, which is headed 'Of Baptism'. Here we read:

> [I]t is the indispensible Duty of such who are baptized, to give themselves up to some particularly orderly Church of Jesus Christ, and to walk in all the Commandments and Ordinances of the Lord blameless: Baptism being an initiating Ordinance (page 21).

2. *Publications by or about Baptist Leaders* - In addition to the official Confessions issued by Baptists, a number of other documents produced by them, or associated with them, also employ the language of 'walking'. One of the earliest examples can be found in the work of John Smyth who writes movingly of the nature of the true church in *Paralleles, Censures, Observations* (1609), employing the 'walking' metaphor within his description of church conduct. As Smyth asserts:

> The visible church hath in it a visible communion, visible & sensible ordinances for men to walk in a visible fayth expressed in the outward declarations thereof in confession & profession of the truth.[21]

A letter written from Thomas Helwys, William Piggot, Thomas Seamer and John Murton to the Waterlander Mennonites in Amsterdam on 12 March 1610 expresses the hope that 'you and wee might walke uprightlie in the waies of God.'[22] Another early example of the use of this 'walking' language is found within records of the church formed by Henry Jacob in London in 1616. The members of the church are described as having 'covenanted togeather to walk in all Gods Ways, as he had revealed or should make known to them.'[23] The same church re-affirmed its commitment to this

---

[21] John Smyth, *Paralleles, Censures, Observations* (1609), p. 18.

[22] MS B 1351, Mennonite Archives, Amsterdam.

[23] ALRPCO, Benjamin Stinton, 'Repository of Divers Historical Matters Relating to English Antipedobaptists' (1712) (D Stinton 1), page 2. This is

covenant in 1630 when it was under the pastoral leadership of John Lathrop. One again language of 'walking' was used, as we read the members of the congregation agreed

> To Walke together in all ye Wayes of God so Farr as he hath made known to Us, or shall make known to Us & to forsake all false Ways & to this the several Members subscribed their hands.[24]

John Spilsberie published *A Treatise Concerning the Lawfull Subject of Baptism* (1643), which uses the 'walking' metaphor a total of thirteen times. Most significantly, Spilsberie offers one of the most thorough discussions of the Gen 17 passage which linked Abraham's walk with God and the making of a covenant between God and Abraham and his seed. He argued that in Paul's thinking this Abrahamic covenant was taken over by the Gentile church and that the demand for 'walking in covenant' was central to the life of true followers of Christ. Spilsberie asserts that the Gentiles 'are called the seed or children of Abraham onely as they walke in the steppes of his faith (page 6)'. The importance of baptism as a sign of this covenant is also emphasized. The ordinance of baptism, Spilsberie argued, 'is an institution of Christ, and contained in the Scriptures, as a rule for the Lords people to walk by in their obedience to him; only so considered it is an ordinance of God' (page 34). Spilsberie also published *Gods Ordinance, the Saints Priviledge* (4 May 1646), where his thoughts along these lines were extended. Spilsberie here described the people of God as those who 'walke by faith in the light of truth', and asserted that the rule of God's written word 'according to which the Saints are to walke, and to judge of wayes and Doctrines, is an infallible rule (page 34).'

A number of publications by Baptists in the 1640s and 1650s used the 'walking' metaphor on their title pages. A good example of this is the pamphlet entitled *Heart-Bleedings for Professors Abominations* (28 February 1650) which was signed by sixteen Particular Baptist leaders, including John Spilsberie, William Kiffen, Thomas Patience and Henry Forty. The title page of the pamphlet (see Figure #1 below) declares that it was issued 'By the *Churches* of *Christ* in *London*, Baptized into the Name of Jesus Christ, and walking together through the Grace of God, in the Order of his Gospel, according to the Scriptures'. The opening paragraph of the pamphlet continues in the use of the 'walking' metaphor with the subscribers

---

strikingly similar to the phrasing of John Smyth's covenant noted above in footnote 2).

[24] ALRPCO, Benjamin Stinton, 'Repository of Divers Historical Matters Relating to English Antipedobaptists' (1712) (D Stinton 1), page 9.

addressing the Christian Churches and describing themselves as 'Having these many yeers, through the grace and free mercy of our God, been kept in the profession of the name of Christ … and finding the exceeding benefit and comfort of walking with God in some measure suitable to what he hath made known to us (page 3)'.

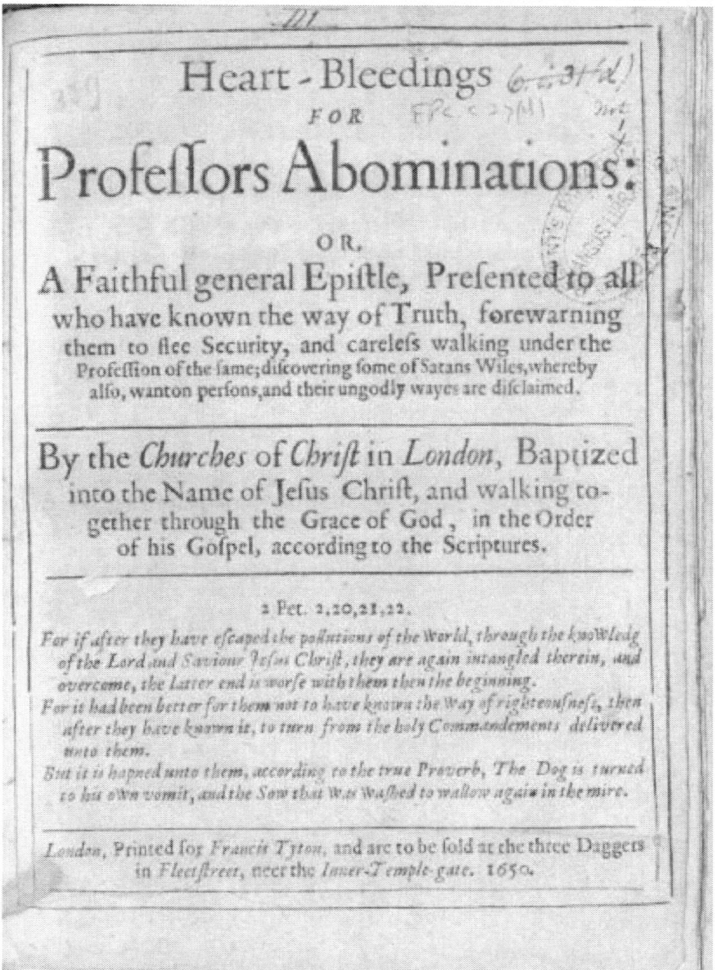

Heart-Bleedings
FOR
Profeſſors Abominations:
OR,
A Faithful general Epiſtle, Preſented to all who have known the way of Truth, forewarning them to flee Security, and careleſs walking under the Profeſſion of the ſame; diſcovering ſome of Satans Wiles, whereby alſo, wanton perſons, and their ungodly wayes are diſclaimed.

By the *Churches of Chriſt* in *London*, Baptized into the Name of Jeſus Chriſt, and walking together through the Grace of God, in the Order of his Goſpel, according to the Scriptures.

2 Pet. 2,20,21,22.

For if after they have eſcaped the pollutions of the World, through the knoWledg of the Lord and Saviour Jeſus Chriſt, they are again intangled therein, and overcome, the latter end is worſe with them then the beginning.
For it had been better for them not to have known the Way of righteouſneſs, then after they have known it, to turn from the holy Commandements delivered unto them.
But it is happned unto them, according to the true Proverb, The Dog is turned to his oWn vomit, and the Sow that Was Waſhed to wallow again in the mire.

London, Printed for *Francis Tyton*, and are to be ſold at the three Daggers in *Fleetſtreet*, neer the *Inner-Temple-gate*. 1650.

Figure #1 – Title Page of *Heart-Bleedings for Professors Abominations* (1650) (Courtesy of the Angus Library and Archives, Regent's Park College, Oxford)

The London-based Baptist pastor and teacher Hanserd Knollys produced *A Moderate Answer unto Dr. Bastwicks Book* (17 July 1645), which speaks on its title page of 'Beleevers who walk together in the Fellowship of the Gospell'. Daniel King, a Baptist preacher in Coventry, similarly used the language of 'walking' in the title of his *A Way to Sion Sought Out, and Found, for Believers to Walk In* (23 March 1650). Thomas Tillam also used the 'walking' metaphor on the title page of his *Banners of Love Displaied over the Church of Christ Walking in the Order of the Gospel at Hexham* (16 January 1654).

Another intriguing example of the 'walking' metaphor is Elizabeth Poole's *An Alarum of War* (1649). This contains a letter written by Thomasine Pendarves in support of the controversial prophetess Elizabeth Poole who had dared to challenge the General Council of the Army over the execution of Charles I. The letter by Thomasine Pendarves (which is signed simply as 'T.P.') was addressed 'To the Congregations of Saints, walking in fellowship with Mr. *William Kiffin*' (page 8). Other examples which show language of 'walking' in fellowship with a Baptist church under the leadership of a named pastor are also extant. A good example is John Atherton's *The Pastor Turn'd Pope* (1654) which was written as an invective against John Pendarves, the pastor of the Particular Baptist church in Abingdon. Atherton and his wife were both members of Pendarves's church, but left because of what they felt were abuses by him as a spiritual leader. Atherton says, 'After I had walked three yeers, or thereabouts, with Mr. *Pendarves* and his company … I went out from them' (page 1). Atherton also notes that his wife 'had sent you and your company word, that she would walk no longer with you in your Way, and left you'. John Pendarves himself used the 'walking' metaphor in his influential *Arrowes Against Babylon* (1656), posing a rhetorical question that speaks to the freedom of Baptists to worship in their own separatist congregations, while alluding at the same time to the military victories of Cromwell which guaranteed that liberty:

> And did not God … put it also into the hearts of our Rulers after great and signall successes given their Armies, to grant liberty to his people to walke according to their light without restraint and confinement to the Parish-Churches? (pages 2-3)

Another interesting example involves Thomas Patient, who was one of the signatories of the 1644 *Confession*, working alongside William Kiffen in one of the seven London churches responsible for issuing the document. In early 1650 Patient went to Ireland where he served as a chaplain to Cromwell's military forces there. Patient combined his activities as a military chaplain with his interest in establishing Baptist churches in the towns and cities of Ireland, first in Kilkenny in the spring of 1650, and then in Waterford where he moved to in 1651. On 14 January 1652 Patient and the church at Waterford wrote a letter to the mixed congregation of Baptists and Independents in Dublin led by John Rogers. The letter was signed by Patient and eleven other members of his congregation. The substance of the letter was a stern exhortation to Rogers and his congregation for their baptismal theology and their open-membership policy. It called for the members of the church who had been baptized as believers to withdraw fellowship from those who had not. The language of 'walking' was invoked eight times within the letter, beginning with an opening statement by the Waterford church self-righteously declaring their own obedience to the Gospel demands: 'The Church of Christ in Waterford, walking in ye Faith & Order of the Gospel, do wish all Grace & Peace to the Saints in Dublin.'

In 1651 Obediah Holmes, who was imprisoned in Boston, Massachusetts, wrote a letter addressed to John Spilsberie and William Kiffen in London, which employed the 'walking' metaphor in its description of the church they pastored:

> Unto the well beloved Brethren John Spilsbury, William Kiffin, and the rest that in London stand fast in the Faith, and continue to walk steadfastly in that Order of the Gospell which was once delivered unto the Saints by Jesus Christ.[25]

The controversial Paul Hobson describes himself in *Innocency, Though Under a Cloud, Cleared* (1664) as 'among the People that walk with Mr. *K[iffen]'* (page 17).

A pamphlet entitled *A Declaration of Several of the Churches of Christ* (2 September 1654) contains a list of 144 members from ten different London congregations who issued the tract in an attempt to counter the establishment of a Court of Triers by Whitehall. The leaders of the ten churches are named and several of the congregations are described using the 'walking' metaphor. Thus, we read 'Of the Church that walks with M. Feak, now close prisoner for the caus[e] of Christ at Winsor-Castle'; 'In the name of the whol[e]

---

[25] John Clark, *Ill Newes from New-England* (1652), p. 17. Apparently Holmes was unaware that John Spilsberie was no longer in London and had departed for Ireland in 1650.

Church that walks with Dr. Chamberlain'; 'Of the Church that walks with Mr Simson'; and 'Of the Church that walks with Mr Jesse'.[26]

Thomas Collier's *The Personal Appearance and Reign of Christs Kingdom upon the Earth* (1657) includes a reference to the 'walking' metaphor as part of his millennial argument, asserting that there is a link between the believers and their Lord:

> Jesus Christ was a pattern in his own person to all his people, in the Gospel-ministration, till his coming, whose life was a life of suffering; he being the Head, his members must walk in the same way (page 9).

Collier also published *A Discourse of the True Gospel Blessedness in the New Covenant* (1659) which likewise catalogues some of the 'duties of the Covenant, and the rules left by Christ for his people to walk by till his second coming' (page 111). A numbered list of duties for individuals and churches is provided. This list includes declarations that the believer is 'To walk holyly in all manner of conversation and godliness' (page 112); 'To walk worthy of that high and holy calling wherewith and whereunto we are called' (page 113); 'To endeavour to walk inoffensively toward all' (page 118); 'To put on the Lord Jesus Christ and to walk in him' (page 118); and the expectation that the church is 'To walke together in love as brethren' (page 121).

In 1673 Luke Howard published *The Seat of the Scorner Thrown Down*, his apology for why he had left the Baptists and joined the Quakers. Howard had been baptized by William Kiffen in London in February of 1644, but soon fell out with them and went in a new direction. He relates that when he decided to separate from the Baptists, 'At that time one of the Preachers asked me (when separated) *Why I would not walk with them?*'[27] The language of 'walking' stayed with him, however, and his conversion to Quakerism was described by Howard as a decision 'to walk in the True Light' (as the sub-title of his pamphlet affirms).[28]

In 1672 John Bunyan published *A Confession of My Faith*, primarily as a justification for his belief in open-membership church polity and his refusal to make water-baptism a bar to fellowship among churches. Bunyan uses the language of 'walking' a total of twenty-one times within the volume,

---

[26] *A Declaration of Several of the Churches of Christ* (2 September 1654), pp. 21-22.

[27] *The Seat of the Scorner Thrown Down* (1673), p. 6.

[28] The 'walking' metaphor was taken up by many Quakers and appears in many of their books and pamphlets.

usually in citations of scriptural passages. He argued for toleration and understanding of those who held different views on the subject of baptism: 'let us love one another and walk together by that glorious rule above specifyed, leaving each other in all such circumstances to our own Master, to our own Faith (page 97). John Bunyan's book prompted a reply by Paul Thomas entitled *Some Serious Reflections on that Part of Mr Bunions Confession of Faith Touching Church Communion with Unbaptized Persons* (1673). William Kiffen wrote an 'Epistle to the Reader' for this pamphlet and took issue with Bunyan's views in favour of open-communion. He too picked up the 'walking' metaphor as part of his counter-argument, suggesting that communion with all saints was indeed a desirable thing, but that 'care must be had in the first place to observe the Rules given by our great Lord, and to walk according to them' (page A5).[29] Bunyan published a response entitled *Differences in Judgment about Water-Baptism No Bar to Communion* (1673). Again 'walking' language is employed by Bunyan in his argument, particularly as it pertains to the conduct of a believer who happens to hold to an open-communion stance. As Bunyan puts the central argument: 'All I say, is, *That the Church of Christ hath not Warrant to keep out of their Communion the Christian that is discovered to be a visible Saint by the Word, the Christian that walketh according to his Light with God* (page 2).' Or again

> I am for Communion with Saints, because they are Saints· I shut none of the Brethren out of the Churches, nor forbid them that would receive them. I say again, shew me the man that is a visible Believer, and that walketh with God; and though he differ with me about Baptism, the Doors of the Church stand open for him (page 97).

Next, we note that William Kiffen and Hanserd Knollys helped organize the first General Assembly of Particular Baptist churches, which met in London on 3-12 September 1689. Representatives from 107 churches throughout England and Wales converged on the capital and sought to forge a new denominational identity and find ways to work together creatively and address some of the problems facing Baptist congregations. Interestingly, in *A Narrative of the Proceedings of the General Assembly* (1689), which reports on this important meeting, we find that one instance of the language

---

[29] The General Baptist John Denne also wrote a response to Bunyan entitled *Truth Outweighing Error* (1973) which makes frequent use of the 'walking' metaphor. For more on this controversy over open-communion, see Robert Greaves, *Glimpses of Glory: John Bunyan and English Dissent* (Stanford, California: Stanford University Press, 2002), pp. 291-301.

of 'walking together' appears. This appears in connection with a declaration about the autonomy of the individual congregations in the midst of co-operation with other churches in the denomination. The passage reads:

> That in those things wherein one Church differs from another Church in their Principles or Practices, in point of Communion, that we cannot, shall not, impose upon any particular Church therein, but leave every Church to their own liberty, to walk together as they have received from the Lord (page 10).

Finally, the Seventh Day Baptist Edward Stennett uses the 'walking' metaphor in his *The Seventh Day is the Sabbath of the Lord* (1697). Stennett declare that 'it is the duty of the World now to believe, and be baptized, and to walk with the Church of Christ which is separated from the world' (page 5).

3. Minute Books of Baptist Churches - The surviving minute books of a number of Baptist churches also demonstrate that the language of 'walking' was in common use by them. There were a variety of ways that this was done. For example, it was not unusual for Baptist congregations in the seventeenth century to describe themselves as people who 'walked together' under the leadership of the person or persons who served as their pastor. A good example is the Devonshire Square Baptist church led by William Kiffen, whose membership lists are included in the extant minute books. Three separate membership lists survive from this congregation, dated 20 February 1668, 3 August 1670 and 6 October 1690. In each list the opening heading declares that the document consists of 'The Names of Those Brothers & Sisters yt have given up themselves to The Lord to walke in his wayes In fellowship together with Bro[ther] W[illia]m Kiffin'.[30] The Maze Pond Baptist church similarly mentions 'the Congregation walking with Brother Robert Steed'.[31] Robert Steed signed a letter written on behalf of the Cripplegate Baptist church to the Bromsgrove Baptist church on 31 March 1695. The letter was a commendation for Richard Claridge, who is described as 'having walked with us in the fellowship of the Gospell and having laboured amongst us'.[32]

---

[30] This is the wording of the 1668 list. The 1670 lists adds the name of Daniel Dyke as a co-pastor with Kiffen, and the list of 1690 adds the name of Richard Adams as co-pastor with Kiffen.

[31] ALRPCO, Maze Pond Church Book (1691-1708), page 31.

[32] ALRPCO, Cripplegate Churchbook (1689-1723), page 10.

The minute book of the Baptist church in Bedford records how John Gifford was called to be their pastor in 1650. Gifford's leadership of the congregation is specifically said to include his 'walk with them':

> [T]hey with one mouth made choice of our brother Gifford to be their pastor or elder, to minister to them in the things of the kingdom of Christ, to whom they had given themselves before: wherefore brother Gifford accepted of the charge, and gave himself up to the Lord, and to his people, to walk with them, watch over them, and dispense the mysteries of the gospel among them[33]

The minute book of Leominster similarly records that on 28 September 1656

> the Church of Christ meeting at brother Joseph Patshall's house in Leominster constituted and the persons undernamed did, after a solemn seeking of God, give up themselves to the Lord and to one another to walk together in all the ordinances of Jesus according to his appointments.[34]

The minute book for the Petty France Baptist Church contains a number of records of people who are admitted into membership with the congregation; their previous church association, under the leadership of another pastor, is described using the language of 'walking'. For example, note the following entry for 16 May 1675:

> Upon ye 16th of ye 3d m[onth] Sister Maulton who had formerly walked with Mr Palmer was received into this Congregation; those with whom shee formerly walked giving Testimony of her good conversation unto ye messengers sent by ye Church to inquire concerning that matter.[35]

Meanwhile, an entry for 18 November 1688 records that 'S[is]t[e]r Sparrow was dismist to Mr Kiffens people upon her desire to walk with them (page 23).

---

[33] Cited in Joseph Ivimey, *A History of the English Baptists, Volume 2* (1814), pp. 21-22.

[34] The Leominster Churchbook as cited in B.R. White, *Association Records of the Particular Baptists of England, Wales and Ireland to 1660: Part 1. South Wales and the Midlands* (London: The Baptist Historical Society, 1971), p. 41.

[35] GLL, Petty France Minute Book – 1675-1701 (MS 20228/1B): page 1 recto.

However, the language of 'walking' was perhaps most frequently used in the church minute books in connection with cases of church discipline.[36] When a member of the congregation behaved in a way that was deemed unacceptable and out of keeping with Christian principles discipline was frequently expressed within the bounds of this 'walking' metaphor. For example, on 3 November 1667 Elizabeth Malbon, together with three of her associates, were disciplined by Kiffen's church for their failure to attend church services regularly (it appears they had gone over to the Quakers). The record of their censure states: 'ye Church considered of ye whole matter together w[i]th theire obstinancie and accordingly Agreede to withdraw from them as persons that did walk contrary to ye Doctrine of Christ.'[37]

The Wapping Baptist church, which met in Old Gravel Lane under the leadership of Hercules Collins, includes a number of references to 'disorderly walking' (or an equivalent phrase) within its Minute Book, clearly taking up the wording of 2 Thess 3:6, 11 as it appears in the KJV. On 30 April 1678 the church disciplined a couple who were members of the congregation: 'It was hear and then Agreed by ye Ch[urch] to withdraw from Tho[mas] Margasine And his wif[e] for ye sine of Drunkenness and Rayling and Striking ______________ and for her disorderly walking.'[38] The church similarly decided to withdraw from Edward Banks on 16 September 1679 'for the sin of disorderly walking and refusing to hear ye Church after sending for 2 or 3 times'.[39] On 28 October 1679 a Brother Hopkins was publicly admonished 'for ye sin of disorderly walking and for leaving of prayer for his family and Idleness.'[40] The church decided to withdraw from Sister Mary Lane 'for ye sin of lying and keeping bad company and walking Scandulusly in ye world.'[41] A Sister Allaway was censured on 30 September 1684 'for disorderly walking not paying what she owed';[42] and the church decided to withdraw from Sister Right on 7 October 1684 'for ye sin of disobedience to her parent and disorderly walking.'[43] The Wapping church decided on 17 November 1685 to withdraw their communion from

---

[36] On this topic, see T. Dowley, 'Baptists and Discipline in the 17th Century', *The Baptist Quarterly* 24 (1971-2), pp. 157-166.

[37] GLL, Devonshire Square Minute Book (MS 20228/1A), pages 9 recto and verso.

[38] Wapping Minute Book (1676-1711): page 3 verso. Thomas Margasine was also disciplined on 19 July 1681 (page 14 recto).

[39] Wapping Minute Book (1676-1711): page 7 verso.

[40] Wapping Minute Book (1676-1711): page 8 recto.

[41] Wapping Minute Book (1676-1711): page 11 recto.

[42] Wapping Minute Book (1676-1711): page 21 recto.

[43] Wapping Minute Book (1676-1711): page 21 verso.

Sister Weeks 'for walking offensively and negligently in not making good her Place & Refuseing to come before ye Ch[urch];'[44] and on 26 May 1698 the church similarly withdrew their communion from Mary Church 'for her disorderly walking and not making Censurence of her word.'[45]

The minute book of the Baptist church in Devonshire Square contains five examples of the 'walking' metaphor being used in disciplinary cases. First of all, on 3 May 1665 the church addressed the behaviour of one of their members, Henry Hills, a long-standing colleague of William Kiffen's who had made a name for himself as a printer during the Cromwellian Protectorate. The minute book notes:

> The Church haveing taken notice of Brother Henry Hills long absence from them and his walkeing at a distance from his place w[hi]ch according to Rule he ought to have continued in amongst them;[46]

Meanwhile on 3 November 1667 the church decided to withdraw from four members 'as persons that did walke contrary to ye Doctrine of Christ w[hi]ch formerly they had received'.[47] The intention was to 'Reclaime them from ye principles of the quakers w[hi]ch they had for some tyme had lived in ye practice of'.[48] Another member of the church, John Westly, was disciplined on 17 January 1669. Several member of the church testified that Westly displayed 'simptomes of his Excesse in Drinking, his walking being such as had saddened ye hearts of ye righteous & opened ye mouths of ye wicked.'[49]

The minute book of the Baptist church in Bromsgrove in Worcestershire recorded that Samuel Jugins was withdrawn from 'for his disorderly walking'. The minute cites 2 Thess 3:6 as the scriptural justification for this action.[50] On 25 May 1695 the Bromsgrove church withdrew communion from Mary Crowe for

---

[44] Wapping Minute Book (1676-1711): page 22 verso.

[45] Wapping Minute Book (1676-1711): page 80 verso.

[46] GLL, Devonshire Square Minute Book (MS 20228/1A): page 5.

[47] GLL, Devonshire Square Minute Book (MS 20228/1A): page 14.

[48] GLL, Devonshire Square Minute Book (MS 20228/1A): page 13.

[49] GLL, Devonshire Square Minute Book (MS 20228/1A): page 15. Westly was also discussed in a church meeting held on 10 May 1669 (page 16).

[50] Bromsgrove Churchbook (1672-1715), page 14 (no date is given for this church meeting but it was between 1674 and 1678).

> 'many disorderly walkes especially in that she in a most tameing manner did abraid ye Widow Cooks that her face ... was handsomer than hers, Intemating as if Thomas Cooks was more taken with hers then his own wife.[51]

The minute book of the Baptist church in Broughton in Hampshire records two cases of discipline for 'disorderly walking'. The first involved a Joane Joyman who was withdrawn from on 24 March 1675 'for walking disorderly as appears against her by a letter from the Devizes'.[52] It is also recorded that on 7 April 1682 the conduct of one of their members over his 'disorderly walking' and involvement with sabbatarianism was addressed by the church meeting.[53]

The minute book of the Baptist church in White's Alley in Little Moorfields records one disciplinary case was addressed at the church meeting held on 5 December 1692:

> Complaint being brought Against Bro[ther] Caune of his Disorderly walking his being often in Drink and Cursing of his wife all which he fell under; it is Agreed that he be set at a distance till he shall reforme his Life and Conversation and the Church shall receave satisfaction therin.[54]

The minute book of the Baptist church at Glasshouse Yard records that the church agreed on 3 July 1693 to discipline Ann Dickeson, who

> Hath bin very remis and negligent of her duty in the Church not being at ye meetng as we think for one yeere or two, that if she cannot be reclaimed from such disorderly walking to be then discharged from her Church membership.[55]

---

[51] Bromsgrove Churchbook (1672-1715), page 57.

[52] Broughton Churchbook (1657-87), page 45.

[53] Broughton Churchbook (1657-87), page 62.

[54] GLL, White's Alley Minute Book (1681-1700): page 84 recto. Brother Caune was eventually restored to communion with the church on 21 April 1693 (GLL, White's Alley Minute Book (1681-1700): page 92 recto), and was quite active as a deacon for several years, but succumbed to drinking again and was censured by the church on 20 March 1699 (GLL, White's Alley Minute Book (1681-1700): page 182 recto).

[55] ALRPCO, Glasshouse Yard Church Minute Book (1680-1740): page 137.

Meanwhile the church tackled a much more complicated case on 17 December 1694 when it brought Sister Weston before the church meeting for discipline. Weston was called to answer

> For marr[y]ing twice out of the Church & sprinkling a Child and not giving the Church satisfaction was ordered to take Care to Walke Circumspectly and to demand her self orderly in Conversation[56]

4. Association Records of Baptist Churches – The surviving records of Association meetings of Baptist churches are also an important source of how the 'walking' metaphor was employed by Baptist leaders. For example, at the Midlands Association meeting held at Morton Hinmarsh on 4-6 June 1656 a query was raised about members serving in the military and whether it was possible for them to 'walk' in faith and be considered a church:

> Question 8: Whether a competent number of baptized believers in a troop or regiment may there walke as a church.
> Answer: wee do not discerne that a number of disciples in a troop or regiment canne there walke as and act as a particular church of Christ as seeing no Scripture to warrant it nor discerning them to be in a capacity to keep close to the rule of the worde in receiving of members, dealing with them in all cases as the matter shall require, and that they are continually liable to be dissolved.[57]

Clearly it was not only the theological principle of the autonomy of the Baptist church to determine their continuing existence, but also the mutual responsibility in caring for the members of the congregation and forging a common life together, that was at stake here.

At the meeting of the Midlands Association held at Alcester on 15-17 September 1657 the question of what to do with believers who had separated themselves from other Baptists on doctrinal grounds and formed a new church was addressed. The essential debate here was between those who were associated with the celebrated Baptist worthy John Tombes of Leominster and held to an open-communion stance as regards church polity, and those who were of a closed-communion stance and advocated separation from Tombes's church. The former group are described in the records as 'the people walking with Mr Tombes' in this debate, whereas the latter are

---

[56] ALRPCO, Glasshouse Yard Church Minute Book (1680-1740): page 155.

[57] Tewkesbury Churchbook as cited in B.R. White, *Association Records of the Particular Baptists of England, Wales and Ireland to 1660: Part 1. South Wales and the Midlands* (London: The Baptist Historical Society, 1971), pp. 27-28.

described as 'the church at Leominster and Hereford that walkes distinct from Mr Tombs'.[58]

At the so called Abingdon Association meeting at Wormsley on 8 October 1654 the nature of the communion between churches within the Association was a prime focus of discussion. The desire that purity be maintained amongst the churches was emphasized, and the language of 'walking' invoked:

> [T]o keepe each other pure and to cleare the profession of ye gospell from scandale which cannot be done unless orderly walking churches be owned orderly and disorderly churches be orderly disowned, even as disorderly walking members of a particular Church[59]

In terms of ecclesiology, what is central to this argument is the assertion that the same symbiotic relationship that exists between the individual believer and his or her own church, also exists between individual congregations and the wider association. Life within a Baptist church is simultaneously lived at both a congregational and an associational level.

The issue of how churches should keep each other informed about the movement of members from one church to another was a matter of discussion for the Association meeting which was held at Tetsworth on 10 June 1653. Here it was agreed that 'when any church hath so received any person and he hath continued some time with them he shall at his returne (upon his just desire) have a testimonial from them of his walking with them.'[60] At the Association meeting which was held at Tetsworth on 20-22 May 1657 a letter was received from the Baptist churches in London. The opening paragraph of this letter employs the 'walking' metaphor as the London-based churches describe themselves: 'The brethren and messengers of the respective churches walking in the faith and order of the gospell in and about London'.[61] Finally, we note that at the Association meeting which was held at Tetsworth on 5-7 April 1659 the church in Kingston raised a

---

[58] Leominster Churchbook as cited in B.R. White, *Association Records of the Particular Baptists of England, Wales and Ireland to 1660: Part 1. South Wales and the Midlands* (London: The Baptist Historical Society, 1971), p. 33.

[59] ALRPCO, Longworth Churchbook (1652-1708), page 3 recto. This record was re-iterated at the Association meeting which took place at Tetsworth on 27 December 1652 (ALRPCO, Abingdon Association Record Book (D/AA/1), page 3 recto).

[60] ALRPCO, Abingdon Association Record Book (D/AA/1), page 4 verso.

[61] ALRPCO, Abingdon Association Record Book (D/AA/1), page 28 recto.

query about what sort of communion could be shared with Seventh Day Baptist churches. The question was framed using the 'walking' metaphor:

> It was the desire of the baptized people of Bledlow, most of which doe now hold the 7th day Sabbath, that ye three churches which did formerly hold communion with them would now give them a meeting to the end that they might [decide how] far they can all walke together or in what [things they] can have communion together.[62]

Representatives of the Western Association of Baptist Churches met at Wells in Somerset on 7-11 April 1656. Following the meeting the thirty churches who attended issued a statement which was signed by Thomas Collier, John Pendarves, and Nathaniel Strange on 12 April 1656. Fortunately, a copy of this statement has survived, probably the copy originally belonging to Andover Baptist Church in Wiltshire. In the midst of a discussion about whether baptism is absolutely necessary to an orderly Church communion, we have the following declaration:

> It much concerns those who professe to walke according to the rule of God in scripture in faithfullnesse to the Lord, that they cleave close to that rule, Act[s] 3.22; 2 Thes[salonians] 2.15, without which they cannot with clearnesse and comfort approve themselves, either to God or men.[63]

5. Memoirs, Wills and Probate Records of Baptists – The 'walking' metaphor also appears in memoirs and testamentary records of Baptists with some regularity. In 1692 Thomas Grantham is recorded as exhorting his friends on his deathbed with the words, 'I recommend you to the Grace of God, that you would walk stedfastly in the Faith of Jesus Christ, as by the Grace of God I have done to this my Live's End'. He also says to them, 'I desire you for the Lord's sake to walk together, and keep the Unity of the Spirit in the Bond of Peace … and walk peaceably with all Men'.[64]

William Kiffen records in his 'Memoirs' (compiled in 1693 when Kiffen was in his seventy-seventh year) how in 1643 he befriended a young man from Wantage named Robert Stiles, and formed a business partnership with

---

[62] ALRPCO, Abingdon Association Record Book (D/AA/1), page 40 recto and verso).

[63] ALRPCO, Whitchurch MSS Letters – A1 (12 April 1656), page 6.

[64] *The Dying Words of Mr. Thomas Grantham* (1692), pp. 1-2.

him to trade in Holland. Kiffen notes that Stiles 'was a member of the same congregation, who walked very soberly'.[65]

The Particular Baptist pastor Hanserd Knollys in his 'Memoirs', published after his death in 1692, described his longstanding relationship with a Baptist congregation in London. Speaking of events which took place in 1648, he employs the language of 'walking' together with them when he says:

> I was then Pastor to a Church which I had gathered two or three years before, in the year 1645, with whom I have walked ever since, except that I was absent from the Church sometimes upon just Occasions, and with their leave, or forced from them by violent Persecution.[66]

Knollys also wrote an 'Epistle to the Reader' for the enigmatic prophetess and hymn-writer Katherine Sutton, whose *A Christian Womans Experiences of the Glorious Working of Gods Free Grace* was published in Rotterdam in 1663. The fact that Knollys penned this commendation has led many to conjecture that Sutton was a member of Knollys's church in London (she mentions her baptism in passing within the document).[67] She does speak of 'walking' with her church at one point in the pamphlet:

> I had a great fit of sickness; and I was inquiring of God, what his mind should be in that affliction: he shewed mee, it was because I did not declare to the Church with whom I walked; those things he had made known unto mee (page 20).

An associate of William Kiffen, the widow Isabel Jones of Wantage, used the language of 'walking' in her last will and testament which was signed and sealed on 11 April 1698. She named Robert Keate, and Elias Clarke, leaders of the Baptist church in Wantage, within her will, appointing them as trustees and bequeathing them twenty shillings apiece. She also left £5 to 'the poor people of the Congregation with whom I walk'.[68]

---

[65] William Orme, *Remarkable Passages in the Life of William Kiffin* (1832), p. 23.

[66] *The Life and Death of That Old Disciple of Jesus Christ, and Eminent Minister of the Gospel, Mr Hanserd Knollys* (1692), p. 23.

[67] See Ian Mallard, 'The Hymns of Katherine Sutton', *The Baptist Quarterly* 20 (1963-4), pp. 23-33; Michael Davies, 'Sutton, Katherine (*fl.* 1630–1663)', *Oxford Dictionary of National Biography*, Oxford University Press, 2004.

[68] TNA, PROB 11/461, page 314 verso.

In 1671 *The Life and Death of Mr Vavasor Powell* was published to honour the life and ministry of this influential Baptist leader who died in 1670. The volume contains a number of references to 'walking', including a direct citation to two of the key Old Testament texts which we noted above spoke of 'walking with God'. This occurs in a section of the volume in which some of Powell's choice sayings and sentences were collected out of his papers and recorded for posterity. Powell is recorded as saying 'The Care of a true Christian – To walk with God. Gen. 5.22, 24 & 6.9, 24, 40'.

Summary

The metaphor of 'walking' to describe the life and conduct of the covenanted people of God is a common one within both the Old Testament and the New Testament, notably within the Pentateuch and the Pauline epistles. The metaphor was one that Baptists throughout the seventeenth century turned to in describing their Christian life, both as individuals and as gathered communities of baptized believers. We have here catalogued approximately fifty examples relating to Baptist life which employ the 'walking' metaphor and grouped them under five interlocking headings. Taken together they demonstrate a creative adaptation of the biblical text by Baptists as they sought to give expression to their life together as a covenanted people committed to walking with God and with each other.

3.

The Fellowship of Christ's Sufferings: Fawcett, Fiddes, and the Tie that Binds

Robert Ellis

Two of the most prominent themes in Paul Fiddes' work are those of divine passibility and ecclesiology. Developed in his first major work on the doctrine of God, *The Creative Suffering of God*, and given particular pastoral and Trinitarian attention in *Participation in God*, the subject of divine suffering has been a constant. Another concern, arguably a growing one, has been ecclesiology. Most clearly and elaborately in *Tracks and Traces*, Fiddes has mined historic Baptist resources to outline an understanding of church which gives a prominent place to the concept of covenant – and in that volume also seeks to make connections between the doctrine of (the suffering) God and God's people the church. Increasingly, he has deployed the notion of participation to speak of the human relationship with God, Father, Son and Holy Spirit.

While the suffering of God has been frequently in view, human suffering has also been explored. Usually, however, this has been in the context of gaining clearer insights, through comparison and contrast, with divine suffering. In this essay I will suggest that notions of covenant and participation also enable us to say something about the fellowship of the church and also more particularly something about human suffering. This will prove a natural extension of Fiddes' thought, perhaps even something he might have said (though better, I am sure) had he turned his attention more earnestly to the topic. As such, amid the currently fashionable talk about 'doing' or 'being church' these ideas will suggest something which ought to be at the core of any such accounts, a thread which connects the nature of God, the essence of church, and the modality and content of the church's mission. My main resources in advancing this argument will be Fiddes' own work and (in what I hope he may regard as true Fiddes-ian style) the life and work of a great Baptist from the long eighteenth century, John Fawcett.

Baptist Accounts of Covenant and the Fellowship of the Church

According to Fiddes' account in *Tracks and Traces*, we may enumerate four interconnected understandings of covenant in English Puritan and Separatist theology, the well of so much Baptist theological thought.[1] First there is the saving 'eternal covenant of grace,' which God has made with all human persons in Jesus Christ. Calvin had been a strong influence in the way this was understood, and for Calvin this covenant was restricted to the elect. The second use referred to a covenant between the Father and the Son, an intra-Trinitarian covenant, through which the Son consented to the Father's will in the mission of salvation. This idea is nascent in Calvin, but developed by seventeenth century writers such as Benjamin Keach, with the striking image of a 'handshake' between the Father and the Son. In some hyper-Calvinistic writers in the eighteenth century this becomes the dominant or controlling understanding of covenant – those who are saved participate in the benefits of this covenant between the Father and the Son rather than being direct participants in the covenant itself.

Thirdly, the term 'covenant' is used to denote that agreement which God makes with his church as a whole, or, indeed, with particular congregations within that whole. There are references here to the Old Testament covenantal wording ('I will be their God and they shall be my people') as well as to New Testament texts on the church where the church is understood to inherit this covenant of God with God's people.[2] Fourth, and finally, 'covenant' can refer to the agreement made between church members at the founding of a congregation – or by new members as they join it. In such covenants members typically make promises of faithfulness to God as well as to one another, the latter often in the language of watching over and walking with one another.

There are many indications that this fourth sense of covenant was an important aspect of Puritan and Separatist understandings of church in the sixteenth and seventeenth centuries, but a key question is the relationship of these various understandings to one another. In particular, what is the

---

[1] See Paul S. Fiddes, *Tracks and Traces: Baptist Identity in Church and Theology* (Carlisle: Paternoster, 2003), pp. 24-31. It is salient to note the live controversies during the seventeenth and eighteenth century over Calvinist understandings of this, and other, doctrines.

[2] Fiddes points out an interesting detail of Calvin's thinking on this notion. Given the early Separatist preoccupation with the purity of the church as God's covenant people, it is worthy of remark that Calvin understood there to be a general covenant with the nation of Israel, while the perseverance granted by the 'Spirit of regeneration' fell only upon the elect – thus explaining the falling away of those who appear to be within the covenant but do not persevere. *Tracks and Traces*, pp. 27-28.

relationship of a covenant made between the members of a congregation, and the covenant which God makes with God's people, or with the church (either or both perhaps being understood as the 'elect'), and which may be grounded in the covenant between the Father and the Son. There is ambivalence in the early Puritans about whether God's covenant of grace is endangered by a breaking of its obligations such that it might be understood as conditional (or 'mutualist') rather than assured and permanent.

Robert Browne (?1550-1633), an influential though enigmatic Separatist, had a great concern for the purity of the church, believing that the Elizabethan settlement was flawed because of 'reminders of popery . . . the incompetence and immorality of her ministers, [and] . . . her very membership was rotten to its core.'[3] He believed that a true church could only be founded upon a 'covenant with the Lord' whereby members also 'gave their consent, to join themselves to the Lord, in one covenant and fellowship together, and to keep and seek agreement under his laws and government.'[4] As might be expected given Browne's typical concern for the purity of the church in keeping the covenant obligations laid upon it and its members, the exercise of spiritual and ecclesiastical discipline was an important part of living out this covenant. So White could say that 'Browne's conviction that the stability of the covenant relationship depended not only upon the grace of God but also upon the obedience of his people in conforming the structures of the Church to his will.'[5] A little later Francis Johnson could speak of the making of a covenant as the 'essence of the Church.'[6]

Browne and Johnson influenced but did not end up within the stream of Separatist life which we can finally call Baptist. John Smyth, however, did. He had been part of the early Separatist congregation at Gainsborough in Lincolnshire which in 1606 or 1607 covenanted together – an event which Fiddes describes as 'formative for Baptist Christians' as 'an Augsburg or a Dort or even . . . a Chalcedon.'[7] White remarked that 'a certain ambivalence' in Smyth's use of the concept of covenant 'became almost characteristic of his use of the term,'[8] with even a study of the context of use failing to clarify whether Smyth was referring to God's covenant with the elect, or the covenant which the believers made with one another in the fellowship of the church. White suggests that Smyth strikes an original note among the early Separatists in the way in which he brings the local and

---

[3] B. R. White, *The English Separatist Tradition: From the Marian Martyrs to the Pilgrim Fathers* (Oxford: OUP, 1971), p. 47.

[4] Browne cited in White, *English Separatist Tradition*, p. 49.

[5] White, *English Separatist Tradition*, pp. 161-1.

[6] White, *English Separatist Tradition*, p. 113.

[7] Fiddes, *Tracks and Traces*, p. 21.

[8] White, *English Separatist Tradition*, p. 128.

eternal covenants together: '. . . in the covenant promise of the local congregation the eternal covenant of grace becomes contemporary and man's acceptance of it was actualized in history.'[9] If this is true it might lead us to wonder whether Smyth's ambivalence about which covenant he is speaking of in his writings is rooted in a move to elide the two so that they become two sides of the one salvific coin. No wonder then that Fiddes can later go on to suggest that his key concept of participation may be a way of bringing together the local and eternal covenants: the human cooperation of the local covenant is, he says, a participation in the eternal covenant of grace.[10]

As already indicated, an important concern among the early Separatists in deploying their covenant language was the discipline, and therefore the purity, of the church. We can see this clearly more than a hundred and fifty years after Smyth in the life and work of John Fawcett. Fawcett was born near Bradford in 1740 and attended the local parish church before being deeply affected by the preaching of George Whitfield after which he associated with Methodists and other dissenters before joining a Particular Baptist congregation in 1758. This was by no means a straightforwardly uplifting experience. 'In the Bradford church where he was a member from 1758 to 1764 he encountered the morbid introspection, interminable grieving and excessive argumentation of the hyper-Calvinist system.'[11] It is worth bearing in mind in what follows that Fawcett's experience of church life was, from the first, neither idealized nor sheltered.

Fawcett was called to be pastor of the nearby Wainsgate church in 1764, and was already displaying indications of his prodigious ability. A remarkable preacher, a scholar, pastor, intellectual, writer, hymnodist, and educator, he was to be massively influential in the developing life of Baptists, especially in the North, towards the end of the eighteenth century. He played a leading role in the revitalizing of association life and the promotion of the newly discovered missionary imperative and organization. His work with ministerial students, teaching, forming and mentoring them in his home, in a pattern which was widespread at the time, meant that he shaped many of the next generation of Baptist leaders. He declined an invitation to become President of the Bristol College in 1792 but he played a leading role in establishing the Horton Academy in Bradford in 1804, the North's own Baptist seminary which in time became Rawdon College. He did all this while remaining, basically, in one place though with different

---

9 White, *English Separatist Tradition*, p. 128.

10 Fiddes, *Tracks and Traces*, p. 46.

11 Ian Sellers, 'Other Times, Other Ministries: John Fawcett and Alexander McLaren,' in *The Baptist Quarterly*, 32/4 (October 1987), pp. 181-198, here p. 183.

roles all his working life.[12] He also opened a day school and a circulating library.[13] All in all, Fawcett was 'a scholarly and able man . . . there were few Nonconformists who equalled him.'[14] Indeed, there were giants in those days.

Fawcett gives his major theological account of the church in *The Constitution and Order of a Gospel Church Considered* published in 1797.[15] The work has a clear polemical purpose and much of it must be read as a critique (sometimes implicit but often explicit) of the Church of England and its Episcopalian system. Fawcett, in typical Baptist manner, looks back to the New Testament church as a prototype and model of ecclesiastical polity. 'The members of the primitive churches were joined together by a holy confederation and mutual consent.'[16] First, the early Christians 'gave themselves to the Lord as his servants . . . and to one another, by the will of God, to walk in fellowship together.' When Fawcett begins to sound as if he is describing the church as a voluntary association, the reader must recall the national church into which he had been born was in his sightlines. 'All societies, and all relations, excepting that between parents and children, are formed by mutual consent, covenant or agreement. No individuals can be formed into a body, or joint society, without something of this kind.'[17] Fawcett, we may assume, while still standing within the Particular Baptist Calvinistic tradition, was not suggesting that churches were formed merely by the aggregation of human wills or decisions. By contrast with the Church of England, which did not include any element of 'mutual consent' (but was, in his contemporary Daniel Turner's phrase, formed by 'outward violence'[18]) it may at first seem like that, but Fawcett also believed that 'the primitive church consisted of persons who appeared, in a judgement of

---

[12] The parallels, and mirror-images, of Fawcett and Fiddes could themselves be the topic for an interesting essay!

[13] John A. Hargreaves, 'John Fawcett', *Dictionary of National Biography*, online at http://www.oxforddnb.com/view/article/9221?docPos=2, accessed 30th March 2014.

[14] Charles Williams, 'History', in *A Brief History of the Baptist Church, Hebden Bridge Yorkshire, With addresses given at the Centenary Services, held November 20th, 1877* (London: Yates and Alexander, 1878.), p. 7. See also David S. Milner, 'The Last Days at Rawdon and the Formation of the Northern Baptist College', online at http://www.biblicalstudies.org.uk/pdf/bq/supplement-1989_021.pdf, accessed on 30th March 2014.

[15] John Fawcett, *The Constitution and Order of a Gospel Church Considered.* (Ewood Hall, Halifax and London: Wills, Johnson, Button, and Martin, 1797).

[16] Fawcett, *Gospel Church*, p. 11.

[17] Fawcett, *Gospel Church*, p. 11.

[18] Daniel Turner, *A Compendium of Social Religion* (Second edition. London: John Ward, 1778), p. 15.

charity, to be the subjects of that divine change which is so often insisted on in the sacred scriptures, as essential to vital Christianity.'[19] In other words, before any covenant is made by the believers, those believers have already become heirs of and appropriated the eternal covenant by which God reaches out in grace through Jesus Christ. The church, and a particular church, is formed by divine initiative of grace rather than human persons coming together in voluntary association. Fawcett distinguishes two senses of the word translated 'church' in the New Testament. There is the concrete local congregation which is neither national nor provincial. But it also denotes 'the whole body of God's chosen people in every period of time . . . Jesus Christ is the head of this mystical body . . . The individuals of it are called, renewed, sanctified, and preserved by him on earth, and shall be glorified with him in heaven.'[20] For Fawcett too, the covenants made by God with believers, and by believers with one another and their Lord, are inseparable.[21]

Divine and human love fuse in the church in the same way as the eternal and local covenants. The human love is the 'divine cement' which binds the fellowship together as the true church is 'knit together in love.' Fawcett goes on, 'A particular gospel church then is a voluntary society, formed by mutual agreement. This transaction implies in it the nature of a covenant, or mutual compact stipulation, for the respective duties and privileges of that relation.'[22] This talk of covenantal duties could sound like a conditional or mutualist understanding of the divine covenant, and Fawcett like many Particular Baptists appears to affirm something like this at the same time as a strong emphasis on God's initiative, grace and faithfulness. This inherent tension or paradox is indicated by Sellers' observation that Fawcett came to 'expound the free offer [of salvation to all] within a broadly Calvinistic setting.'[23] It was the hyper-Calvinists who dissolved this paradox by stressing the divine initiative at the expense of the human response instead of holding the two in creative tension, as the Scriptural witness does. In so doing they gave Calvin's thought a rigidity and a centre which it did not have itself[24], and Fawcett is among those Particular Baptists who pull back

---

[19] Fawcett, *Gospel Church*, p. 8.

[20] Fawcett, *Gospel Church*, p. 4.

[21] See Fiddes, *Tracks and Traces*, p. 42.

[22] Fawcett, *Gospel Church*, p. 12.

[23] Sellers, 'Other Times', p. 183.

[24] 'It cannot be over-emphasised: faith in predestination is a long way from being the centre of Calvinism; much rather is it the last consequence of faith in the grace of Christ in the presence of the enigmas of experience.' Paul Wernle, quoted in Francois Wendel, *Calvin* (London: Fontana, 1965), p. 265. This view is supported by Alister E. McGrath: see, e.g., *Christian Theology: An Introduction* (Oxford:

from this error. The 'respective duties and privileges of that relation' referred to here will almost certainly refer to the duties owed by Christians to their Lord, but will most definitely also include those duties owed by the believers who have covenanted together to one another. These obligations, to God and to one another, we might also regard as being not simply congruent with one another but also having a relationship of coinherence, like the eternal and local covenants from which they derive. To meet one's obligations to the fellowship is to meet one's obligations to the Lord; meeting one's obligations to the Lord means nothing apart from walking with and watching over one's fellow believers.

The Sharing of Covenant Love and Participation in God

One of the major Particular Baptist figures of Fawcett's day was the hyper-Calvinist John Gill. Gill pastored a Strict Baptist congregation in Southwark from 1719, and moved with the fellowship to Carter's Lane in 1757. This illustrious congregation had been pastored by Benjamin Keach and would in time become New Park Street Chapel and then the Metropolitan Tabernacle where Spurgeon presided. Gill was one of those hyper-Calvinists who disconnected the 'eternal' and 'local' covenants: characteristically, divine initiative was separated from human response. Fiddes describes his position and its consequences like this:

> Gill shows no interest in linking the 'covenant of grace' with the church covenant. Gill's locking up of God's covenant-making within the persons of the Trinity results in a view of the local church covenant which is modelled thoroughly in a secular contract of human obligations; 'like all civil societies' the union between members is made by 'voluntary consent and agreement' in which they 'propose themselves a church.' Gill, notably, refrains from using the traditional phrase 'give themselves to God' in this discussion, urging only that members 'give themselves up to the church.'[25]

Fiddes goes on, drawing principally on the work of Karl Barth, to connect the local covenant of the church with the eternal covenant of grace, and specifically with the Second London Baptist Confession's (1767) Trinitarian understanding of it. This Confession speaks of the eternal covenant as 'a transaction between the Father and the Son about the Redemption of the

---

Blackwell, 1994), pp. 396-7 and *A Life of John Calvin: A Study in the Shaping of Western Culture* (Oxford: Blackwell, 1990), p. 168.

[25] Fiddes, *Tracks and Traces*, pp. 34-5.

Elect.'[26] Admitting that Barth does not use the language of covenant to describe God's commitment (election) to be the God-for-us in Jesus Christ, Fiddes argues that we can see 'the making of covenant with Jesus Christ, the representative human son, as being 'given in' the eternal generation of the divine Son from the Father.'[27] God in Christ is therefore, for Barth, elected and elect, and Fiddes argues that this 'double election' may also be seen as a 'double covenant' of love, and so our own human covenant making – such as that between church members when they covenant with one another in response to the God's gracious covenant initiative – is taken up into God's own eternal covenant making. 'Church is what happens when these vectors intersect, and God in humility opens God's own self to the richness of the intercourse.'[28]

In this way Fiddes suggests that the making of covenant between fellow believers is itself a mode of participation in the life of the Triune God. As such it may be elaborated alongside other such movements of participation which Fiddes describes, such as an act of forgiving and the pastoral act of articulating and embodying God's forgiveness,[29] prayer[30] and the sacraments,[31] and also in human suffering.[32] Doubtless we could suggest more such movements of participation, such as acting for justice and with compassion.

If we take Fiddes' insight into our covenant-making as a participation in the life of God back to Fawcett's account of the covenant we will find this illuminating. Among the benefits of church membership, Fawcett suggests that various 'incitements to holiness' are given, and that 'virtuous and gracious affections are excited by Christian society.' His illustration may give some indication of his gift for preaching: 'Kindled coals, if placed asunder, soon grow cold; but if united together, they quicken each other, so as to keep up a lasting heat.'[33] Thus the fellowship of the church permits, enables, and encourages mutual support between believers, that 'they may exhort and teach one another daily . . . comfort, strengthen, and edify one

---

[26] Fiddes, *Tracks and Traces*, pp. 26, 78-82; 'The 1677/89 London Baptist Confession of Faith. Thirty-Two Articles of Christian Faith and Practice with Scripture Proofs. Adopted by the Ministers and Messengers of the General Assembly Which Met in London in 1689', VII/3. Online at http://www.ccel.org/creeds/bcf/bcf.htm, accessed on 30th March 2014.

[27] Fiddes, *Tracks and Traces*, p. 79.

[28] Fiddes, *Tracks and Traces*, pp. 79-80.

[29] Fiddes, *Participating in God* (London: DLT, 2000), pp. 208, 215.

[30] Fiddes, *Participating in God*, p. 136.

[31] Fiddes, *Participating in God*, p. 281.

[32] Fiddes, *Participating in God*, p. 162.

[33] Fawcett, *Gospel Church*, p. 15.

another in love'[34], though this mutual care is actually the care of Christ which they mediate to one another, and the nourishment received at the Lord's table becomes a sign and instance of this.

The church in covenant also directs its own affairs, including with regard to the disciplining of members which must sometimes be part of the 'watching over' one another.[35] Here we see again more than an echo of the early Separatist concern for the purity of the church. The believers must also elect their own officers – bishops (sometimes called elders or pastors) and deacons.[36] The believers have a responsibility towards those they elect to these offices: the pastor, for instance, should receive encouragement, love, sympathy in affliction, obedience, provision of their needs, and be supported in prayer.[37] The pastor or bishop, in turn, has responsibilities towards the other members of the fellowship as the 'governor and guide' of the flock. He (Fawcett's use of the pronoun is not meant to be inclusive) is not to 'lord it over'[38] the congregation but to teach the message of grace and live graciously, though Fawcett has more to say on the 'person specification' than the 'job description,' showing an interest in formation which has a contemporary ring.

We will have more to say about the mutual obligations of the community in a moment, but already a clear picture is emerging. The fellowship is bound together by a covenant commitment which has its origin in God's covenant of grace. Together they mediate to one another the sustenance of Christ as the vectors of the two covenants intersect (in Fiddes' phrase) and the community of the church shares in the life of the Triune God.

Human Suffering and the Fellowship of Believers

I noted earlier that Fawcett's experience of church life was by no means straightforwardly happy. His time in membership in Bradford exposed him to some of the stresses and strains of church life, and in pastorate too he knew such moments. The realism is implied when discussing in *Gospel Church* the objection that might be made to entering into covenant relationship with a local congregation, that the church fellowship is not 'exactly answerable to my wishes.'[39] Such a person, Fawcett suggests in a way which seems uncomfortable to a reader accustomed to the contemporary

[34] Fawcett, *Gospel Church*, p. 16.

[35] Fawcett, *Gospel Church*, pp. 25-27, 46-50.

[36] Fawcett, *Gospel Church*, pp. 28-31.

[37] Fawcett, *Gospel Church*, p. 37.

[38] Fawcett, *Gospel Church*, p. 31.

[39] Fawcett, *Gospel Church*, p. 18.

practice of 'shopping around' for churches, might find 'many imperfections, many improprieties and irregularities.' However, Fawcett avers, 'if you refuse to unite with a gospel church till you find one free of all defects, you may live in the neglect of the divine ordinances till the day of your death. And if every one were to act on the same principles that you do, there would be no visible church of Christ existing in this world.'[40] Fawcett knows that no church is perfect, and that no congregation will meet all our individual preferences. This is true even of a congregation to which one ministers for a whole lifetime, as was the case for him.

As the chapel at Wainsgate was regularly packed with enthusiastic listeners to Fawcett's sermons, he decided that larger premises were required and plans were made to remove to a new and larger chapel to be built nearby. But these plans did not find favour with all, and a difficult period followed as groups within the fellowship debated and, indeed, contested the plan. As Charles Smith observes: 'There were obstructives in those days. A section of the church opposed the building of a new and larger place of worship. While the dispute was proceeding, Mr Fawcett, who had pupils residing with him, received notice to quite the farm he was renting.'[41] Fawcett relocated to a neighbouring valley, remained as pastor at Wainsgate, but also opened his home to a new Sunday evening meeting which gathered there. In time, it was finally agreed to build a larger meeting house up the road in Hebden Bridge, but in addition to rather than instead of the Wainsgate Chapel which remained. In 1777 Fawcett and a goodly company of members from Wainsgate were dismissed to 'plant' the new congregation there. The two congregations remained close, and Fawcett was the guest preacher when a new Wainsgate chapel was finally opened in 1815. Neither this mark of reconciliation, nor the constructive corporate decision to plant a new congregation with the much-loved Fawcett as its pastor, should blind us to the stress and acrimony which must have been experienced through this protracted episode.

In fact, just before this incident, he did very nearly move. In 1771 John Gill, aforementioned hyper-Calvinist of Carter's Lane, died. In seeking his replacement the congregation there invited the young Yorkshireman Fawcett, then thirty-two, to 'preach with a view.' They did things differently then: Fawcett stayed in London for nine weeks, and preached no fewer than fifty-eight times to the Carter's Lane faithful.[42] At the conclusion of which he received a call to the pastorate there. This call was not only to a large and prestigious congregation but was also a call to a higher material reward. His salary at Wainsgate and Hebden Bridge never exceeded £25 per annum.[43]

---

[40] Fawcett, *Gospel Church*, p. 18.

[41] Charles Smith, 'History', p. 5.

[42] Charles Smith, 'History', p. 3.

[43] John A. Hargreaves, 'John Fawcett.'

Carter's Lane would have multiplied that several times. Fawcett accepted the call and preparations for his family's move to London were made. The day came, the farewell sermon was preached, and the wagons loaded with the Fawcett's belongings. Then, so the story says, in the farewell tears both John and his wife were overcome with sadness and Mary Fawcett exclaimed 'Oh John, John, I cannot bear this, I know not how to go!' He replied, 'Nor I, either, nor will we go.' And the wagons were unpacked, and Fawcetts remained in Yorkshire. [44] The story is touching enough, but there was more, giving a reason for its frequent re-telling well over two hundred years later.

Fawcett had been something of a hymn writer throughout his ministry. Sellers considers his contribution to Baptist hymnody to stand alongside that of Anne Steel, Beddome and Stennett. Sellers speaks of an astonishing development of literary style in his mature work, given that Fawcett was largely self-taught. Earlier work showed problems of scansion and appeared to be poor copies of the hymn writers he himself admired such as Watts, Cowper and Wesley. In due course, writes Sellers, 'a plain, straightforward vocabulary and imagery emerge, well suited to blunt northern tastes'[45], along with sophisticated metres and nuanced content. He wrote for the church's young people, for various liturgical moments, and kept returning thematically to the atonement, and to the joy of belief and wretchedness of unbelief.

But following the aborted move to Carter's Lane Fawcett (according to tradition, though contemporaneous accounts are not available) wrote the hymn with which he is probably today most closely associated. 'Blest be the tie that binds' came directly from this experience of going and then staying, and constitutes a reflection upon the reality of Christian fellowship in the covenanted community of Christ's people. In his 1782 hymnal[46] it appears below the heading 'Brotherly Love' and reads as follows:

I.

Blest be the tie that binds
Our hearts in Christian love;
The fellowship of kindred minds
Is like to that above.

---

[44] This story which can be found in a number of variations on the internet, such as this account by Robert D. Kalis, 'Blest be the tie that binds,' online at http://www.joy-bringer-ministries.org/hymns/BBTTTB.pdf, accessed on 30th March 2014. As indicated, it must be conceded that none of these accounts appears to be contemporaneous, and there remains the possibility that some creative re-telling has taken place.

[45] Sellers, 'Other Times', p. 186.

[46] John Fawcett, *Hymns adapted to the Circumstances of Public Worship and Private Devotion* (Leeds: printed by G. Wright and Son, 1782), p. 188.

II.
Before our Father's throne
We pour our ardent pray'rs;
Our fears, our hopes, our aims are one,
Our comforts and our cares.
III.
We share our mutual woes,
Our mutual burdens bear;
And often for each other flows
The sympathizing tear.
IV.
When we are called to part,
It gives us inward pain;
But we shall still be joined in heart,
And hope to meet again.
V.
This glorious hope revives
Our courage by the way;
While each in expectation lives,
And waits to see the day.
VI.
From sorrow, toil and pain,
And sin we shall be free;
And perfect love and friendship reign
Thro' all eternity.

The pain of parting referred to in the fourth verse may refer directly to the hymn's provenance, and the parting in view here is not simply the removal of a family from Yorkshire to London but also those partings which more permanently blight human lives with grief. The beginning and end of the hymn have an equal focus on features of the eternal covenant: on the Father's throne, and on the future hope. The middle of the hymn has a clearer focus on the singers, on their sharing of one another's burdens, and the affection shared between them which means that parting is painful. What is the nature of the 'tie that binds'? Any reader of the *Gospel Church* will have no doubt that it is a reference to the covenant entered into by believers in the fellowship of the church. But there is an ambiguity here once more, and we recall also that this company of believers covenanting together have first been 'subjects of that divine change which is so often insisted on in the sacred scriptures, as essential to vital Christianity' and that they 'are called, renewed, sanctified' by their Lord. They are not only bound together by the covenant into which they have entered, but together they are bound into the covenant of grace by God's gracious election in Jesus Christ. Their covenanting together enables a participation in the eternal covenant of grace

Fawcett's language in the hymn resounds with mutuality, and the mutuality of 'kindred minds' in the congregation 'is like to that above.' In *Gospel Church* he could write that 'The Church of God is sometimes called the kingdom of heaven, and most certain it is, that nothing in this world bears so near a resemblance to the heavenly state.'[47] Once more there is an ambiguity: is this 'heavenly state' the company of the redeemed in heaven, or is this a reference to the divine life, Father, Son and Spirit, such that, as some of our contemporaries want to affirm, the church is 'in his likeness'[48], a community modelled or in imitation of – or a participation in – the triunity of God? Fawcett's language is not clear but such a reading which sees the fellowship of the church as 'like' the trinitarian fellowship of God is not inappropriate.

The second verse of the hymn suggests that, whatever our individual circumstances, we share three things in common: in coming 'before our Father's throne' we share a dependence upon God (else why would we be praying?), and we share also, in common humanity, fears and hopes, comforts and cares; we also share a common sense of purpose. From here the third verse examines the depths more searchingly. Fear and cares are one thing, but now we can speak of the sharing of 'mutual woes' and 'mutual burdens.' At such moments, because of the closeness of this fellowship, the tears will flow as we experience one another's hurts as if they were our own. Indeed, in such a fellowship, they are our own.

Earlier I suggested that the covenant entered into by believers in the fellowship of the church was essentially related to the eternal covenant of grace; that the offering of support in the name of Christ was in fact the care of Christ mediated through his people, and that the enacting of the church covenant not only relates the believers to the eternal covenant but draws them into the divine life, enables a participation in God. We can argue now that the sharing of 'mutual woes' and the bearing of 'mutual burdens' is also an entering into the life of the Triune God, a participation in the divine life.

Fiddes' discussion of human suffering has often identified it as both requiring an understanding of God as passible and shedding light on that passibility.[49] But Fawcett's work, and in particular this hymn, suggest an alternative logic in which the experience of *shared* human suffering itself in the fellowship of the church, is itself an analogue for and a participation in divine suffering – 'is like to that above.' In the fellowship which is shared, and in the participation in one another's sorrow and woe, the bearing of one another's burdens, Christian believers mediate and enact the presence of

---

[47] Fawcett, *Gospel Church*, p. 13.

[48] E.g. Miroslav Volf, *After our Likeness: The Church as the Image of the Trinity*. (Grand Rapids: Eerdmans, 1998).

[49] See Fiddes, *The Creative Suffering of God* (Oxford: Clarendon 1988), pp. 31-37, and *Participating in God*, pp. 155-163 and 170-178.

God in human suffering and point to the larger redemptive suffering of Christ.

In constructing an argument for a suffering God Fiddes suggests that 'at the most basic level it is a consolation to those who suffer to know that God suffers too, and understand their situation from within.'[50] He goes on to note that, while our experience of human comforters can give similar consolation, it is important for the comforter not to be overwhelmed or crushed by their empathetic entering into our suffering. But the focus in this discussion is very much on the relationship between the human sufferer and the suffering God, rather than on the experience of sharing our mutual woes. It is when discussing the re-creative but painful process of forgiveness and reconciliation that Fiddes examines the way in which one person might enter into the feelings of another – with both forgiver and forgiven being disturbed and made vulnerable.[51] He can speak of this as a 'journey of empathy.'[52]

Fawcett's account of the nature of Christian fellowship foregrounds the sharing of joys and troubles. Alongside the 'duties of worship and discipline' church members have other responsibilities, and 'the chief of these may be summed up in that sincere and mutual affection which is so often insisted on in the New Testament, under the name of brotherly love'[53] – the heading, it will be recalled, given to 'Blest be the tie.' This fulfils the law, and is the working out of Christ's redemption in the believers. 'The members of Christian churches are so to walk in love, as to bear one another's burdens, to pour out constant and fervent supplications one for another, to visit one another for spiritual edification, to relieve one another in necessity, to use hospitality without grudging, to be pitiful, courteous, and kind-hearted to one another.'[54] To achieve this, Fawcett indicates that a high priority must be given to making and being at peace with one another, so that they should 'be subject to one another in all humility' and avoid various kinds of destructive behaviours including 'evil-surmising' and 'evil speaking.' The sharing among believers should be frank and open, and (as on Fiddes' journey of empathy) in this sharing believers may be disturbed and vulnerable. 'They ought, with freedom and simplicity, to communicate one to another their spiritual experiences; the trials, temptations and difficulties they meet with in the way, and the supports, comforts and deliverances with which they are favoured . . . By this means Christian sympathy is excited, so that we rejoice with them that do rejoice, and weep with them that weep.'[55] Those who neglect such fellowship place themselves at a considerable

[50] Fiddes, *Creative Suffering*, p. 31.

[51] See Fiddes, *Creative Suffering*, p. 159.

[52] See Fiddes, *Participating*, pp. 201-207

[53] Fawcett, *Gospel Church*, p. 52.

[54] Fawcett, *Gospel Church*, p. 53.

[55] Fawcett, *Gospel Church*, pp. 54-5.

disadvantage in living the Christian life. Elsewhere he has already cautioned the reader, citing Eccl 4:10: 'Woe to him who is alone when he falleth.'[56] Furthermore, the reality of such fellowship is evidence for Fawcett that we are 'dwelling with [God] for ever'.[57]

The enactment and embodiment of the covenant obligations which believers owe one another within the fellowship of the church, the giving of mutual care, the sharing of woes and the bearing of burdens is, then, more than a taking up of the duties within a 'voluntary society': it is a dwelling with God. This participation in one another's suffering becomes a participation in God. The fellowship of the church is moreover, nothing less than the fellowship of Christ's body, for Christ is the head of the 'mystical body' and the love shared among believers is the '*divine* cement' by which the fellowship is 'knit together in love.' One further way of thinking of this sharing of mutual woes is therefore to think of it as the fellowship of Christ's sufferings – as hinted at in 2 Cor 1:5, Rom 8:17, 1 Peter 4:12 and most tellingly (and enigmatically) at Col 1:24 where Paul says 'I am now rejoicing in my sufferings for your sake, and in my flesh I am completing what is lacking in Christ's afflictions for the sake of his body, that is, the church.' Paul elsewhere links the present experience of suffering for believers with the anticipated or already present experience of sharing in Christ's resurrection. With Fawcett's account in mind we may see the shared suffering of believers in the fellowship of the church as a sharing in the suffering of Christ ('for the sake of his body, that is, the church'), so that they too might share his risen life. The ecclesial community, through its mutual and empathetic caring and shedding of the 'sympathizing tear', transforms the suffering of believers as it enters into the fellowship of Christ's suffering and the experience of his resurrection, as it becomes caught up in movements of divine empathetic love so that the enactment of the local and the eternal covenant coinhere.

Concluding Remarks: The Sharing of Suffering as the Modality and Content of Mission

Fawcett makes a clear link between the close fellowship of the kind we have been considering and the progress of the gospel and the church's mission.[58] 'See how they love one another', Tertullian reports the pagans as remarking

[56] Fawcett, *Gospel Church*, p. 16.
[57] Fawcett, *Gospel Church*, pp. 53.
[58] Fawcett, *Gospel Church*, pp. 56-58.

around 200 CE.[59] Fawcett certainly believes that the winsomeness of both the gospel and the local community of believers is enhanced by a witness to mutual care and the sharing of one another's sufferings. Fawcett the evangelical rejoiced in the joy of believers and in the fellowship of the church. The medium and the message are not so easily separated as we sometimes pretend (or hope!).

Contemporary discussions of church, at least among practitioners, often focus on models of church organization and models of mission, on structure or activity rather than the quality of common life. Attractional or incarnational? Inherited or pioneering? But beyond such simple (and perhaps simplistic) polarities, Fawcett and Fiddes challenge us to consider something more fundamental about the essence of church – the quality of its fellowship and the nature of its common life. Part of our Baptist heritage has been to understand the local church as a body of believers under the authority of Christ, who covenant to walk with and watch over one another in a deep sharing in common life. Such an enacted local covenant connects and coinheres with the eternal covenant through which God in gracious love shares our joys and pains in Jesus Christ and through the presence of the Spirit who 'intercedes with sighs too deep for words.'[60] *This* is what it is to be church: to live out such a life of fellowship with integrity amid the ups and downs, giving and taking, bitter arguments and sweet agreements, and so 'dwell in God' together.

To a world often struggling to be at peace with itself the church fellowships, in whatever form they may be constituted, may then become a model of communal life which points to 'a more excellent way.'[61] As such, the quality of fellowship which Fawcett sketches gives a clue about the way we are church but also about the way we do mission: by being such a people. And not such a people turned in upon ourselves, but communities turned outward to their communities in compassionate service and loving concern. Mission is pastoral care turned outwards, and the sharing of cares, woes, and burdens which Fawcett enjoins upon his readers (the sharing of which is a dwelling in God) is offered in the humility of which he also often speaks to those around as well as within. As such the 'sympathizing tear' points us towards both the mode and the content of our message. A message which will also point to the One who shares our sufferings and transforms it utterly, the Triune God of cross and resurrection.

---

[59] Tertullian, *Apology*, 39. Online at: http://www.ccel.org/ccel/schaff/anf03.iv.iii.xxxix.html, accessed 30th March 2014

[60] Rom 8:26.

[61] 1 Cor 12:31.

4.

Veiled Presence: The Risen Christ in Spurgeon's Great Communion Hymn and Baptist Communion Rituals

Stephen Finamore

Preamble

Professor Paul Fiddes has written on an astonishing range of themes and subjects. He is able to engage creatively with presentations across all theological disciplines. On the occasions I have engaged with him it has always seemed to me that he knows more than I do about areas that I had thought were my specialism and in which he claimed only to dabble. In the light of this I feel both honoured to be asked to contribute something to a collection of essays being published in Paul's honour, and a sense of trepidation that I have been daft enough to accept. These feelings are accentuated by the fact that I have agreed to write on the theme of the Lord's Supper; a matter on which I learned so much from Paul during my years as a ministerial student at a time when he was the College Principal. It always interested me that Paul was prepared to make use of well-known hymns in the course of his theological reflections.[1] In addition, in his work on Baptist life, Paul explores the theological ideas, helpful and unhelpful, which underpin aspects of Baptist ecclesial practice.[2] So, in reflecting on our understandings of the Lord's Supper using the lenses of a hymn written by a distinguished Baptist figure and of some of our traditional communion rituals, I feel I am taking a leaf out of Paul's own book.

Introduction

We are sometimes taught that one of the attributes of God is omnipresence. The writer of the old song may have boasted 'I've *been* everywhere, man',[3]

[1] For example, in his book *Past Event and Present Salvation: The Christian Idea of Atonement* (London: Darton, Longman and Todd, 1989), he cites hymns by C. F. Alexander (p. 140) and Isaac Watts (p. 150).

[2] See, for example, Paul S. Fiddes, *Tracks and Traces*: *Baptist Identity in Church and Theology* (Carlisle: Paternoster, 2005).

[3] Geoff Mack, 1959. My italics.

but Christians insist that God *is* everywhere. Stephen Tomkins gently lampoons our religious language when he writes,

I once heard a true story about this church in some village which was doing everything right but just wasn't growing. So they sought the Lord about it. They sought him by day, and they sought him by night. And then in the morning they found him – he was everywhere, just as he always is, so that was nice.[4]

Of course, the Church wants to claim that God is everywhere while at the same time insisting with the Psalmist that God's presence is something that needs to be sought[5] and simultaneously believing that God has promised to be present to God's people in specific ways in particular circumstances.

In the light of this, the Church's belief in the divinity of Christ causes some apparent tensions when it is allied to our convictions about his bodily ascension. The risen Christ is God and human. He has a human body. A glorified body, certainly; a spiritual body, if the Apostle is to be believed;[6] but a body for all that. How can one who is embodied be everywhere? Luther, depending on, and probably extending the scope of, the doctrine known as the *communicatio idiomatum* or the communication of attributes, which states that, 'in view of the unity of Christ's Person, His human and divine attributes, experiences, etc. might properly be interchanged'[7], insisted that it is legitimate to speak of the ubiquity of Christ's ascended body.[8] Yes, he is located in the heavens at the right hand of the Father but he may also be spoken of as being present by his Spirit always and everywhere.

If we grant that this is so, and it should be noted that Zwingli, among others, has questioned the argument,[9] what might be different about a gathering of two or three in Christ's name?[10] Or for that matter about the Lord's Supper? If it can be said that Christ is present in the human heart, in a daisy or in a sunset, what difficulty can there be in saying that he is present in bread and wine? Is it wiser to speak of a spiritual rather than a bodily

---

[4] Stephen Tomkins, *My Ministry Manual by Gerald Ambulance* (London: SPCK, 2002), p. 6.

[5] Psalm 27:7-9.

[6] 1 Cor 15.

[7] J. N. D. Kelly, *Early Christian Doctrines* (5th edition) (London: A&C Black, 1977), p. 143. And see Bernard Reardon, M. G., *Religious Thought in the Reformation* (London: Longman, 1981), who writes of Luther that he allows the full significance of the *communicatio* in other words that the divine and human natures of Christ are 'so intimately related that the attributes of the one may be expressly predicated of the other.' p. 80.

[8] For a contemporary Lutheran perspective on this issue, see Robert W. Jenson, *Systematic Theology*, *vol 1*, *The Triune God* (Oxford: OUP, 1997), p. 206.

[9] Reardon, *Religious Thought*, p. 116 n. 38.

[10] Matt 18:20.

presence? And is it better still to speak of a *sacramental* physical presence? This language begs all kinds of questions but leaves open the possibility of speaking of a real bodily presence which is not understood in the usual categories of science and geography.

There is an interesting discussion of these issues in Robert Jenson. He points out that modern understandings of the cosmos prevent us from understanding that Christ's body occupies space within the created universe. For God, the whole created order is but one place and the risen Jesus shares this relation to created space. The natural objection to this position is that an entity with such a capacity can scarcely be called a 'body'. Jenson argues that since Jesus is the Logos of God, his self-understanding must determine what is real and therefore it is possible to assert, building on the Apostle Paul's use of the term 'body of Christ' to describe both the church and the Eucharistic elements, so that:

> We must learn to say: the entity called the body of Christ is whatever object it is that is Christ's availability to us as subjects; by the promise of Christ, this object is the bread and cup and the gathering of the Church around them.[11]

While this argument may cohere with some aspects of the Apostle's teaching, it is not evident that it can adequately account for all of it; Paul's comments on the nature of the resurrection body in 1 Corinthians 15 and his own concerns about being found 'naked' in 2 Corinthians 5, suggest a perspective which would struggle to limit the understanding of the resurrection body, and therefore the body of the risen Jesus, to the Eucharistic elements and the gathered Church alone. Nevertheless, Jenson offers a helpful way of understanding the particular presence of Christ in the Eucharist.

Of course, an answer that can be offered to any and to all of these questions must rely on the idea that there are different ways in which Christ is present in different times and places and that there are differences in the way in which that presence is apprehended by creatures. The church believes that Christ has promised to be present in certain ways in particular circumstances. His presence will be mediated to his people when defined things happen. One of these is in the Lord's Supper. This does not mean that Christ's presence cannot be mediated at other times or in other ways, or that the promise can be treated presumptuously or without the presence of sincere and faithful prayer. However, it must surely mean that when the Supper is celebrated, we are offered a focussed moment in which we may legitimately expect that the presence of Christ will be encountered.[12]

---

[11] Jenson, *Systematic Theology, Vol* 1, p. 205.

[12] See the argument of John Colwell, *Promise and Presence; An Exploration of Sacramental Theology* (Carlisle: Paternoster, 2005).

The Bible suggests that there are certain ways in which such a presence might be apprehended and the Baptist tradition has worked with such ideas while at the same time drawing on developments of these in other streams of the Great Church of which it is a part. Rather than offer a general survey, this essay will focus on two things and ask what they might say about the ways in which the risen Christ is present when the Supper is celebrated: firstly, a communion hymn written by a significant Baptist figure and its subsequent revision; and secondly, traditional Baptist communion practices.

The hymn offers an example of Baptist devotional language. It provides a useful means of investigating how a significant Baptist figure, his congregation, and no doubt many others, understood what was happening when they met around the Lord's Table. The practices, the things churches actually do, are of interest because repeated rituals have an impact on people's understanding of themselves and their communities. The two things, the words and the activity, offer two lenses through which we can observe both the way Christ's presence in communion is understood and the impact it might be having on how people relate to one another and the ways in which they behave. So, our concern is the presence of the risen Christ in the Lord's Supper; what Baptists sing devotionally about this presence, the rites or symbolic actions they participate in when they practice this presence, and what all this might teach us about the impact Baptists expect the presence of Christ to make on their shared lives and, perhaps, on the world.

However, before considering the hymn and practices, it seems appropriate to pause to consider a biblical text that might help frame the discussion, and then to say something about the Baptist tradition out of which the hymn, the practices and this reflection on them have all emerged.

Biblical Reflection

In the final Chapter of his Gospel Luke recounts the story of an encounter between two disciples and the risen Christ. The astonishing conclusion of the account is that in the very moment of spiritual apprehension, the bodily encounter is foregone. The evangelist writes, 'When he was at table with them, he took bread, blessed and broke it, and gave it to them. Then their eyes were opened, and they recognized him; and he vanished from their sight.'[13]

While Biblical scholars debate the nature and extent of the text's allusions to either the Last or the Lord's Supper, there seems little doubt that Luke is offering an echo of the events in the upper room. The presence of the risen Jesus is real and yet it is both allusive and elusive. He makes himself known but not in ways that readily lend themselves to analysis or

[13] Luke 24:31.

explanation. This is a form of presence that is always true yet always just beyond reach, both physical and mental. Christ reveals himself and is yet hidden.

Baptist Diversity

In common with Christians of other traditions, Baptists have struggled to account for their experience of the presence of Christ in the Lord's Supper.[14] One stream of thought among us strains to outflank Zwingli by advocating what seems to be a doctrine of the real absence of Christ from the Eucharist. This position appears to be driven by two main concerns. Firstly, there is the view, probably derived from the Enlightenment, that the spiritual cannot be mediated by the material and indeed that the two should on no account be confused or mixed. Secondly, there is the dysfunctional angst which so benights our tradition that it causes us to panic about any doctrine, tradition or practice which might be understood as being in any way Catholic. On this view, the bread and wine are not symbols, they are *mere* symbols; the elements are not signs, they are *only* signs; they are not even tokens, they are *just* tokens: the adjective (or other modifier) has truly become the enemy of the noun. And yet even among advocates of such positions there seems to be an embarrassed recognition that something more is going on; Baptist people will insist on experiencing Christ in the Supper and no amount of their being slapped down by their pastors with reminders that it is all just a memorial can prevent this from happening. Other streams within Baptist life are more devotional, more content to explore the experiential, more open to acknowledging a real presence when communion is shared. One example of this is found in the hymn set out below.

A Communion Hymn

The hymn is not found in the Baptist collections of 1933[15] or 1962[16]. It was, however, through one of the few truly wise decisions made by its compliers,

---

[14] There is an interesting incident in a David Lodge novel which acknowledges this. The context is a Catholic event at which the mother of a child with Down's syndrome says, 'When my little girl, she's mentally handicapped, wanted to go to Communion with the rest of the family, I didn't see why not. She's always been very interested in the mass, very reverent. Some busybody, a woman in the parish said, "But does she really understand what it's about? Could she explain?" I said "Could you?" That shut her up.' *How Far Can You Go?* (London: Penguin, 1982), p. 237.

[15] *The Baptist Church Hymnal.*

revived in the 1991 collection, the oddly-named *Baptist Praise and Worship*. So far as I can ascertain, the original words were these.[17]

AMIDST us our Belovèd stands,
And bids us view His piercèd hands;
Points to His wounded feet and side,
Blest emblems of the Crucified.

What food luxurious loads the board,
When at His table sits the Lord!
The wine how rich, the bread how sweet,
When Jesus deigns the guests to meet!

If now with eyes defiled and dim,
We see the signs but see not Him,
Oh may His love the scales displace,
And bid us see Him face to face!

Our former transports we recount,
When with Him in the holy mount,
These cause our souls to thirst anew,
His marr'd but lovely face to view.

Thou glorious Bridegroom of our hearts,
Thy present smile a heaven imparts:
Oh, lift the veil, if veil there be,
Let every saint Thy beauties see!

The writer is, of course, the great nineteenth century preacher, Charles Haddon Spurgeon, who exercised a long and successful ministry from the Metropolitan Tabernacle at the Elephant and Castle in South London.[18]

Since discovering the edited version of this hymn in *Baptist Praise and Worship*, I have been intrigued by Spurgeon's theology of the Lord's Supper. In my mind the great evangelist is associated with controversy with the Tractarians over the issue of baptismal regeneration. In seeking to distance Baptists from the idea that infant baptism serves to bring about the new birth, Spurgeon seemed at times to limit its meaning to that of a

---

[16] *The Baptist Hymn Book.*

[17] C.H. Spurgeon, compiler, *Our Own Hymn Book*, (London: Passmore and Alabaster, 1866). The hymn was headed 'Jesu's Presence Delightful'.

[18] Peter Morden discusses the hymn in *'Communion with Christ and his people': The Spirituality of C. H. Spurgeon* (Oxford: Regent's Park College, 2010), pp. 183-4.

memorial to an event which had already occurred. I assumed that he must have held a similar position with respect to the Lord's Supper. I suspect I was mistaken or at least that his position was more nuanced than many may have assumed. After all he was, as Walker reminds us, on this issue as on others, a Calvinist.[19] Where some of Spurgeon's allies in the battles with the Oxford Movement embraced a thoroughgoing Zwinglianism, he himself allied their memorialism to 'a grasping of Christ in the present'.[20]

According to Grass and Randall, Spurgeon preferred to speak of the Supper as an ordinance because he was concerned about some of the implications of sacramental language. Roman Catholic concern for the corporeal presence of Christ amounted to a lamentable desire to know Jesus 'after the flesh'. Yet when it came to the language of devotion, Spurgeon was able to speak of eating the body and drinking the flesh. Indeed as he prayed, eyes closed, at the Table, the great preacher sensed the footfall of Christ and he opened his eyes almost expecting to see his Master.[21]

Some of these thoughts are reflected in his hymn. And we shall see that in devotion and poetry he is prepared to say more than might be imagined.

AMIDST us our Belovèd stands,
And bids us view His piercèd hands;
Points to His wounded feet and side,
Blest emblems of the Crucified.

What food luxurious loads the board,
When at His table sits the Lord!
The wine how rich, the bread how sweet,
When Jesus deigns the guests to meet!

In the opening stanzas of his hymn Spurgeon asserts the real presence of Christ in the church as it celebrates Communion. There is no pseudo-Zwinglian avowal of a real absence. Instead the church is encouraged to sing of a crucified and risen Christ whose presence at the Supper is wholeheartedly affirmed. As Peter Morden affirms, 'Spurgeon believed Christ was powerfully present at what was his table'.[22] The question of the nature of this presence is not addressed. We are not explicitly told that it is

---

[19] Michael Walker, *Baptists at the Table* (Didcot: Baptist Historical Society, 1992), pp. 164-181.

[20] Walker, *Baptists at the Table*, p. 172.

[21] Morden *Communion with Christ*, p. 71.

[22] Tim Grass and Ian Randall, in Anthony R. Cross and Philip E. Thompson (eds), 'C. H. Spurgeon on the Sacraments' in *Baptist Sacramentalism*, (Carlisle: Paternoster, 2003), p. 178.

bodily nor that it is spiritual.[23] However, since Christ is said to adopt bodily poses - he is stated both to stand among us and to be seated at his Table to meet his guests - it is not unreasonable to surmise that the presence is bodily or may legitimately be pictured as being so. Of course it is the language of poetry and of devotion and it is not fair to push the images too far. Nevertheless, the author seems to be unembarrassed by the idea of Christ's presence being imagined in bodily terms.

Furthermore, the risen Christ draws attention to the marks on his body confirming that it is legitimate for the gathering to envisage Christ's presence in bodily terms. This also suggests that Spurgeon was part of a tradition that encouraged the believer to reflect on the fact that the risen Christ yet bears the effects of his once-and-for-all self-offering. Other examples are found in the words 'those wounds yet visible above in beauty glorified' from *Crown him with many crowns*, and Wesley's affirmation that 'the dear tokens of his passion, still his dazzling body bears' from *Lo! He comes with clouds descending*.

The second stanza ends with the idea that the Table is a meeting place between the risen Jesus and his guests. Spurgeon understands the Supper as a context in which there might be an encounter between Christ and his people. Furthermore, since Christ is present and reminds those gathered of his sufferings for their sake, the language is not only that of remembering. Nor is it only that of expectation though the language of luxury suggests a banquet to come. Furthermore, it is not simply the language of pietistic, prayerful attention. It is about meeting. It is personal and it is real.

If now with eyes defiled and dim,
We see the signs but see not Him,
Oh, may His love the scales displace,
And bid us see Him face to face!

Of course, while Christ's presence is affirmed, there is an understanding that it may not be experienced. Those who sing the hymn pray that every saint might encounter the Belovèd in the course of the ritual. There can be no presumption that the experience of his presence will be accorded to all; it is possible that some may see the bread and the wine without 'seeing' Jesus. However, the hymn writer longs that Christ's love would be experienced in such a way that he be truly encountered. And this encounter is no matter of intellectual assent, it is the face to face meeting associated with an I-Thou relationship. The prayer is that anything that prevents the communicant from

---

[23] Of course there is a biblical precedent for refusal to be drawn on this issue. When the Apostle describes his ascent to Paradise in 2 Cor 12:2-4 he twice insists that he does not know if the experience was bodily or not.

encountering the risen Jesus, here instantiated by the scales which are yet to fall from some eyes, be removed.

Of course, the elements are referred to as signs. However, there is no sense that they are signs rather than the reality they represent. They are a means by which that reality, the presence of the Host, might be encountered. Only eyes defiled and dim stop at the signs and see nothing beyond, beside, through or in them. To be in such a position is to miss the point of the event and prayer is offered that such a condition be overcome. The author is a Calvinist and there is quite rightly no suggestion that the encounter may be achieved through any effort on the part of the believer. The removal of any scales is an achievement of the love of God; all is grace.

Our former transports we recount,
When with Him in the holy mount,
These cause our souls to thirst anew,
His marr'd but lovely face to view.

No remnant of this verse remains in the heavily edited version of the hymn that appears in *Baptist Praise and Worship*. What is interesting is that there is no particular suggestion that the communion service is itself a memorial. Instead, the allusion to the Transfiguration[24] encourages the participant to use the occasion of the Supper to reflect on past experiences of Christ's presence in order to generate a desire to encounter him in the present. And the meeting is depicted in terms of a face-to-face meeting.

Thou glorious Bridegroom of our hearts,
Thy present smile a heaven imparts:
Oh, lift the veil, if veil there be,
Let every saint Thy beauties see!

The final stanza offers some rich devotional language and the suggestion that the present encounter around the Table is proleptic. It is a taste in the present of a greater and fuller encounter that remains future. A heaven is imparted here.[25] The hymn ends with a reference to the veil. This may be an allusion to the Temple veil which hid from sight the inner sanctuary; or it may be intended to bring to mind the related veil of 2 Corinthians 3 and to present the idea of the risen Christ as the new Moses. The next possibility is

---

[24] The words 'holy mount' strongly suggest a reference to the King James Bible's translation of 2 Peter 3.18 where, Spurgeon would surely have understood, the Apostle is recalling his experience of Jesus's transfiguration.

[25] Paul has, of course, written very helpfully on eschatological themes in his book *The Promised End: Eschatology in Theology and Literature* (Oxford: Blackwell, 2000).

that this is a development of the bridegroom imagery and the veil should be understood as one that covers the groom's face until the moment comes when he is revealed in all his beauty. The last interpretation has considerable appeal because Spurgeon often preached from the Song of Songs allegorizing the words of the lovers so that they came to express the love between Christ and his bride, the Church.

Of course the image may be deliberately polyvalent. All these possible interpretations are ways of speaking about the hiddenness of God's glory. It is, I suppose, a little like the elusive and allusive presence of the risen Christ in Luke's story. As the Apostle claims, using a slightly different image, 'now we see in a mirror, dimly, but then we will see face to face.'[26] If the Temple veil is at all in view in Spurgeon's thinking then he may be recalling that at the death of Christ the veil was torn in two so that all might gaze upon the beauty of holiness.[27] This inner shrine, the very presence of the divine, may now be accessed through bread and wine in the Lord's Supper. There is a sense in which the elements veil the presence but another in which they do not. The final prayer is that insofar as there is any further work that God needs to do to enable his people to encounter the Christ who is already present, that this be done. And the prayer is that this be not the privilege of some special part of the people of God but the experience of each and every believer who participates.

The implication of all this seems to be that from God's perspective there is nothing that separates the gathered church from its Redeemer; he is truly present to them. However, there may be some deficiencies in the believer that prevent this from being experienced. In the poetic language of the hymn these are pictured as scales that prevent one from perceiving something that is in truth present. The metaphor is presumably derived from the experience of the Apostle Paul.[28] There may also be a veil which might or might not need to be lifted and again we are reminded of the elusive and allusive nature of Christ's presence.

The Hymn's Revision

It is interesting to note the changes made by the editors prior to including the hymn in *Baptist Praise and Worship*. The revised text reads as follows;

Among us our beloved stands
and bids us see his nail-scarred hands
points to his wounded feet and side

[26] 1 Cor 13:12.

[27] Mark 15:38 and parallels.

[28] Acts 9:18.

blessed emblems of the crucified.

When at his table sits the Lord
what glorious food adorns the board
when Jesus comes his guests to meet
the wine how rich, the bread how sweet.

If now with eyes earthbound and dim
we see the signs but see not him
then may his love the veil displace
so we may see him face to face.

Minor changes are made to the first verse. The second stanza is reorganized with line order being changed but the overall sense maintained. The third verse is largely retained. The eyes that fail to see are now categorized as earthbound rather than defiled. This suggests that they are failing to look heavenward or with spiritual insight rather than that they have been spoiled in some way. The focus has moved from our past sin, expressed in the idea of defilement, to our current attitude, articulated as being tied to this realm rather than to a heavenly one. It might not be too much to say that the theocentric original has given way to an anthropocentric revision.

An even more interesting difference is that the veil of the fifth verse is imported in place of the scales of the original. It is the veil which must now be displaced. In other words, the scales which represent some deficiency in the believer give way to a veil which, presumably, is set in place by God. Where Spurgeon both acknowledges the veil and yet questions its reality, the revised hymn accepts that it is there, even while praying for its removal. Having made this change the editors then remove the last two stanzas thus omitting both Spurgeon's thoughts on the appropriate use of memory and his hints at realized eschatology.

The new version is a fine hymn and it is probably true that parts of Spurgeon's text were in need of revision. Nevertheless, it seems that something has been lost even if I am grateful to the compilers for re-introducing the hymn to British Baptist congregations. On the other hand, it may be that something is gained in the revised version. The link between the veil and the elements which is implicit in Spurgeon is made more apparent. This connection seems worthy of further consideration.

A Veil for the Presence?

First of all, there are suggestions in the Letter to the Hebrews that the flesh of Jesus is related to the Temple curtain. We are told that we may enter the sanctuary with confidence because Jesus has opened a way 'through the veil, this is his flesh'.[29] While some exegetes are anxious to avoid the implications of this statement, some theologians have found the idea to be a rich one and have made use of it in their thoughts about the Eucharist. Wesley's Christmas hymn, *Hark the herald angels sing*, states the idea boldly; 'Veiled in flesh the Godhead see'. This is not an attempt to deny the truth of the humanity of Christ but to affirm the reality of his divinity. In addition, it is possible to read it as an indication that the flesh of Christ may be understood as being like the veil of the Temple behind which was the presence of God. This line of thought might then be applied to the communion elements which, when the believing community gathers and focuses its mind on the great actions of God, become veils which either hide or reveal the divine presence, or both. The hymn's use of the veil metaphor draws on this rich idea that Jesus's flesh was a veil which covered the presence of God and suggests that the bread and wine may have a similar function.

Next, the use of the image of a veil is connected to the Catholic tradition that the body of the ascended Jesus is present in the elements in veiled form. Aquinas concludes one of his Eucharistic prayers with these words, "Most loving Father, grant that I may behold for all eternity face to face Your beloved Son, whom now, on my pilgrimage, I am about to receive under the sacramental veil, who lives and reigns with You, in the unity of the Holy Spirit, God, world without end. Amen."[30]

The doctrine of transubstantiation teaches that after the consecration of the elements Christ's bodily substance is veiled in the accidents of the bread and wine. Spurgeon manages to allude to a similar idea without resort to any Medieval version of Aristotelian philosophy.

No doubt there are great differences between Aquinas's understanding of the Eucharist and that of Spurgeon. The good doctor held to the doctrine of transubstantiation which had been affirmed at the 4th Lateran Council in 1215. Spurgeon emphatically did not share such a belief. However, transubstantiation is but one way of explaining a belief in the real presence of Christ in the Eucharist. It is possible to hold the same belief but to account for it in other ways; indeed, it is possible to hold the belief and to offer no explanation at all for such a mystery. Luther, for example, affirmed the real presence of Christ while refusing to account for it in terms of transubstantiation. McGrath summarizes his position; 'It is not the doctrine of transubstantiation which is to be believed, but simply that Christ really is

---

[29] Heb 10:20 (my translation).

[30] http://www.ourcatholicprayers.com/aquinas-before-communion.html, accessed 21st August 2013.

present at the Eucharist. This fact is more important than any theory or explanation.'[31]

Aquinas's discussions of the issue are quite complex and are not altogether straightforward to pin down. His opinions are perhaps more nuanced and more subtle than he is sometimes given credit for, either by his Protestant critics or his Catholic advocates. At one point he acknowledges the objection,

> Further, no body can be in several places at the one time. For this does not even belong to an angel; since for the same reason it could be everywhere. But Christ's is a true body, and it is in heaven. Consequently, it seems that it is not in very truth in the sacrament of the altar, but only as in a sign.

His response to this is that,

> Christ's body is not in this sacrament in the same way as a body is in a place, which by its dimensions is commensurate with the place; but in a special manner which is proper to this sacrament. Hence we say that Christ's body is upon many altars, not as in different places, but 'sacramentally': and thereby we do not understand that Christ is there only as in a sign, although a sacrament is a kind of sign; but that Christ's body is here after a fashion proper to this sacrament, as stated above.[32]

This is an argument for sacramental presence which is a different order of being from any others. This should not be taken to mean that the presence is anything other than real; Aquinas is most insistent that the substance of Christ's body and blood are indeed present even while those things appreciable by the physical human senses have remained the same.

However, Aquinas acknowledges that Christ's body is not present in quite the same manner as other bodies may be present; it is spiritually present, 'that is, invisibly, after the manner and by the virtue of the spirit.'[33] He later expands on this theme to say that Christ's body is indeed present but not after the manner of dimensions, which means, 'not in the way in which the dimensive quantity of a body is under the dimensive quantity of place.'[34] Later he adds that 'in no way is Christ's body locally in this sacrament'.[35]

---

[31] Alister E. McGrath, *Reformation Theology: An Introduction*, (Oxford: Blackwell, 1999), p. 177.

[32] *Summa Theologica* 3.75.1.

[33] *Summa Theologica* 3.75.1.

[34] *Summa Theologica* 3.76.3.

[35] *Summa Theologica* 3.76.5.

Colwell summarizes Aquinas's position by saying:

> to speak of this sacramental presence is to say something entirely distinctive, something entirely other than any spatial presence: Christ's presence here is unique; he is present here in a manner in which he is present nowhere else; he is present here 'sacramentally'. For Thomas, as for the tradition he represents, Christ is spatially (or locally) present in heaven, at the right hand of the Father; he is present at the Eucharist, therefore, in an entirely different manner...'sacramentally' rather than spatially.[36]

Calvin, while not prepared to tolerate the idea of transubstantiation, affirms the work of the Spirit in mediating Christ's presence through the bread and wine.[37] Furthermore, he acknowledges a secret conversion so that something more than bread and wine is present.

> For when they say that a secret conversion takes place at consecration, so that it is now something else than bread and wine, their meaning, as I already observed is not that these are annihilated but that they are to be considered in a different light from common food, which is only intended to feed the body whereas in the former the spiritual food and drink of the mind are exhibited. This we deny not.[38]

In the same passage, speaking of the ancient writers, he affirms that 'All clearly and uniformly teach that the sacred Supper consists of two parts, an earthly and a heavenly.'

Clearly, Calvin has a robust doctrine of the presence of Christ in the Lord's Supper and it is not unreasonable to suppose that the same would have been true of Spurgeon. While this is not to say that either of them would have been content to be associated with Aquinas, this may have as much to do with their objection to transubstantiation as it was taught in their days, as it has to do with the detail of Aquinas's arguments. All may have been content to affirm that there are circumstances in which it is legitimate to affirm that in the Lord's Supper the elements veil the true presence of Christ.

---

[36] Colwell, *Promise and Presence,* p. 168.

[37] Calvin, *Institutes* 14.17.33.

[38] Calvin, *Institutes* 14.17.14.

True Presence

It is not my purpose to dwell further on the arguments of the past. Instead I wish to affirm that Christ is present when his people gather and that one of the means by which that presence is experienced is the Lord's Supper. In the Supper his presence is given a focus, signs are given which are visible and tangible, that affect the physical senses and mediate the promises of grace and divine presence and communion with the Saviour. Spurgeon's hymn clearly expresses the ides of the presence of Christ in the Lord's Supper and does so in a manner that is not dissimilar to some of the devotional language of Aquinas. However, I am also interested in the ways this access to Christ's person which is claimed by these different traditions, is manifested in practice. With this in mind I turn to a reflection on the role of food within culture and current Baptist practice of the Lord's Supper.

Reflections on Meals in Culture and in Church

It is possible to argue that, broadly speaking, there are two ways in which humans relate to one another. We might categorize these as the household and the market place. It may be appropriate to add a third to which resort is taken when relationships in the other two break down: the battlefield. The household is where we engage with members of our own family and others who share the same domestic space. It is marked, where it has not become dysfunctional, by co-operation and the sharing of resources without conflict. The members of households sit down with one another and food resources are distributed without competition and on a broadly equitable basis. Table manners have evolved to reinforce this pattern and to ensure that conflict is kept to a minimum. Outside the household, in what we might call the market place, the situation is very different. People find themselves in competition with one another for limited resources. Most human cultures have rules to control the conflicts that are generated and people may accept some degree of responsibility for the welfare of others, but there is no presumption that resources are to be equitably shared or that a person has a particular responsibility to ensure that strangers are fed. Where the rules intended to control conflicts prove inadequate, violence occurs. If, for whatever reason, markets are not perceived as facilitating an appropriate distribution of limited resources, attempts may be made to adapt the legal and other frameworks within which the markets operate. If these fail then attempts may be made to resolve the issues on the battlefield.

On the other hand, when hospitality is exercised, the rules that apply to the family are extended temporarily to a member or members of another family. People no longer relate as they might in the market, still less as on a battlefield, but instead relate, at least temporarily, as members of the same family. The sharing of a meal can generate profound emotions because it involves the exchange of spheres. One of the reasons that the Eucharist is so significant is that it offers, in theory at least, the sharing of resources on the household model by an enormous number of people. In principle the invitation is limitless. All are invited to engage with one another as family rather than as competitors. It is not simply that a state of enmity has been resolved so that there is peace instead of violence; it is that the battlefield and the market place both give way to the family table.

This resonates with the idea that the great reconciler Christ is the host at the communion Table. Where he takes charge women and men are invited to relate to one another in new ways. The traditional language is that of sisterhood and brotherhood and this reflects a change in the way people engage with one another; a way modelled on the household rather than the market. It is an example of the permanent offer of hospitality to strangers. Where communion works in this way, the presence of Christ is experienced as he breaks down barriers and changes the way in which humans engage with one another.

In the Gospel according to John, Jesus speaks from the cross to his mother and to his friend. He says to her, 'Behold, your son!' and to his friend he says 'Behold, your mother!'. The friend then takes Jesus' mother into his own home.[39] Perhaps one point of the story is that at the cross of Jesus people become family and so change the way in which they might be expected to relate to one another. In the Lord's Supper the death of the Lord is brought actively to mind. Those who participate become family members and the ritual of sharing reinforces the idea that they relate to one another in a new way.

Although Baptist practice is often criticized and compared unfavourably with Eucharistic practice in other traditions, there are nevertheless a number of significant theological ideas that it exemplifies.

Reflections of Contemporary Baptist Eucharistic Practice

Firstly, Baptists traditionally insist that the deacons gather with the Minister at the Table. At first sight this looks for all the world like the top table. It is as though the patterns of hierarchy so familiar from elsewhere are being reinforced. However, this turns out to be the servants' table for the deacons will go out into the congregation to serve others. Furthermore, the Minister, whom some might have assumed to occupy the pinnacle of the implied hierarchy, then serves the servants upon their return. The Minister in turn will be served by a deacon. All are served by others. The whole thing can be read as a parable of the transformed relationships found in the Kingdom of

---

[39] John 19.27.

God as expectations are confounded. It is not uncommon at festival times for roles to be reversed in some ways. There is a tradition in the British Army that at Christmas those with commissions serve food to the rest. Baptist churches act out this parable as the normative way of marking communion. And this is intended to represent in a public rite the way in which these relationships work in practice. The risen Christ is understood to be the host at the Table and so one of the marks of his presence is the subversion of expectations where social hierarchies are concerned.

Secondly, many Baptist churches will wait until all have been served before anybody eats or drinks. A key characteristic of a shared meal is thus retained. No hierarchy is tolerated. All are equal and so they eat and drink as one. There is no question of one person being allowed to eat or drink before others; unity and equality are demonstrated. Again, the ritual, in addition to everything else that it conveys, represents and defines the way relationships are intended to function within the community. Again, the presence of the risen Christ guarantees equality.

Next, the resources are shared equally and without competition. Again, something significant is said about the nature of the relationships between the participants. This is not a community in which a lion's share will go to the wealthy or the powerful. There will be no contest for resources. Instead, distribution is based on what is perceived to be God's economy. Perhaps reference should be made to the story of manna with which God fed the Israelites in the wilderness.[40] Intriguingly, this is the story to which Paul turned when we was encouraging the Corinthian Christians to respond generously to the needs of the Jerusalem poor so that there might be equality or fair balance.[41] Perhaps this is something that Baptist congregations may be manifesting when they share the bread of heaven in the Lord's Supper. The risen Christ prompts equal sharing among those who gather.

A further interesting practice, though one which may be dying out, is the taking up of a communion offering to be given away to those in need within the church. This was one way in which members accepted their responsibility for one another as family. It was an acknowledgement that this responsibility extended beyond sharing around the Table to ensuring that there were funds available to the pastor and deacons that could be used to support those in particular need. In those churches where this tradition has lapsed the officers will usually have access to a church fund which can serve a similar purpose but it may be that something significant has been lost through the separation of this concept from the family table.

Finally, when Baptists share in Communion, there is bread and wine to spare. All who wish to share have been served, and yet there is an abundance left over. It is not put aside for future use or consumed by the priests; it is the

---

[40] Ex 16.

[41] 2 Cor 8:14.

overflow and may simply be returned to the created order whence it came. This is an acted parable of grace. There is enough for all and still there is more. This is a meal to which the whole world is potentially invited and it is therefore vital for it to be very clear that there is sufficient for all who are present and still plenty left for those who have yet to respond to their invitation. The communion service is thus a sign of God's continuing mission in the world and the universal offer of God's kingdom. All these are ways in which the transforming, reconciling and challenging presence of Christ is experienced by the community that celebrates the Supper.

Conclusion

There is something to be said for the view that the debates of the past about the way in which Christ is present in the Supper have missed the point. Whatever differences Christians of different traditions may have, there ought to be scope for agreement around the idea of the 'veil'. As our brief Bible study suggested, there are times when Christ is present and yet his presence is hidden and elusive. As Spurgeon suggests, our sinful humanity may find it difficult to fully grasp a presence which from heaven's perspective could not be more real. And yet in part, through a veil darkly, we do encounter the Belovéd and in our devotion we may understand that presence in bodily terms.

What also matters is that the presence of Christ is known by the effects he has upon those gathered. Of course he is present to nurture and to console, to minister his presence. But he is also present to demonstrate that he makes things new, that he radically changes the way people relate, that he shares grace and abundance and this is where Baptist practice offers something. This is not always appreciated among Baptists let alone our ecumenical partners. However, it does point to the subversion of the ways of the world and offers a picture of the kingdom of God in which all the resources of earth and heaven are shared equally and without conflict. And it encourages us to prepare ourselves in the present for our own struggle as we seek to be faithful to the one who urges us to pray that the kingdom will come and who promises that the prayer is heard and is being answered.

There are signs in the Baptist tradition of words and practices which strongly suggest the conviction that the risen Christ meets his people at the Communion Table. This is something that is strongly suggested in Spurgeon's hymn. Furthermore, our practices not only reflect that presence but also point to its impact on our shared lives in the present as well as pointing us towards God's future. Thus, these instances of our hymnody and our ritual point to the presence of the risen Christ in the Lord's Supper experienced as a loving, intimate relationship, and to the fact that such presence is understood as a summons to act out the impending reign of God.

5.

Encountering Christ: Zwingli, Signs and Baptists around the Table

Ruth Gouldbourne

It was an evening part way through a conference taking place at Luther King House. Three of us, Paul Fiddes, myself and one of our leading younger theologians were sitting round the fountain, with glasses of red wine, watching the stars. And they were talking about poetry. I had long loved poetry, but it had faded from my attention through the press of other demands. As I listened to them talk about the importance of language, its capacity to evoke that which is more than itself, and indeed more than us, there was a strong sense that more was present than just the words spoken and ourselves. I rediscovered a desire for poetry that night. But I also discovered more; I was given a new way of thinking about language itself, and our capacity to encounter what is more than us when it is mediated through relationship and words used with care.

That this conversation involved Paul is no surprise; his awareness of and careful use of language is one of the significant gifts that he has offered us over the years. And that attentive use of language has brought us theology of creativity and humility. Underlying the exploration in this paper is the memory of that night – of the power of language and its capacity to point us beyond, and my gratitude to Paul for his engagement with Baptist identity and in particular sacramental theology in ways that illuminate our self-understanding, and our ability to be understood and to engage with the wider church.

It is a truism, but nonetheless painfully obvious, that one of the most bitter ironies in the history of the church is that the place where we are called to discover and demonstrate our unity in Christ has become the centre of controversy, conflict and even mutual killing. To gather at the Table of the Lord and share bread and wine is above all to demonstrate our oneness in Christ, and to experience the depth of our divisions and separation in the church. It was of course always so – Paul's words to the church in Corinth suggest that splits in the congregation had their most visible expression in the division between those who could eat and drink their fill, and those who were hungry and struggling.

And the history of the relationship between different Christian traditions has all too easily been played out in disagreements about and exclusions from the Table; the (albeit largely manufactured) suspicion when it became clear that Tony and Cherie Blair had a practice of coming to the Table together even when technically belonging to different 'communions' (in itself an interesting linguistic give-away) demonstrated the ways in which this division and perception of division remains potent. Among the many gifts that Paul Fiddes has offered both Baptists and the wider Christian community has been that of dialogue and invitational explanation, which has been part of the ongoing journey to find a common life that is truly reconciled; one that means we can meet at the Table. That we have not yet got there is no reason to give up. That we have people like Paul who can do what needs to be done is hope that we do not need to give up.

However, it is not only between Christian traditions that there is an experience of separation. It happens within traditions too, and Baptists have by no means been immune to this. Historically, we have had the creativity to have a different focus for the fight. Rather than arguing about where and how Christ is present – the concern that usually dominates the discussion elsewhere – Baptists in their most visible disagreement have argued about which Christians should be present, should the Table be open or closed.[1] Ecumenically, of course, this has perhaps been the aspect that has had the most impact, as it has been the one that has divided us not only among ourselves, but from other believers, as we have effectively unchurched fellow Christians.

Though this is the best known of our communion disputes, we have also had differences of opinion about what is happening, about the nature of the practice, and this shows no sign of abating in the current generation. Indeed, we might say, as certain parts of our tradition are recovered and made more visible, this debate has intensified.

Memorialism and Baptist Theology

In 'The Church as Eucharistic Community'[2] Paul Fiddes has discussed the ways in which early and developing Baptist theology drew deeply on Calvin's theology. Fiddes goes on in that chapter to explore ways in which Baptist theology and practice can contribute to the understanding of the wider church. However, as also he points out, it is not only Calvinistic theology that has shaped our understanding of the Eucharist; we have also been – perhaps even more deeply – shaped by the teaching of Zwingli, and his theology of memorialism and sign. In the nineteenth century this became

[1] For a full discussion of this, see, for example, Michael Walker, *Baptists at the Table* (Didcot: Baptist Historical Society, 1992).

[2] Paul S. Fiddes, *Tracks and Traces; Baptist Identity in Church and Theology* (Carlisle: Paternoster, 2003), pp. 157-192.

the dominant thinking, perhaps, as Fiddes points out, in reaction to the Oxford Movement, and the fear of the priestcraft that it was held to embody.

The 'popular' version of Zwingli's theology that has fed deep into our tradition is that, in the bread and wine, we are offered signs and reminders of the body and blood of Jesus on the cross. So, for example, in *Radical Believers*, we get the following formulation;

> Baptists have always viewed the Lord's Supper as a memorial meal, and based their interpretation son the words of Jesus 'Do this in remembrance of me'….In eating the bread and drinking the wine, we remember Jesus and in particular remember him in relation to his death … The Lord's Supper however, cannot be a *mere* memorial meal, not least because the Saviour who died is also the Lord who rose. As we remember Jesus we become aware of his presence with us even now. … 'We feed on Jesus by faith' (Jn 6:56-57) is a biblical metaphor expressing the fellowship which Christians have with their Lord. Although Christ does not come nearer to us in the bread and wine, we through eating bread and drinking wine may come nearer to him. Luke tells us that the couple of the Emmaus Road recognised Jesus in the breaking of bread (Lk 24:30-31)
>
> That experience has been repeated in the lives of many Christians since. For what is true of worship in general is true of the Lord's Supper in particular; as we 'draw near to God' (Heb 10:22) we discover ourselves caught up into heaven itself and join with the great multitude around the throne.[3]

The discussion then goes on to cover issues of 'the foretaste of heaven' and 'community', each of which have been deeply important in our history. But the issue I want to engage with here is that our experience so often so far outstrips our theology. 'We become aware of his presence with us even now' and 'we may become nearer to him' are all ways of trying to say something more than our dominant mode of memorialism will easily let us articulate. I suggest that in our current formulations of the Zwinglian aspects of our tradition we have allowed ourselves only meagre rations; in discussing the Table as a place of remembering, we have missed something of the richness of the meal offered here, and as a result, our imaginations and our responses are starved of nourishment.

Although Beasley-Murray is very clear that this theology of memorialism is rich and full, it is not always expressed or experienced that way. And in those who talk to us about our theology, contrasting it with other more 'sacramental' understandings, it can even be phrased as 'mere

---

[3] Paul Beasley-Murray, *Radical Believers: The Baptist Way of Being the Church* (Didcot: BUGB, 2nd edition, 2006), p. 31.

memorialism', suggesting that it has little depth. Even when we are trying to explore richness in the context of memory, we appear constantly to run the risk of making memorialism something diminished; almost of accepting 'mere memorialism' as a sufficient description of what we do. The minimising of what we do in sharing bread and wine – which I am characterising in this discussion by the term 'mere memorialism' or 'just remembering' – lowers our expectations unhelpfully and unhealthily.

If we focus too much on 'simply remembering' we run the risk that all we do is call to mind – and only to mind, not to will or imagination – a small part of the gospel story. We locate what is happening entirely in what has happened, focusing entirely on what took place however many thousand years ago on a hill a long way off, among people we only know through hearsay, and actually on an account that is – if we are going to place our focus there – historically contested.

Even more significantly, we disconnect what we are doing in eating and drinking from the life of our community, by focusing on our individual 'remembering', 'calling to mind' and we fail to explore and develop the connections between what we do in the eating and drinking and our life in the variety of our contexts. Thus, a minimal version of this memorialist theology can bring us to the point at which sharing bread and wine has little or no content, and indeed is more or less abandoned. Offered only the meagre rations of a 'mere' theology, we are not fed for life and are left hungering for something we may not even have been given the words to name. And even if it is not abandoned in practice, it is in danger of becoming something we do because Jesus told us to, without any more reason than that. Clearly, this is the reason par excellence, but when it is simply that we do this to obey, not because in obeying, we are led deeper into faith and life, then the mechanistic aspects that dominate demonstrate the same worst excesses of the *ex opere operato*[4] theology that we – and those who espouse such a theology – profoundly want to reject.

My other concern with 'mere memorialism' is its overwhelming subjectivity. Again, a significant part of our witness has been that grace draws a response from us, and that that response is a valid and significant part of the life of discipleship. Much of our understanding of sacrament draws deeply on the importance of response, and the significance of its place in encountering grace. Our whole theology of baptism depends on the conviction that in baptism we both express faith and encounter grace. In the same way, our theology of Eucharist at least implicitly, and often explicitly states that any encounter with Christ that happens draws on – and perhaps depends on – *our* remembering, *our* faith, *our* activity.

---

[4] Literally, 'by the work performed'; that is, that grace is conferred through the sacramental action regardless of the virtue or faith of either priest or recipient. The sacrament, in itself, confers grace, it is not a sign of grace conferred.

While it is deeply – and I believe rightly – embedded in our tradition that our response is important and is part of the way that God works in us, the over-emphasising of it, that I suggest can develop from a theology of 'mere memorialism', can lead us into unhealthy places. What about the days when I am – for reasons of, for example, grief, or weariness, or depression, unable to 'generate' any response other than a commitment to be present. What happens when through illness, I am unable to 'remember' as I did, for example, if I suffer from dementia? What happens when, in times of deep confusion, I find it hard to 'remember' with any conviction of personal connection? In any of these – or the many other scenarios when my humanity and brokenness means that I am not approaching the table in a state of mind and heart that I might at my best aspire to – do I have to resign myself to the reality that I will not meet with Christ?

Clearly, experientially, I do not. Many of us know with gratitude those occasions when, coming to receive bread and wine without any conviction of our *own* 'real presence', yet still we know we have been met by a real presence which is not us. A minimal memorialist theology does not easily account for such experience – and therefore, I suggest, is open to revision and challenge. We may find, in exploring the direction in which Zwingli's reflection on language points us, a capacity to speak with more power on what we experience to be true but all too often and too easily minimise in our theologising.

The need to find other formulations and ways of discussing what we are doing has opened up other theological approaches to us. This has been not only from the recognition that we belong to wider community and there is therefore a broader tradition of understanding of Table theology open to us, but also through the uncovering of another tradition within our history. With the publication of such discussions as *Baptist Sacramentalism and Baptist Sacramentalism 2*,[5] and John Colwell's work *Promise and Presence*[6] there have been attempts to offer contemporary Baptists an alternative, or perhaps a corrective to what has been portrayed as 'memorialism', supposedly derived from the Zwinglian tradition, and which can be so limiting of our language in relation to our experience.

That such an approach is not uncontested is demonstrated in the publication of such books as *Baptist Sacramentalism: a Warning to British*

---

[5] Anthony R. Cross and Philip E. Thompson (eds), *Baptist Sacramentalism* (Carlisle: Paternoster, 2003) and *Baptist Sacramentalism 2*, (Carlisle: Paternoster, 2008).

[6] John Colwell, *Promise and Presence; An Exploration of Sacramental Theology* (Eugene, OR: Wipf and Stock, 2011).

Baptists.[7] It is however, a demonstrable part of our tradition. But it is also true to say that it is not the dominant part certainly of our current tradition.

Therefore, I want in this paper to engage with Zwingli's theology in a way that I hope will open up some of the richness, the 'fatness' available to us from it, in order to offer a way towards a more robust, a more nourishing theology of the Table alongside others that people have been exploring. In the spirit of my glorious memory of listening to a discussion of poetry, and its capacity to take us beyond because of the power of its language, I suggest that we might work with Zwingli as he works with language and discover here more food for the journey.

Zwingli in Historical Context

Zwingli was writing in a very particular context. He was arguing with a dominant worldview which understood the bread and wine of the mass to be – or rather, to become, through the words of the institution uttered by the priest – truly the body and blood of the crucified Lord. Thus, the sacrifice of Calvary was re-presented on the altar, each time the mass was celebrated. Such a theology depended on the Aristotelian philosophy of substance and accident; that the substance was the true being, and the accident the formal presence in the physical world of any 'thing', and that in the miracle of transubstantiation, the substance, the true being of the bread and wine are miraculously transformed into the true being of Christ's body and blood, while the accident, the experienced presence in the physical world, remained bread and wine.

Against the prevailing traditional view, Zwingli argued in three ways. He argued theologically. He argued that any theology that suggested – or stated – that what was done at the altar in any way repeated what happened at Calvary was a theology that undermined the once and for allness of the sacrifice on the Cross. This conviction, shared with the majority of the Reformers is one of the deepest divides between reform and the older tradition.[8]

---

[7] David H. J. Gay, *Baptist Sacramentalism; A Warning to British Baptists* (Biggleswade: Brachus, 2011).

[8] See for example, the eighteenth article of *The Exposition of the Sixty-seven Articles by Huldrych Zwingli* in trans. H. Wayne Pipkin and Edward J. Furcha, *Huldrych Zwingli Writings, Vol 1* (Pennsylvania: Pittsburgh Theological Monographs, Pickwick Publications, 1984), p. 92: 'That Christ who offered himself up once as a sacrifice is a perpetual and valid payment for the sin of all believers … Thirdly [the Article] affirms that his death is a perfect sacrifice; that he, having been sacrificed once, cleanses all sin for all eternity and that it need not be repeated like the sacrifice of the priests who preceded him.'

He argued philosophically. He argued that because Christ's body is human, and because a human body has a certain kind of physical reality, it cannot be present both at the right hand of the Father, as stated in Scripture, and on the altar in the mass. In this, he was working as a good humanist, engaging the new philosophy that challenged the previous assumptions. The move away from an Aristotelian world view, and indeed the very beginnings of the early modern disposition towards what eventually becomes known as 'the scientific method' is evident here in his approach. And again, though he pursues it with a particular vigour, he is not distinctive in this.[9]

He also argued philologically. It is not possible to read any great distance in his Eucharistic writings without becoming aware that he roots his argument not only, and perhaps not even mainly in philosophy or theology, but in the words and in the way that the words are used[10]. He argued that, when the words that Jesus spoke at the Last Supper were properly understood, there was no suggestion of transubstantiation or real presence, but that the emphasis fell on remembering. This is where his distinctiveness is most evident, and it is where, I suggest, if we read him carefully and follow the trajectory he indicated, we can find the more robust theology I am arguing for.

To work with language was central to Zwingli's theological approach. He was a theologian within the sixteenth century humanist tradition, which took language and the careful use of language seriously. And it is clear from his own writings that this was central to him. In one of his major works on Eucharistic theology, *Letter to Mathew Abler Concerning the Lord's Supper,* in 1524, he writes a long passage on the meaning and on the gender of the Greek words in the gospel account of the Last Supper, and climaxes with this:

> I think the hinge of the matter is to be found in a very short syllable, namely in the word 'is', the meaning of which is not always given by 'is' but sometimes by 'signifies'.

After a series of examples, he continues

---

[9] Among other places, he tackles this in his challenge to Luther, in *Friendly Exegesis, that is, Exposition of the Matter of the Eucharist to Martin Luther* in Pipkin and Furcha, *Huldrych Zwingli Writings, Vol 2*, p. 312: 'You tell us also that one and the same voice can be heard by many people, etc, and that all the more can Christ do the same thing with his body, which is the same body, namely in all bread which is eaten in the supper. An again you bring forward a dissimilarity. You have not yet shown that anybody has ever been in various places at once, and all the things you bring our as similarities are really opposites'.

[10] Pipkin and Furcha, *Huldrych Zwingli Writings, Vol 2*, pp.127ff.

> Christ says I am the vine, and yet he is not a vine, but showed the character of a vine. It is therefore evident that this word 'am' cannot be taken for 'being' at all, but for 'I signify' or 'I represent' so that the meaning is I signify or represent the vine or show its character.

With more examples of this meaning of 'is' he then comes to the Matthean account of the Last Supper.

> Now to take up Christ's words in Matt 22:26 'Jesus took bread etc saying 'take, eat, this is my body which is given for you' Put signifies for 'is' here and you have 'Take, eat, for this which I bid you do will signify to you or remind you of my body which presently is to be given for you' for he adds immediately 'This do in remembrance of me'.[11]

Over and over again, in his drive to discover and explain a new theology of the Eucharist, Zwingli follows this pattern with a close reading and careful analysis of the words used and what they signify.

Reading him carefully we become aware of two things. Firstly that he is indeed exploring a new theology, and secondly that language and signification are central to what he is doing. While this might make an interesting historical corrective to those who suggest that Zwingli taught a theology of 'mere' sign, the significance of the discussion is in how that might deepen our theology of the table and give us more nourishment.

Combining Zwingli and Sign Theory

My way in is to consider his use of language in general, and his concept of signify and sign in particular. Zwingli is not a contemporary specialist in linguistics, but in these terms, and in the way he engages with the complexities of language and its use, he does offer us a linguistic way of approaching how we do this thinking.

The term 'sign' is central to contemporary linguistic analysis and exploration. This originates in the writings of Ferdinand de Saussure[12], and has been developed in several ways, especially in the work of Peirce.[13] We do not need to go too deeply into the intricacies of these theories for this

---

[11] Pipkin and Furcha, *Huldrych Zwingli Writings, Vol 2*, p. 138-9.

[12] See, for example, Ferdinand de Saussure, *Course in General Linguistics*, trans. Wade Baskin, eds. Perry Meisel and Huan Saussey, (New York: Columbia University Press, 2011).

[13] Thomas Short, *Peirce's Theory of Signs*, (Cambridge: Cambridge University Press, 2007).

discussion. Sign theory is the consideration of how signifiers (for example words, but not only words) convey meaning, the signification. The discussion of how signs work, and how meaning is communicated is detailed and indeed contested. But there are three common features through most theories.

Firstly, a sign operates by pointing to that which is beyond itself, and in a referential way making it present. The sign, as it were, stands in for what is absent and indicated. In this way, it mediates that which is to be communicated. The sign only has content insofar as there is something for it to signify, and that that something is not present. The sign points to and in that sense mediates what is not there to the receiver. So, to take a trivial and obvious example, a road sign directing me somewhere only operates as a sign when the place I want to go is not the signpost itself, and does exist. If I am already there, I do not need the signpost. The signpost links me to the place I am trying to reach by representing it to me, making it present to me in this particular way.

Secondly, for a sign to be effective – that is, for meaning to be communicated – there must be a transmitter with intentionality to communicate and a receiver with willingness to receive, who share a system. Returning to our road sign, it is only an effective sign of direction if that is in the intention of the person who puts it up. And it only works if I look at it and pay attention to what is going on.

And thirdly, the signs themselves are arbitrary; that is, they convey meaning only within the system, not by something inherent in themselves. The road sign is, in itself, paint on metal. There is nothing in the paint or the metal that can tell me where to go. It only works because I know how to decode it, and have an understanding of the roads and how the sign relates to them.

I suggest that using these basics of sign theory as a way of interpreting what we are doing at communion, in line with Zwingli's trail, we will open up further theology that will nurture us.

Zwingli was writing for his context, a context of a deeply sacralised world view, in which the presence of God was not, on the whole, doubted. The discussion and indeed argument was to do with how and where this presence was to be discerned. He was also writing in a context in which a well-boundaried community shared a common narrative that shaped not only their thinking, but also their practice. It was a changing situation – hence the need for a new theology. Simply the change in philosophy had necessitated a change in theological approach.

And our world view is different again. The dominating worldview within which and against which we write does not locate the divine in bread and wine – or indeed, in almost anything. Our world, far from representing or even mediating the divine to us is, rather, deeply de-sacralised. Most of us, most of the time, do not expect to meet God. In deep contrast to Zwingli's context, far from locating, and perhaps dangerously limiting Christ's presence to bread and wine consecrated by a priest duly ordained within the hierarchy, we operate in a context in which for the majority of those we live among meeting Christ is not on the agenda, in bread and wine, or in any other way. And we are not immune to such assumptions.

And, far from living with the experience that Zwingli could assume, of a coherent community, bound together by shared story and ritual and boundaried by the sacramental practices, we live in a highly fragmented society, with competing stories, a lack of common rituals and a profound mistrust of boundaries. Within that we are also aware of a deep longing for belonging in meaningful ways, a seeking for relationship and a need to create moments of connection. Alongside this is also the mistrust of authority and an almost unquestioned assumption of autonomy and self-generation. Thus, though Zwingli's insights may have brought us life and possibility, they also speak to and for a different world. To reappropriate them, and find new possibility in them is a proper challenge for us to accept.

In his discussions of bread, wine and what is going on at the Table, he makes great play of trying to understand the meaning of the words and the way they are used. Indeed, he actually plays with the term 'signify' at one point, in a discussion about the nature of sacrament, in which he is disputing the traditional use of 'sacrament' and insisting that its original meaning is not what is currently implied.[14] More to the point, he spends much of his energy in discussion in exploring what words mean in this particular usage, and the complexities of language. This is particularly obvious in his writing to Luther, *A Friendly Exegesis*, in which, he ends up by arguing that language as a whole is primarily non-representational.

He is not a Saussurean or any other kind of linguist, but he does reflect on questions that also inform sign-theory and semiotics. Thus, it is an appropriate interplay of ideas to bring the one to bear on the other in our quest to speak theologically in our situation. The sign points beyond itself and re-presents something that is not present. In a desacralised world, the sign of bread and wine points us towards something beyond ourselves. That there is more than that which we see and touch (and measure), a position which is insisted on by 'sign' , can open up for us a much more robust understanding of presence and encounter than the minimal one indicated by 'this helps me to remember'. If the bread and wine are signs, then they are signs of something – something that is beyond us, outside us, and not dependent on our conceptualising or understanding.

---

[14] Continuing the discussion on Article 18, Pipkin and Furcha, *Huldrych Zwingli Writings, Vol 1*, p. 99: If then the body and blood of Christ is a sign of a holy thing, I should really like to know what it signifies and if it only signifies, how can it be a sacrifice?

Zwingli rejected the idea of transubstantiation because he insisted that the body of Christ could not both be present at the right hand of the Father *and* on all the altars in the world. In Fiddes' chapter The Church as Eucharistic Community, he engages with this understanding and points out its weaknesses. But even with these weaknesses, there is something significant here. For the Christ who is present in heaven and therefore not on the altar is the Risen and Ascended One; that is – the Christ to whom the signs point is not the dead and gone crucified One, but our Living Lord. Thinking this way about bread and wine as signs gives some content, for example, to the phrase 'we become aware of his presence'. We are aware of it because it is pointed out to us, and mediated to us by the sign. And what we are aware of is not our memory (or fantasy) of the cross on the hill outside Jerusalem, but the living presence of the Resurrected One. At the heart of a sign understanding of Eucharist is not death, or rather, not only death, but death and resurrection as the whole work of God in Christ.

Similarly, if we consider the second aspect, the intentionality of sign, then we also find a fruitful area for reflection. Signs operate because the one enacting the sign intends to communicate, and the one receiving the sign has the capacity to interpret it within the agreed system. The communication in the bread and wine, if we are exploring it within this framework, is not that which we generate by our attention or our calling to mind, or even our faith. It is that which is intended by the signer – God the Father – and conveyed through the action of the Spirit. Such a framework of understanding does not become entirely objective (a complaint that can be levelled against a more 'sacramental' approach) since a sign does not complete its communication without the intention on the part of the receiver to receive and understand. There is a place, a role for our faithful response and 'reception' of what is given. In our reception, we encounter the Risen Christ – not because he is present *in* the bread and wine, but because they are for us the sign of his Living reality. But the intentionality of communication remains with God.

And so, again, our theology of the Table is rescued from too much dependence on what 'I' can make happen through my faithfulness or remembering, while at the same time not committing us to a priestly-led theology which depends on a hierarchical understanding that is untrue to our ecclesiology. An understanding of communion as that in which God communicates is hardly revolutionary – but it has been an aspect of the theology of what is happening when we share bread and wine which we have had a tendency to minimise or lose sight of, perhaps only paying lip-service to it. By taking seriously 'sign' as a model for talking about this, we have space for the intentionality of God, *and* for the place of our own faith and response. And more than that, we ensure that our theology of what is going on is truly Trinitarian. God the Father is communicating with us. What is communicated is the encounter with the Risen Christ. And we encounter this through the Spirit-given capacity to receive and 'understand.' John V.

Taylor's theology of the Go-Between God[15] gives us a language for understanding the Spirit's role in allowing us to receive and 'decode' the signs of bread and wine (along with all the other ways that God communicates with us.) Thus, approached in this way, we move beyond 'I remember – and perhaps encounter – Jesus' into an encounter with the Trinity, both given to us and evoked within us. To ground our Eucharistic theology in Trinity, rather than in 'remembering Jesus' is to allow its richness and depth to draw us ever deeper into the ongoing life and love of God.

It also links our theology of Eucharist more firmly to our theology of baptism. In baptism we can see that the grace of the Father in bringing us to new life, the call to follow Jesus as disciples and the work of the Spirit in our ongoing sanctification means that a thorough theology of baptism is deeply Trinitarian. Even more than that, in our incorporation into the Body which is the church, we are drawn into the community life of God, the love that is given and received and thus constitutes the Trinity – the kind of theology that Fiddes explores in *Participating in God*[16]. By identifying a Trinitarian reality in our Eucharistic theology as well, we can uncover and develop the link between baptism and Eucharist.

We also challenge the isolationism that is one of the dominant characteristics of our contemporary context. A Trinitarian theology of Eucharist immediately moves us from individualism into relationship as the dominant pattern of understanding what we are doing. And a sign reading of our practice can take this further. In a world in which individualism and the consequent isolation is the dominant experience, and indeed expectation, the arbitrariness of the signifiers can in fact be a community building practice. Arbitrary signs carry meaning because of an agreed system. The system must be shared for the signs to be powerful. To be involved in such a system one must know it – which is a linguistic way of restating the theological truth that we tell and retell the story of the faith to build community as we share its meaning and its practice. That the bread and wine mean nothing on their own insists that we explore the story together and so build community and draw closer to one another, thus creating the challenge to autonomy that is central to being church.[17]

This in turn becomes a challenge in various ways; to our willingness to explore the complexity of 'the system' – the gospel story and its call on our life and character, our capacity to communicate that to others, both those within the faith (in some form of catechumenate perhaps – we cannot

---

[15] John V. Taylor, *The Go-Between God* (London: SCM Press, 1972).

[16] Paul S. Fiddes, *Participating in God: A Pastoral Doctrine of the Trinity* (London: DLT, 2000).

[17] For a fuller and more developed exploration of this aspect, see 'The Church as Eucharistic Community' in Fiddes, *Tracks and Traces*, esp. pp.169-170.

assume that the system of meaning which makes sense of bread and wine is clear and understood) and in mission. Wesley's description of a converting ordinance is a powerful recognition of the communicative potential of bread, wine, words and action. Reading Eucharistic practice through Zwingli's theology textured by sign theory gives us, I suggest as creative and fruitful a way of engaging the worldview of our context as Zwingli developed for his in the sixteenth century.

I started this paper with a memory – a memory of an encounter which in itself was transformative, and which drew me into an awareness of words and their capacity to take us beyond ourselves. This essay is an attempt to reflect on linguistics, the poetry of communion and the reality of an encounter beyond words but enabled by such signs It is offered as a tribute to one whose creative thinking and attentive use of words has opened up these possibilities for many of us.

Zwingli was not a proto-sign theorist, nor a forerunner of de Saussure. He was a theologian who worked earnestly in his own time and context, taking seriously the philosophical questions of the world-view that dominated and bringing them to bear on Scripture, and Scripture to bear on them, in the life of the community open to the leading of the Spirit. As such, he offers us not a once-for-all meaning of our practice at the table, but tools which, far from minimising what we are doing and sharing, open all sorts of possibilities in the growth of our faith and the development of faithful relationships across traditions. He took language seriously, as something to be reflected on and used faithfully, considered prayerfully and understood as a gift of God and a means to God. He engaged n controversy, and argued with vigour. He was resistant to anything that might be seen as sloppy or lazy thinking. He wrote with energy and conviction, for the benefit of the faithful. He was restless in the best sense, and he believed that seeking God, seeking truth and seeking clarity belonged together.

His intention always was to point those he wrote for towards the more that is God and the life in God. As such, to reflect on his thinking as we honour Paul Fiddes seems more than fitting.

6.

Still Blessing the Tie that Binds

Brian Haymes

In February 1986, at the invitation of the Yorkshire Baptist Ministers, I gave five lectures on Baptist Principles and Practice.[1] This was not my first venture into issues of Baptist Identity but I was eager to share with others concerns about the developing life of the denomination in the 1970s and 80s, not least in face of the increasingly wide diversity of beliefs, practices and loyalties among us. I welcomed that diversity then and now but it caused me to wonder about what actually held us together. That, for me, has always been a question of theological identity.

I was concerned about Baptist Identity for two reasons. One was the fact that from the first my ministry had been set in ecumenical contexts where the theological sense of my identity was challenged.[2] Were my theological reasons for being Baptist good enough? If they were good enough then they were worth developing and sharing with the whole church. The second is harder to pin down but related to the changes taking place among British Baptists which pressed the questions of identity because it was growing less clear just who we were and what held us together. In those years I felt the force of growing party spirits as never before. I was probably naïve in that regard, Baptists having had a long history of splits and separations. We began with divisions, Particular and General, and our on-going history has only accentuated that in the wide variety of Baptists groups throughout the world. Was that our identity, in fact? Some Baptists seemed cavalier about it all, others played up their party spirit determined to win, rejoicing in their distinctiveness from others who took the name Baptist. I found that, then and now, hard to understand theologically and painful emotionally. Surely the Church of Christ sharing the life of the Triune God was more than the odd alliance or union of discrete independent congregations as appeared at times to be the practice? This seemed to deny the claim that we were a fellowship

---

[1] At the request of those attending the Conference the lectures were published by the Yorkshire Baptist Association under the title *A Question of Identity: Reflections on Baptist Principles and Practice.*

[2] My first pastorate was in a notable ecumenical context with the most active exploration of local church unity I have ever known. At the time of the YBA lectures I was Principal of the Northern Baptist College, a member of the ecumenical Northern Federation for Training in Ministry as it was then known.

of believers.[3] What did we believe? And did that hold us together or was there something or Someone else that made us one? Was it only utilitarian and organizational factors that united the Union?

One of the Yorkshire Baptist Association lectures was entitled 'The Importance of Right Belief'. I referred to the early Baptist practice of drawing up Confessions, exercises by which they sought to explain themselves to themselves and others. There was an educational, devotional and ecclesial purpose behind these texts. They often claimed to show that Baptists were part of the great Christian Church, holding the faith of that one Church as they drew on other Protestant Confessions and the older Catholic Creeds. However, such Confessions were never offered as final and timeless statements of faith. They positively invited reflection and revision. They definitely did not have the status of Creeds although they set out to show that the Christian faith is what it is and not something else. In no sense were the Confessions equal to Scripture in their importance. The seventeenth century alone saw several such Confessions and it is obvious that it would have proved to be difficult if not impossible even then to create a solitary united work. There never was a golden age of Baptists sweetly agreeing in all things.

None the less, I suggested that the task of drawing up a Confession now might be an important thing for us to do. We were within a few years of the new millennium and this would be a good gift to bring from the past to the present rising generation. I acknowledged that such a Confession, if it could ever be drawn up, might be divisive, misused and even given too high a status. I was aware that there were those, from several sides, who came to theological disputes with an adversarial attitude, a bitterness of spirit which earlier generations spoke of as the *odium theologicum,* leaving a bad smell. I was also conscious that such work might turn congregations in on themselves, the church talking to the church, but I was seeking an active exploration of the Faith and a deepening of our life in Christ. Drawing up a Confession might help us do that.

The response to this suggestion was almost entirely negative. There was a fearfulness which asserted that such an activity would split the denomination by bringing to light divisions already there.[4] In practical pastoral terms those

---

[3] This recalls the significant book by E. A. Payne, *The Fellowship of Believers: Baptist Thought and Practice Yesterday and Today* (London: Carey Kingsgate Press, first published in 1944, enlarged edition in 1952).

[4] During the years of my ministry there have been several active groups all with their own agendas for reform, among which have been, for example, The Baptist Revival Fellowship; The Baptist Renewal Group; Mainstream, the politically most active group seeking to ensure key roles were filled with appropriate people. There were other forms of division as what came to be called post-denominationalism grew. Increasingly, any denominational loyalty came at least second place to a

anxious about my suggestion were probably right but my concern was only heightened by this question, is it really impossible for us to talk about the Faith together without falling out? Is this the one and only empirically verifiable matter of identity among Baptists? This remains for me a crucial question, more significant than those to do with the reorganization of structures to which we have given so much time and energy. Why do we divide and adopt a party spirit, becoming adversaries, determined to win? We cause one another pain in spite of the fact that we know that the faith we personally hold is a feature of our identity and that to have it questioned is more than suffering a moment of intellectual discomfort. Is it nervousness or over-confidence that leads us to give and receive wounds? Why do we so quickly forget, as H. H. Farmer put it, that there are forms of the Faith too confident to be true, lacking all modesty before God, any awareness of the unspeakable 'Godness' of God?[5] If we really cannot talk about the faith together and share the life of prayer and action with mutual trust and accountability, without competitively falling out, then is there not something embarrassing about our claims to be a gospel people proclaiming the good news of reconciliation? Have we lost all sense of mutual belonging and accountability before God? The question remains, where is the unity of the Union?

Let me be clear. I had never longed for some final statement of faith to which we must all sign up as Baptists, an approach that I would hardly acknowledge as Baptist at all! I recognize that plurality of conviction is always going to be a feature within the church of Christ. Indeed, I take this to be a sign of blessing before God who destroyed the work of those who would build one language and structure to dominate the world.[6] What I was asking for was the steady shared reflection on and restatement of the Faith among Baptists that would deepen our life together as part of the great coming church of Christ, so strengthening our shared sense of mission in God, our partnership in the Gospel, for the sake of the world.

One who did see some merit in the idea of a contemporary Confession was George Beasley-Murray. He knew first-hand the diversity of Baptist convictions, having taught in Europe and America. There and here he had experienced personal attacks on his views and integrity. He knew of the American Baptist Convention's Commission on Baptist Identity and its report (1987) which he described as 'stimulating' and a 'splendid attempt'.

---

personal choice among the growing groups of independent congregations on offer. Issues of leadership, ways of worship and music seemed to be particularly significant in making these individual choices. People looked for the church of *their* choice.

[5] H. H. Farmer, *The Healing Cross: Further Studies in the Christian Interpretation of Life* (London: Nisbet and Co. Ltd, 1938), p.vii.

[6] Gen 12:1-9.

He thought that making such a Confession was important for God's sake, for our sake, for the sake of other Christians and for the sake of the world. He argued:

> Every generation has to appropriate the gospel for its own day. The Spirit of the Lord is at hand to enable his people to do that very thing. The need is clearly present and so is the Lord. Then let us go to it. Let us look and listen and then communicate what we see and hear. In so doing, we may yet rise to bless the Church and the world with the vision of God.[7]

Such a plea for 'visionary theological thinking' warmed my heart but no attempt was made to discuss the proposal of a new Confession any further. As far as I was aware the whole idea had fallen flat and has remained so.[8]

However, I myself had come to a change of mind. With others, I reached the conclusion that 'it would be a retrograde step to initiate a new search for a Confession of Faith as a "covenant document"'.[9] Sharing an exercise that could quickly become 'wrangling over words' (1 Tim 2.14) is not the way to deepen the unity of our life in Christ and our effectiveness in discipleship together. However, two developments in particular I saw as important and hopeful.

One was the coming into being of a new department in the organization of the Union, the Faith and Unity Executive. There had been a significant series of committees working on ecumenical matters, writing reports on Baptist engagement with the ecumenical movement[10] and responding to *Baptism, Eucharist and Ministry.*[11] There had been a notable tradition in the Union of creative thoughtful reports on the doctrine of the church, issues of

---

[7] George Beasley-Murray, 'Confessing Baptist Identity' in David Slater (ed.), *A Perspective on Baptist Identity*, edited by David Slater (Mainstream, 1987), pp. 75-88.

[8] The only other comment on the idea came from John Colwell in his George Beasley-Murray lecture at the Assembly of 2008, published as 'Catholicity and Confessionalism: Responding to George Beasley-Murray on unity and distinctiveness' in *Baptist Quarterly* 43, Jan 2009, pp.4-23. Colwell expresses surprise at Beasley-Murray's interest in such a proposal.

[9] See Richard L. Kidd (ed.) *Something to Declare: A Study of the Declaration of Principle* (Oxford: Whitley Publications, 1996). It was the joint work of Paul Fiddes, Michael Quicke, Richard Kidd and Brian Haymes, all serving at that time as Principals of English Baptist Colleges.

[10] *Baptists and Unity* (London: BUGB, 1967).

[11] *Baptism, Eucharist and Ministry* (Geneva: World Council of Churches, 1982).

ministry and ordination and other matters[12]. Another working group focused on the Child and the Church[13] but here, organizationally, was a new initiative that recognized that regular reflection on the faith was important for the life of the Union. A key creative member of this Executive was Paul Fiddes who moderated the Doctrine and Worship Committee. Soon there appeared unashamedly theological papers for discussion by churches, Associations and Colleges.[14] These were and remain important contributions to Baptist thinking and identity. They received a mixed reception in Council, Colleges and Associations. Predictably a variety of theological views were taken but at least there was a theological discussion going on although the issues were seldom given the full attention they deserved. It cannot be claimed that local churches were drawn creatively into all this, a response reflecting the growing lack of interest in matters denominational to be found in some congregations and groups. As often is the case, the attitude and ability of the local Minister was decisive. The changing negative attitude to all things denominational was not easily to be overcome.[15]

The second development focused on the fact that, in the last thirty years, there have been groups of people seeking to understand Baptist ways of living theologically in the conviction that this is an essential part of the renewal we seek. This work has issued in several publications and conferences. At the centre of this, again, has been Paul Fiddes and the theological concept of covenant. I believe that these writings, while still not widely read in the denomination, are an immensely creative resource for those who know we must above all think seriously about God. One reason why I moved from the hope of a new confessional document to exploring more thoroughly this theme of covenant is that *covenant* in the Bible is

---

[12] Roger Hayden (ed.), *Baptist Union Documents 1948-1977* (London: Baptist Historical Society, 1980).

[13] All the time, of course, individual writers and small self-selecting groups were producing books on Baptist issues: Ernest Payne, George Beasley-Murray, Neville Clark, Alec Gilmore and many others. There were also 'service' books: *Orders and Prayers for Church Worship; Praise God; Patterns and Prayers for Christian Worship,* all published with the support of the Baptist Union. These, along with a series of hymn books from the Psalms and Hymns Trust were ways by which our shared life was preserved and enhanced.

[14] *Forms of Ministry among Baptists. Towards an Understanding of Spiritual Leadership* (Didcot: BUGB, 1994); *The Nature of the Assembly and the Council of the Baptist Union of Great Britain* (Didcot: BUGB, 1994); *Believing and Being Baptized. Baptism, so-called re-baptism and children in the church. A discussion document by the Doctrine and Worship Committee of the Baptist Union of Great Britain* (Didcot: BUGB,1996).

[15] In the most recent restructuring of the Union the Faith and Unity Executive has ceased to be.

fundamentally about relationships, a feature of the story and journey of salvation which cannot finally be fixed in any document.[16] Studying the theme of covenant and finding forms of life that reflected its depth and energy would be an important way by which we, as Baptists, might understand our vocation, our contribution to the ecumenical adventure in obedience to Christ, our unity in Union. Paul Fiddes' attention, with others, to this biblical theme of covenant set a trajectory which it is urgent for us to follow as a recovery and renewal of Baptist life.

Covenant is a rich theme in the Bible. Covenants are made by and with God, with nations and by nations, with individuals, with creation. Paul Fiddes suggests there are four threads of significance in the theme as used in early Baptist Confessions: the eternal covenant of Grace; transactions between persons of the Trinity; agreement God makes with his church; agreement undertaken and signed by church members.[17] There are, therefore, both vertical and horizontal aspects of covenant. What I particularly wish to underline is the biblical emphasis on *God's initiative* in making and keeping covenant. It is God in Trinity who calls and elects. It is the divine love that seeks, gathers and saves. Hence the origin in any local congregation of God's people lies not in human decisions but in the gracious call of God, the call to participate in nothing less than the life of God. This emphasis on the initiative of God is a feature of many early Confessions and is clearly stated in the Baptist Union Document *The Baptist Doctrine of the Church* (1948) where it affirms that 'churches are gathered by the will of Christ and live by the indwelling of his Spirit. They do not have their origin, primarily, in human resolution'[18].

The emphasis on *covenant* as the work of God is an important challenge to any suggestions of a human centred voluntary nature of the church, that is, the church as something we choose, form, grow, maintain and own. Of course, there is a necessary human response to the divine initiative but this also is theologically a work of the gracious God. Any diminishment of this good news of God can lead to congregations gathering around a favourite preacher or leader, or a particular expression of some doctrines, or the quality and kind of music or the undoubted joy of special human friendships. That these are important features of the contemporary church there can be little doubt as people seek the church of their choice. But if that is all then the church has ceased in an essential way to be the church, that company called of God, gathered in Christ, united in the Spirit, sharing the life of God.

---

[16] Paul Fiddes, *Tracts and Traces: Baptist Identity in Christ and Theology* (Milton Keynes: Paternoster Press, 2003), p. 9. This book is the single most significant work of Baptist theology to have appeared in at least the last four decades.

[17] Fiddes, *Tracks and Traces,* pp.25ff.

[18] Hayden (ed.), *Baptist Union Documents*, p.6.

The church in its local, regional, national, and universal expression is not, therefore, a voluntary society in the first and defining instance. It lives as it began under the call and rule of Christ, by the grace of God, in the power of the Spirit.

Contemporary British Baptists, children of their age and cultures, are nothing if not pragmatic. We have a wariness of 'theology' for we can fear that it is remote, academic, out of touch with the realities of life, not least in the church. That the pastor be first a theologian is not often the priority in the profiling of a sought-for leader, unless of course, that theology is prescribed and fixed, a formula to which the preacher must adhere. But theology as shared thought, speech, and action before God known in Jesus, is crucial to the life of the church. Without it, we may reduce our 'calling' to what works to fulfil an intention which meets our hopes and desires (mission?) but is not necessarily what God wants at all. Thus, I have always been anxious whenever pragmatism has shaped our structures, with no clear sense that they reflect our calling in God and for God. At the heart of this are matters of spiritual discernment, of trust, of what we believe is the good news of God. What our structures reveal is what we actually believe about God and the church. We are in need of a deeper unashamedly theological vision.

The kind of primary stance I wish to take is magnificently expressed in the recent Baptist World Alliance Report on Baptist-Catholic Conversations entitled *Baptists and Catholics Together: The Word of God in the Life of the Church.*[19] Its first decisive bold statement reads:

> The One God exists from eternity in a life of relationships, in a communion (*koinonia*) of three Persons, Father, Son and Holy Spirit. Jesus Christ, the eternal Son, is the Word of God as God's self-communication of self-giving love. Jesus Christ is thus God's self-revelation who draws us into communion with God's own triune life and into communion (*koinonia*) with each other. This means that the Word of God in the church in the fullest sense is Christ himself who rules as Lord in the grace and power of the Spirit.[20]

This beginning with God seeking partnership with humankind has practical implications, ones which challenge some common assumptions held by many present day congregations. Attention to the theme of covenant

---

[19] The full report is published in *American Baptists Quarterly* Volume XXXI Spring 2012, no. 1. Paul Fiddes was the Co-Chair of the Joint International Commission.

[20] *Baptist and Catholics Together: The Word of God in the Life of the Church*, paragraph 7, p. 34,

http://www.vatican.va/roman_curia/pontifical_councils/chrstuni/Bapstist%20alliance/rc_pc_chrstuni_doc_20101213_report-2006-2010_en.html.

helps us to discern more positive and wholesome features of our calling under the Lordship of Christ. I wish to use the rest of this essay to reflect further on this and some of the practical implications.

The God who encounters us in Scripture is God seeking partnership and unity. God calls humankind to share the divine purpose for all creation. Even in God's 'inner life', if we may so dare to put it, we find the relating of love and life which God calls us to share. The intensity of the divine desire is seen in the incarnation, the birthed humanity, death, resurrection and ascension of Jesus Christ. No one is ever compelled into that relationship, although it remains a given in promise. We are awakened to it by grace, by the work of the Spirit. Hence, we come to baptism not simply because we have decided for Jesus as if that individual decision is the ground of our salvation. We come because we are called. We have been sought and found. It is all of grace.

We are baptized into Christ, being dead, buried and alive in Him. We begin, by the Spirit, to share already the life of the resurrection of which the risen Christ is a foretaste. We are part of a new humanity, one not determined by issues of nationality, economics, colour or gender (Gal 3:28, Col 3:11), not even by theological partisanship (1 Cor 1:10-17). God's covenant, although initiated by God always has horizontal implication. We belong together because we share the life of God, in Christ, through Christ, by the power of the Spirit. Dividing walls of suspicion and hatred have been torn down in the cross of Christ, the image of the invisible God, the firstborn of all creation, the one in whom all things in heaven and on earth were created, the one who was before all things and in whom all things hold together, who is the head of the Church (Col 1:15 - 20).

In contrast, our contemporary western culture is predominantly individualistic, as if my personal choice and freedom (my right) is the fundamental reality of my life. Legal contracts, not trusting covenant relations, are the way we have come to live together. When such individualism marks the church then it is as if salvation is some private personal deal with Jesus (accepting Jesus as my Lord) and being a Christian is joining a church of my choice, should I so choose to join anything. Of course, believers' baptism affirms the essential personal response we are invited to make to the call of God but the calling and baptism is into the covenanted community of love in Christ, into the church of which Christ is head and Lord. If Christ is ever to dwell in our hearts through faith, if we are ever to know the love of Christ that surpasses knowledge, then it will only be with all the saints, those others in Christ. This is the burden of the apostolic prayer (Eph 3:14 -21). What would the Union be if this was the ground of our belonging and life? If we have difficulty in being one, then who or what are we putting in the place of Christ?

Those who think that baptism is so individual that it has no implications of shared life and accountability with others, no involvement of fellowship and practical membership are wrong. Allowing the persistent individualism of our culture to have such an effect on our common life in Church has had serious deleterious effects. It has weakened local congregations, not just numerically, but because, reflecting the consumer culture, it has allowed a distorted sense of being in Christ to prevail. It mirrors our contemporary attitudes but not the sense of being the called community of the New Testament. It is not Baptist.

Moreover, this covenant theme of shared understanding of life under the rule of Christ has further ecclesial implications. It is sometimes affirmed that Baptists hold to the autonomy of the local church. This is both gloriously right and hopelessly wrong. 'Autonomy' is self-government. Each independent congregation is autonomous. Is that really a primary way of describing the local congregation? Do we think of ourselves as a union of independent self-governing congregations?

This may be gloriously right when the emphasis is on a local congregation living under the rule of Christ, that is, when it is not self-governing! What else could it be if it were indeed the church? In this sense, Baptists have understood that each congregation has the responsibility and privilege to discern and obey that sovereign rule of Christ. No other congregation, organization, Bishop or Apostle can tell them what to do. In their covenanted life together they have the freedom from others given by Christ to seek and serve the will of Christ alone. That, however, requires a great depth of discernment, open-mindedness to the Spirit's guidance, a strong hold on the teaching of Scripture and that kind of modesty which is a mark of spiritual maturity. The good news is that to this community assembled in Christ's name, he is present and his rule can be sought, learned and obeyed.

However, all this goes hopelessly wrong when independent isolating congregationalism becomes a kind of principle to be defended. It shows itself in a refusal to listen to others, a selfishness of ownership, a loyalty to policies and parties other than Christ. The doctrine of the independence of the local congregation with regard to all others is a distortion. Those baptized in Christ are brothers and sisters, all over the world, which also means those living in the next street who, we say, 'belong to another fellowship'. Is Christ so divided? Do we really think Christ will say one thing to this congregation and something contradictory to another? Might not Christ be desiring to speak with us through these neighbours? If we are baptized into Christ, then this is the one Christ, head of the one church who meets us as and where we are, in many places, under many different conditions. We belong together because we belong to Christ. He makes us one, the tie that binds our hearts in Christian love. The loss of regional, associational and national life together is often bemoaned among Baptists these days.[21] Could this be because we fail to discern the fullness of Christ and in consequence our belonging in the one catholic and apostolic church? I have serious reservations about the assertion in the Declaration of Principle that 'each church has liberty, under the guidance of the Holy Spirit to interpret and administer His (Christ's) Laws'[22]. For that discernment we need the resources we do not often avail ourselves of, of wisdom and insight, of knowledge and tested discipleship. We need the Christ who meets us in one another, present and past. We are called to be mutually accountable to one another in Christ. If we had stronger theological convictions about our essentially shared life in Christ, and then worked at local, regional and national expressions of that life, we would draw nearer to being a more faithful part of the one catholic and apostolic church. The issue is not about forms of life that give for effectiveness according to our desires but in what ways we share together the calling of God, living as God's people, shaped not by our programme but by shared participation in the life of the triune God.

In this sense, issues of Baptist identity are but a small instance of the larger fundamental question about being the Church of Christ, the one covenanted communion of saints. I have often thought that a shared study through the denomination of the meaning and practice of baptism would be a means to our mutual renewal in Christ. This would cause us to reflect on those practices and habits which focussed on and expressed the great good news of the calling of God which is ours together, baptized into Christ. After all, the gospel *telos* is nothing less than the healing and sustaining of loving relationships in all creation in and through Christ and 'healed relationships of love participate in nothing less than the Trinitarian life of God, which Christians know as communion'.[23] What prevents us Baptists from practising that?

As I shared Baptist life from the 1950's onward I discovered that a well-known favourite hymn among Baptists was John Fawcett's 'Blest be the tie that binds our hearts in Christ love'[24]. It was sung at local church

---

[21] As are local Baptist Minister's meetings. The author can recall Dr Arthur Dakin say in 1961 that fellow Baptist ministers will forgive us almost anything except not non-attendance at the Fraternal. It was said in all seriousness.

[22] For the full Declaration of Principle see Kidd (ed.), *Something to Declare*, p. 10.

[23] Gerald W. Schlabach, *Unlearning Protestantism: Sustaining Christian Community in an Unstable Age* (Grand Rapids, Michigan: Brazos Press, 2010), p.158.

[24] The hymn, by John Fawcett (1740-1817) can be found in *Baptist Praise and Worship*, number 472. Paul Fiddes reflects on the hymn in *Baptists and the Communion of Saints. A Theology of Covenanted Disciples,* written with Richard Kidd and Brian Haymes (Waco, TX: Baylor University Press, 2014).

Anniversaries, District, Association and Baptist Union Assembly meetings and many an occasion of baptism. When eventually I was to attend Baptist World Alliance meetings in the 1990s I found that this was the international Baptist anthem, sung with passion and gratitude for our common life in Christ. But in the 1990s, as I was more of a travelling preacher and a President of the Union in the UK, I found this hymn was forgotten and out of favour. It was, of course, old, which condemned it immediately to some ears, and local music groups had never heard of it anyway. They suggested an alternative and so we sang 'Bind us together, Lord, with cords that cannot be broken'[25].

I have often reflected on this small particular change in our common life as British Baptists. Does it indicate anything significant? Did one generation know something that we have almost forgotten? There is a difference. One affirms a great conviction, celebrating the tie that binds as the gift of God. The other, for all its doctrinal verses, sounds more like a prayer. Are they two sides of one coin, affirming what God has done and then expressing our hope that God might do what we cannot do and give us what we find so hard to achieve? Is there a difference between the singular 'tie' and the plural 'cords'? Has something happened to Baptist identity such that once we sang in praise of the unity and fellowship we had received in God but now have lost such that we have to pray for a unity for which we can only long in the face of our many diverse expressions?

There are those Baptist historians and theologians who think that there has been a shift in emphasis. Philip Thompson is one who claims that '[t]he primary datum of Baptist theology in the twentieth century has been the human being'[26]. He detects a change in focus from God to humanity taking place during the eighteenth and early nineteenth centuries. It was a move:

> from a theocentrism which was concerned to preserve the twofold freedom of God (namely, the freedom from any sort of control and freedom for the use of the created order in the ongoing work of redemption) to an anthropocentrism which is concerned primarily to protect the rights and capacities of human beings[27].

He argues that in the early Baptist documents used for confessional or catechetical purposes the statements began with God's nature, not with humankind or the Scriptures as was the case in Reformed writings. I am not

---

[25] The hymn, by B. Gillman, can be found in *Baptist Praise and Worship*, number 471.

[26] Philip Thompson, 'Towards Baptist Ecclesiology in Pneumatological Perspective' (PhD Thesis, Emory University, Atlanta, GA, 1995) unpublished, p. 234.

[27] Thompson, 'Towards Baptist Ecclesiology', pp. 325-26.

enough of an historian of doctrine to judge the argument but he is not alone in suggesting a general change in emphasis in theology which comes with the Enlightenment into which evangelical church life has undoubtedly heavily bought. Such might explain the slippage from an emphasis on God's sovereignty to human concerns, such as freedom and rights. It might explain why the concerns of church survival and growth, issues of leadership and finance, in local, regional and national expressions of our common life, have taken precedence in our agendas over the good news of the kingdom of God, the *missio dei* in which the church is called to share.

I have come to the conclusion that a significant weakness of our denominational life in the last half century has been essentially theological. The forms of evangelicalism we have largely espoused, with their individualistic character, privileging subjective authority over communal forms, separating salvation from ethics, encouraging personal customized expressions of spirituality, these simply do not have the resources to construct a full living ecclesiology enabling us to be the Church. We have undergone various forms of organizational restructuring, various bandwagons have come and rolled away, but the heart of the problem has been in our limited understanding of our shared life in God. We have lost the strong ecclesiological convictions and practices that reflected our convictions about the Gospel of God in Trinity who calls and makes us one. Do we still bless the tie that binds our hearts in Christian love?

One theologian who has attempted more than most in these years to keep our emphasis on God and our shared life in God is Paul Fiddes. His wisdom, friendship and partnership in the gospel have meant more than I can say. His reaffirmation of the theology of covenant is full of discernment and insight. I offer this short essay as a gift of gratitude to Paul, Baptist Minister, learned Professor and faithful Confessor of the Faith.

7.

The Founding and Development of the Baptist World Alliance

John Briggs

Early Developments

Congregations in Association

Baptists as a congregational denomination srongly affirm the competence of the local congregation, duly assembled in accordance with principles deduced from Scripture, to be, under the guidance of the Holy Spirit, the whole church in that place, competent to appoint its own officers, to celebrate the sacraments, to exercise discipline of its members, and to determine its mission in the world; all this without any external interference, from the state, or any sacerdotal hierarchy, or from any superior church council or synod. Such basic considerations presented the present author with problems when he was invited to contribute an essay on 'The Synod of 1905' to a volume of essays descriptive of the Conciliar History of the Christian Church. Clearly, the idea of a 'world synod' was not a concept that Baptists encompass within their ecclesiology, for the travel of authority within Baptist life is in an upward, not a downward, direction: from the local upwards, from covenanted church members to covenanted congregation, freely joining in covenant with one another in district, regional, and national associations, not downwards from some international authority via national councils to local congregation.

However whilst Baptists have historically found it difficult to give a determining authority to any organisation other than the local church, their leading theologians, though not every local congregation, have always insisted that the competence of the local church has to be balanced by the duty of such local bodies to associate with others for purposes of fellowship, advice and support, mutual affirmation of the apostolic faith, and mission in the world. For example, E. A. Payne affirms:

> Associations, Synods, Unions and Assemblies of churches are not to be regarded as optional and secondary. They are the necessary expression of Christian fellowship, a necessary manifestation of the

> church visible. The local congregation is not truly a church if it lives an entirely separate life.[1]

Arguments then for other than local groupings have generally been developed by attempts to try and extend the principles of local church government to the larger unit, but with great caution, though from the earliest years General Baptists had a vision of the church which was wider than the local. Thus their Orthodox Creed, drawn up in 1678 and printed in the following year, affirmed of General Councils, consisting of the properly appointed representative of the churches that these same churches 'appearing there by their representatives, make but one church'[2]. Yet, when the Baptist Union was founded in Great Britain, it was initially a union of ministers and churches, with associations and colleges added later. Final authority remained located in the local church, the Union eschewing 'all manner of superiority and superintendence over the churches; or any authority or power to impose anything upon their faith and practice'[3]. However much the need to associate is stressed it remains that Unions, conventions and assemblies do not have the authority to impose their will upon the local congregation, rather they will offer advice, their only sanction being in the most serious of cases to separate from an offending congregation.

Such theological convictions explain why the foundation document of the Baptist World Alliance seems to say more about what the Alliance should *not* do that what it *ought* to do. Whilst later versions of its constitution were to fill out the minimal statement of purpose agreed in 1905, the authority of local churches, national unions, conventions, associations and mission boards remained protected.

Roots and Origins

When the first Congress of what was to become the Baptist World Alliance met in London in 1905, consciousness of the Baptist family as embracing world dimensions had been growing for at least a hundred years. Indeed, even in the seventeenth century there was a consciousness of the danger of a sectarianism which failed to acknowledge that other churches were also, in their own ways, serving the *missio dei*. The problem was how to relate and protect cherished convictions as to Baptist distinctives, whilst recognizing a wider Christendom. Thus, the General Baptist minister, Thomas Grantham,

---

[1] E. A. Payne, *The Fellowship of Believers [Enlarged Edition]* (London: Carey Kingsgate Press 1952), p. 31.

[2] W. L. Lumpkin and Bill J. Leonard, *Baptist Confessions of Faith [2nd Edition]* (Valley Forge, PA, 2011), p. 338.

[3] E. A. Payne, *The Baptist Union: A Short History* (London: Carey Kingsgate Press, 1958) p. 25.

as early as 1671, pleaded for a pan-Baptist Assembly: 'I could wish that all congregations of Christians of the world that are baptized according to the appointment of Christ would make one consistory at least sometimes to consider matters of difference among them.'[4]

From 1790 to 1802, John Rippon, pastor of the Carter Lane Church in Southwark, which would later be transformed into London's Metropolitan Tabernacle, edited *The Baptist Annual Register.* The periodical aimed at introducing Baptists to one another. Thus to details about the English associations, and news of the Welsh, Scottish and Irish churches, he added news of Baptist life in North America. 'An interchange of kind offices between the English and American Brethren, since the last war, has', Rippon argued, 'produced a pretty general wish on both sides [of] the Atlantic, of enjoying a more comprehensive knowledge of each others' circumstances,'[5] in order to stimulate mutual assistance and prayer. To this he appended '*A Catalogue of the Professors and Ministers among the Baptists within, and out of the United Netherlands for 1791,* to which he added details of churches in Prussia, Poland, Lithuania, Saxony, the Rhineland, Switzerland, France and Russia.[6] The difficulty for the historian is that none of these several hundred listed churches in continental Europe were Baptists; rather they were Mennonite congregations conceptualised by Rippon as part of a larger Baptistic cousinage. *The Baptist Annual Register* carried a dedication printed on an unnumbered page after the title page:

> to all the baptized ministers and people in America, England, Ireland, Scotland, Wales, the United Netherlands, France, Switzerland, Poland, Russia, Prussia and Elsewhere … in serious expectation that before many years elapse (in imitation of other wise men) a deputation from all these climes will meet probably in London to consult the ecclesiastical good to the whole.

More immediate to 1905 were developments in Britain and the USA. The success of the modern missionary movement had already developed significant Christian communities in Asia and the Caribbean with promising developments moving forwards in Africa, in which Baptists from autonomous churches in the Caribbean, alongside Baptists from Britain and America, were playing an important part, demonstrating that they were not just part of a mission field but were independent churches working out their

---

[4] Thomas Grantham, *Sigh for Peace*, [1671] pp. 132-3, cited by Clint Bass, *Thomas Grantham, (1633-92) and General Baptist Theology* (Oxford: Regent's Park College, 2013), p. 67.

[5] J. Rippon (ed.), *The Baptist Annual Register for 1790,* 1791, *Advertisement,* p. 4.

[6] Rippon, *Baptist Annual Register*, 1790-93, 1793 pp. 303-318.

own missionary responsibilities. Moreover large numbers of Baptists from both the United Kingdom and continental Europe had migrated to North America and the British dominions taking their churchmanship with them. In the late nineteenth-century developments in transportation, in the form of railways and steam ships, made it possible for great preachers to foster these expatriate communities by frequent preaching visits. Advances in mass literacy and printing technology encouraged not only the hearing but the reading of sermons and other religious literature right across the world with telegraph lines and submarine cables making possible virtually instant communications within the developed world.

In such a context international Christian organisations such as the worldwide YMCA, [1855], the International Lessons Committee of the World Sunday School Convention, [1874], Christian Endeavour, which became international in 1885, and the Student Volunteer Movement for Foreign Missions [1885], together with the emergence of several World Christian Communions, all bore witness to a willingness of churches to organise themselves on a global basis.[7]

In North America, starting in Brooklyn in 1882[8], a series of annual 'Baptist Congresses for the discussion of Current Questions' was organised. Any member of a Baptist Church could become a member of the congress with rights of addressing those assembled, but there were to be no resolutions, statements, or motions to vote upon, but significantly these congresses were supported by Baptists from both the northern and the southern states, together with leaders from black churches. Those involved in these meetings were averse to undertaking legislative functions and thus provided a body of opinion, it has been claimed, that favoured the loose structures with minimum ecclesiological commitment that characterised the BWA when it was founded in 1905.

In Britain, in January 1901 a subcommittee of the Baptist Union was appointed to consider what might be done 'to promote a closer union between the Baptists of the colonies and ourselves' in response to requests for such a mechanism from South Africa and Australasia. Thus Silas Mead in presenting a memorial from the seven Australasian unions, representing

---

[7] Ruth Rouse and Stephen C. Neill (eds), *A History of the Ecumenical Movement, Volume 1* 4th Edition, (Geneva: WCC, 1993), pp. 599ff, and 613ff. Baptists were in fact quite late in this process: the first Lambeth Conference was held in 1867, Presbyterians instituted a world body in 1875, the Methodists in 1881 and the Congregationalists in 1891; of the principal Christian World Communions only the Lutherans came after the Baptists in founding their world body in 1923.

[8] For the immediate antecedents of the BWA I am indebted to Craig A. Sherouse, 'The Formation of the Baptist World Alliance' in L. A. Cupit (ed.) *Baptist Faith and Witness: The Papers of the Study and Research Division of the Baptist World Alliance 1995-2000* (McLean, VA: BWA, 1999), pp. 150-168.

20,000 Baptists in Australia and New Zealand, avowed: 'We long for a closer intimacy between the parent Union at home and our Colonial Unions.' Thankful for the visits of such distinguished preachers as Alexander Maclaren and John Clifford, they expressed a desire for a continuing interchange of visitors.[9] The Council also acted on a request from Pastor Reuben Saillens of France that the Baptist Union liaise with the American Baptist Missionary Union to provide English-language preachers for the forthcoming Paris Exhibition.[10]

Given this background, the Baptist Union Assembly in 1901 resolved to introduce an 'Ecumenical Session' at its fall meetings in Edinburgh. At the time the term 'ecumenical' was being used in terms of international relations among Baptists rather than of dialogue with other Christian denominations. This task was undertaken in 'recognition of the oneness of the English-speaking Baptists and with a view to provide among them yet more of brotherly sympathy and mutual happiness.'[11] Baptists in the British colonies and the USA were invited to send delegates to this gathering of English-speaking brethren. However, continental Baptists heard of this initiative and expanded an 'English-speaking' occasion to one which also included themselves. As a result, seventeen people from the USA, Canada, Jamaica, Australia, South Africa, and five European countries, attended, and twelve of them were asked to give five-minute talks at the evening session in October outlining their home situations. Alexander Maclaren thanked them for their contributions in 'sharing like precious faith with ourselves'.[12] The *Baptist Magazine* opined: 'It is to be hoped that one result of this unique session will be to tighten the bonds which bind Baptists together in whatever part of the world they are found.'[13]

This process of networking demonstrated clearly how badly some sort of an umbrella organization was needed, an idea which was pressed by a number of American leaders, and in particular by Dr J. N. Prestridge who spent most of his career in Kentucky where he founded *The Baptist Argus* which urgently canvassed the idea of an international Baptist organisation. Not surprisingly, he spearheaded the North American contribution to the 1905 Congress. Returning to the USA he significantly changed the name of his paper to *The Baptist World.*[14]

---

[9] *BU Council Minutes* (January 1901), pp. 2-3.

[10] *BU Council Minutes* (April, 1900), p. 19.

[11] *Baptist Union Handbook* (1901).

[12] *Baptist Union Handbook* (1901).

[13] *The Baptist Magazine* (1901), p. 519.

[14] R. Pierard (ed.), *Baptists Together in Christ, 1905-2005,* (Falls Church, VA: Baptist World Alliance, 2005), p. 15.

Translating the Global Vision into Reality

For its part Britain provided both inspiration and organisation. The October 1904 Council of the Baptist Union of Great Britain and Ireland, meeting in Bristol, passed a resolution inviting representatives of the world-wide Baptist family to meet in London in the following July. Inspiration came from the revered figure of an aged Alexander Maclaren, world-famous preacher-expositor, who presided over the Congress. Organisation was headed up by J. H. Shakespeare, ably assisted by W. T. Whitley, the denomination's most energetic historian. Maclaren was described as possessing 'features, stern and ascetic, sometimes melting into tenderness, or irradiated with a playful kindliness'. By contrast Shakespeare described Clifford, who acted as vice chairman, as 'the hero of the world battle against priestly aggression, superstition and tyranny in every form'.[15]

Under Shakespeare's leadership, the mechanics of the Congress had been arranged by a UK preparatory committee of some sixty members, including eight women, and embracing the interests of both the union and the missionary society. By contrast the committee which was formed at the Congress to produce draft rules for a continuation body had 8 US members, 2 Canadians, 4 from the UK together with one from Australia and one from continental Europe. It included no women and had only one black member. Several women did, however, address the founding Congress including the redoubtable Nannie Helen Burroughs, a black leader, secretary of the Women's Auxiliary of the National Baptist Convention, who also spoke at an open-air gathering in Hyde Park. Mrs N. M. Waterbury, who had served as chairperson of the interdenominational committee for missionary co-operation in the USA, and several women serving as missionaries in Asia and Africa, called attention to the extensive work being undertaken by Baptist women in educational, evangelistic and medical work overseas.

Without any existing membership lists or indeed criteria for membership, or knowledge as to who, from amongst the great Baptist family, would attend the Congress, it was almost impossible to predict quite what the membership of the Congress would be. The Baptist family in the USA was already split into those within the regular tradition, a number of primitive groups, which resisted all attempts to extend the witness of the local church through the founding of religious societies to extend tract distribution, missionary endeavour, Sunday School activity etc., and those influenced by the landmark movement, which identified only those churches exhibiting Baptist polity and practice as genuinely Christian, and who therefore

---

[15] *BWA Congress,* (1905), pp. vi –vii.

eschewed any association with other than Baptist churches.[16] Such attitudes made it unlikely that such groups would have an interest in a body as widely embracing as the new Alliance promised to be, but positions were not as yet altogether defined. The BWA itself imposed no credal tests on membership: the preamble to the constitution simply referred to 'Churches of the Baptist Order and Faith', whilst the membership clause opened the possibility of membership to 'any general union, convention or association of Baptist Churches'[17].

The Congress of 1905

Discovering One Another

In the event 26 countries, from Finland in the north to New Zealand in the south, were represented in London in 1905. Of the 3,000 delegates attending, some 2,500 came from the four United Kingdom nations but are unlisted in the record.[18] Though the listings are incomplete, it seems that rather more than 300 delegates came from North America. In excess of 100 represented continental Europe, some 20 – mainly lay – came from Australasia, 14 from South Africa, 7 from the Caribbean and Central America, whilst China, India, Japan and Africa were for the most part represented by missionaries.[19]

---

[16] W. H. Brackney, *Historical Dictionary of the Baptists* (Lanham, MD: Scarecrow Press, 1999), pp. 248-50, 336-7.

[17] *BWA Congress* (1905), p. 241.

[18] The following nations responded to the Roll Call: Austria-Hungary, Denmark, Finland, France, Germany, Italy, Netherlands, Norway, Russia, Sweden, including the Orebro Mission, the United Kingdom, including the Unions of Ireland, Scotland, and Wales and with the Strict Baptist Mission also present, China, India, Japan, the Congo, South Africa, USA [with representatives from a number of state conventions and national organisations including the National Baptist Convention, Southern Baptist Convention, Regular Baptists - North, Lott-Carey Convention, some diaspora Scandinavian State Associations and certain German Baptist Churches/State Associations], Canada [including some German Baptist groups], Mexico, The West Indies, Australia, New Zealand, South America [Brazil]. The Franco-Belgian and the Franco-Swiss Associations were also present, and Jamaica and Puerto Rica were separately represented. There were also individual delegates present from Belgium, Bohemia, the Cameroons, Ceylon, the Congo, Costa Rica, Estonia, Grenada, Switzerland, and Trinidad. *BWA Congress* (1905), pp. xiv–xxviii, 4-18.

[19] *BWA Congress* (1905), p. 11 A delegate named Nlemyo, who by chance was in England helping W Holman Bentley with his OT translation, was able to

Americans came from both northern and southern states, and from the black conventions, whose representatives were agreeably surprised by the welcome they received in London by a population apparently colour-blind.[20] Considerable stress was placed on the strength of the denomination in the USA which was seen as an argument in favour of the separation of church and state and against the imposition of religious establishments. Other delegations, for example the Danish, paid tribute to the support received from British Baptists when they had been persecuted by the Danish state. Persecution was unfortunately still part of the European scene, not least as experienced by Baptists and other evangelical groups in Romania and in Russia[21].

John Clifford believed that Christ was being exalted in their proceedings: 'His place is supreme in the life of the individual, supreme in the life of the Christian Church, and supreme also and ultimately in the life of the world.' The witness of those present who had suffered for their faith was an eloquent testimony to 'soul liberty', language which signified that Christ was the 'one absolute Authority' in the religious life, with the believer 'free from everybody else'. If this were so then Clifford deduced that soul liberty was 'leading on to political liberty'.[22] Judge Willis, then President of the Baptist Union, declared the Congress to be 'a Pentecostal gathering' representing that same strength of numbers and diversity of race and language as was present at the first Pentecost.[23] The delegates were clearly very optimistic with regard to the impact of Baptist witness around the world: they were, by any calculation, a growing movement. Shakespeare described the assembled experience of all the delegates as 'an achievement of faith which must be added to the eleventh chapter of Hebrews'. Those gathered represented a family of some 6 million Baptists world-wide, though Shakespeare exaggerated in suggesting 'almost every land upon earth is represented by members of the Baptist community.' Adding Sunday School scholars, adherents and others who associated with the Baptist cause suggested a world-wide community strength of at least twenty million, forming 'the greatest Protestant evangelical communion on earth as we certainly are in the influence we have on Christian thought and activity.'[24] Lest anybody doubt that Baptists stood in the tradition of the historic orthodox Christian faith and of the Holy Catholic Church as something much larger than that

---

represent Congo. Similarly, the Revd M. C. Mason of Tura, an American missionary who spoke for India, was accompanied by an Indian boy; p. 10.

[20] *BWA Congress* (1905), p. 12.

[21] *BWA Congress* (1905), p 5. Pastor Ohrn of Norway also spoke of persecution and imprisonments in the past but the vitality of lay witness in the present. p 7.

[22] *BWA Congress* (1905), pp. 8-9.

[23] *BWA Congress* (1905), p. 2.

[24] *BWA Congress* (1905), p. 1.

which the Roman Catholic Church can claim for itself, all present were invited to affirm their faith by repeating the Apostles' Creed, line by line, as led by Maclaren.[25] Such an act, he suggested, would rid the world of considerable misunderstanding and quell a good deal of slander.

A Vehicle for Baptist Togetherness

The most significant act of the first Congress was to set up a vehicle to give permanent expression to world-wide Baptist fellowship, and so the Baptist World Alliance was born. It would not, it was emphasised, aspire to being a super-church: it was to be a forum for fellowship, an agency of compassion, a voice for liberty, an instrument for evangelism, and a channel of communication.[26] Shakespeare commented, 'We have travelled far when it has become possible to federate the great Baptist community for common purposes, and as a demonstration of the fact that there is now in existence, and to be reckoned with, a Baptist world consciousness.'[27] Little attention was given, it has to be admitted, to those members of the Baptist family, not inconsiderable in number, who did not wish to join such a body: the strength of the fellowship achieved across so many boundaries was much more significant.

Several speakers were invited to speak to that Baptist understanding of Christian faith that bound the members together. J. D. Freeman of Toronto, in giving the keynote address on 'The Place of Baptists in the Christian Church', argued 'The Baptist denomination is not an accident or an incident, nor an experiment; it is the normal development and permanent embodiment of a great Christian principle', which he defined as 'An acute and vivid consciousness of the sovereignty of Christ, accompanied by a steadfast determination to secure the complete and consistent recognition of His personal, direct and undelegated authority over the souls of men.' In this there could be no action by a proxy: 'There can be no sponsorial performance of religious obligations ... It is no more possible for one person to believe or disbelieve in another's behalf than to go to heaven or hell for him. There must be personal repentance, personal faith, personal confession of Christ's name.'[28] From such convictions, which laid the axe to all sacramentalism and all sacerdotalism, Baptists were represented as an 'Anti-ritualistic People'[29]. Salvation was not dependent upon any ceremony or any

---

[25] *BWA Congress* (1905), pp. 2-3, 20.

[26] W. B. Shurden, *The Life of the Baptists in the Life of the World: 80 years of the BWA* (Broadman Press, Nashville:1985), pp. 13ff.

[27] *BWA Congress* (1905), p. ix.

[28] *BWA Congress* (1905), p. 23.

[29] This was a theme to which Baptists made constant reference. See e.g. A. T. Robertson's address on 'The Spiritual Interpretation of the Ordinances' at

action of a priest, but rather came 'by the direct impact of the Christ-life upon the human soul.' The danger here was that in opposing the exaggerated role of priest and sacrament Baptists could too easily deny to themselves their proper use and benefit.

The logic of the separation of church and state was a natural deduction from Baptists' definition of themselves as 'Champions of Soul Liberty', by which Freeman meant, the right of any individual to 'exemption in matters of faith and conscience from all coercion or intimidation by any earthly authority whatsoever',[30] a principle to be universally applied with an altruistic interest in the religious freedom of all, whatever their creed. 'The world must not be permitted to forget what the Baptist doctrine of soul liberty, broadening into the conception of personal liberty and finding expression in the ordinances of civil liberty, has wrought for the political emancipation of mankind.'[31] From all this, he deduced Baptist advocacy of a 'Spiritual Church', that is a church defined by a 'regenerated church membership', which deliberately determined to exclude from its life and substance those who were not regenerate. Such a church under the authority of scripture had to be a missionary church committed to world evangelisation.[32] Freeman, who was not afraid to speak frequently of the sovereignty of God, was nevertheless quite ready to condemn that older view of sovereignty, which, he claimed, 'sterilised the Church', for 'Hyper Calvinism, running near to fatalism, had chilled evangelical enthusiasm. From such a theological obscurantism, with its sad consequence of religious quietism, Carey brought deliverance.'[33]

Mission to All

J. T Forbes of Glasgow, speaking of 'The Attitude of Baptists to the Working Classes', argued that since 'the only new humanity is twice-born', Baptists were right to focus on their spiritual work. But since love of God cannot be separated from love of our fellow men, other activities were also essential, and Baptists must not be over-partisan in what they prioritised in

---

Philadelphia in 1911. Sacramentalism, he argued, was 'the lazy man's religion.' 'The battle of Paul's life was just this. He preserved spiritual Christianity against the demands of the ceremonialists. He met terrific opposition as did Jesus, as did Stephen, and for the same reason. The intolerance of those who mistake the symbol for the reality is always bitter.' BWA Congress (1911), pp. 120-4.

[30] *BWA Congress* (1905), pp. 22-23.

[31] *BWA Congress* (1905), pp. 25-26.

[32] *BWA Congress* (1905), pp. 27-29. This relationship between the idea of Soul Liberty, not a term naturally deployed by British Baptists, and the Spiritual Church, Clifford reaffirmed at Philadelphia in 1911, *BWA Congress* (1911), p. 59.

[33] *BWA Congress* (1905), pp. 27-28.

this respect. 'Questions of education and disestablishment are of necessity political. But questions of land and housing, of the repatriation of the people on the deserted country, have as much to do with morals and religion as either of them; and they cannot be touched without touching politics'. The 'no politics' rule was not to be used selectively.[34] E. Y. Mullins of the Southern Baptist Convention was concerned to argue that whilst the gospel must not be confused with the demand for social change, equally the gospel must not be divorced from social reform.[35] Here he was directly addressing some of his fellow Baptists from the American South who argued that only preaching – not education or health care or relief work – was the missionary task of the church.

Mission in the Context of Other Faiths

In several respects this first Congress was quite adventurous, as for example in tackling the issues of world faiths, contemporary mission practice, and modern criticism. Richard Glover was given the challenging title, 'The inadequacy of Non Christian Religions to meet the needs of the World'. Boldly Glover introduced his theme by averring, 'the title of my subject must not be held to imply a belief on my part that the salvation of God is limited to those exclusively who know the Gospel story.' Affirming that it was not for the church to limit the Holy One of Israel, he contended that Abraham knew no more than many heathen when he became the father of the faithful'. He argued that God was not only the God of the Jews but of the heathen also, though compared with the noon-day light of the Gospel, the heathen only enjoyed a starlight experience. Accordingly the greatest need of the heathen world was the gospel, and the greatest duty of the Christian world to utter it. Only the religion of the Bible provided a worthy conception of God and spoke of a saviour accessible to all people.[36]

> It meets all the longings of our heart that God should save; and all the reverence of our reason that he should refuse to save cheaply; and all the instincts of our being that he should save us from the curse by sharing it – for sharing sorrow seems to be the one secret of securing it, both for God and man.[37]

The Revd Silas Mead from Australia objected to the language of 'the heathen', preferring to speak of missionary work amongst 'the Nations'; he pleaded for more respect for Asian religions: 'The religions of the

---

[34] *BWA Congress* (1905), pp. 265-6.

[35] *BWA Congress* (1905), p. 278.

[36] *BWA Congress* (1905), p. 65.

[37] *BWA Congress* (1905), pp. 65ff esp p. 67.

East, as they now stand before us translated into our English tongue, forbid our regarding these nationalities as non-intelligent, though mistaken in their religious ideas. Their literature commands the respect of our ablest scholars, however much we dissent from their teachings'. It was important that mission supporters should take every opportunity to inform themselves about other world faiths. Christ was able to overcome error for his own purposes:

> It is He who will abstract from Buddhism whatever of good there is in it; He will gather out of Mohammedanism what is just and true in its mass of teachings. It is He who will dissolve out of Confucianism what in that system is worthy. Yes, He will deduce from idolatry itself the principles of worship and sacrifice which he wrapped up in its contortions; He will deduce from all true science and philosophies and from all nature's forces what will contribute to make his kingdom come'.[38]

A similar emphasis can be seen in the counsels of J. G. Brown of Ontario's Foreign Mission Board, who argued that missionaries should seek to master the culture of those to whom they witnessed, 'gladly recognizing whatever truth their religion may contain, and making it the basis for the larger and fuller revelation which Christianity brings, by refraining from wounding their feelings by making mockery of their superstitions, by preaching Christ rather than denouncing heathenism'.[39]

A Challenge from China[40]

Timothy Richard, speaking from his experience in China, commended a strategy of holistic mission seeking to meet the needs of 'the whole man, body and soul', saving him 'from hell in this world as well as in the next' rather than pietistically focussing on salvation for the soul only, and that after death.[41] Richard commended a focus on general education challenging the whole nation on issues of religion and ethics, rather than concentrating on Sabbath instruction of a religious minority. Essential to such a strategy was the deployment of indigenous Christians rather than expatriate missionaries, as the main agents of direct evangelism. He believed that the

---

[38] S. Mead, 'Missionary Methods-Australian', *BWA Congress* (1905), esp. p. 86 and p. 92.

[39] J. G. Brown, ' Foreign Mission Methods – Canadian', *BWA Congress* (1905), pp. 92-8 esp. p. 93.

[40] T. Richard, 'The Awakening of China and the Duty of the Home Church', *BWA Congress* (1905), pp. 110-116.

[41] *BWA Congress* (1905), p. 114.

strategy should be unashamedly elitist. With a nod at Romans 13, mission executives should seek to win the support of 'God's appointed rulers', religious leaders, and those who had the most influential positions in education, including university vice-chancellors, a position he was shortly to grace himself.[42] Similarly, he advocated the exploitation of the indigenous press rather than the foreign pulpit. And for good measure he commended a search for universal peace rather than the ratcheting up of taxes to maintain competing standing armies. For his preferred strategies he claimed the blessing of the Spirit, whilst designating the methods he criticised, as those that have 'failed in the past'[43].

His final plea was for ecumenical action. The Baptists were relatively late in discovering one another as a world fellowship. Could not this be turned to advantage in seeking to move beyond denominational boundaries to united protestant action. 'Cannot this Baptist World Congress decide now to take an advanced step in this direction, and begin a federation of the six great denominations at work in China – Episcopalians, Methodists, Presbyterians, Congregationalists, Lutherans and Baptists – into one co-operating force as far as possible; for God will not judge us by our creeds so much as by our fruit.'[44] Unless this be done, then Confucianism, Buddhism, and Taoism will – notwithstanding divine elements in each – through ignorance continue to oppress the people of China. 'God calls for the establishment of the Kingdom of God in all the earth in this generation. Where are the volunteers?'[45] Certainly, not among those churches in North America who were already declaring themselves against the whole enterprise of seeking Christian unity.

Biblical Scholarship

If the members of the Congress did not shrink from reflecting on the peculiar problems presented in developing an appropriate missiology for the new century, they were also bold enough to examine a number of topics relating to the study of the Bible in the context of modern thought, including the approaches of higher criticism. Although the title for this session in the programme was conservatively expressed as 'Constructive Work in Biblical Study', in the report this became 'Biblical Criticism.'[46]. This subject Principal Marshall of Manchester College identified as having to do with issues of authorship [including the possibility of multiple authorship], the dating of the writing of texts, and the credibility of the record. Marshall

---

[42] *BWA Congress* (1905), p. 114.

[43] *BWA Congress* (1905), pp. 114-115.

[44] *BWA Congress* (1905), p. 115.

[45] *BWA Congress* (1905), p. 116.

[46] *BWA Congress* (1905), pp. xxxiii & 128.

concluded that by deploying the critical method, in company with relevant archaeological discoveries, for example, in an examination of the story of Abraham, positive affirmations could be made. 'What has been disclosed suffices abundantly to show that we are not dealing with romance, or myth, but with substantial historical traditions'.[47]

Milton Evans from Pennsylvania was equally confident that New Testament criticism served to move the reader away from the bare form of scripture and the familiar and hallowed language there to be found, to a real engagement with the search for truth and meaning.

> As modern historical inquiry more vividly presents to the imagination the truly human nature of the incarnate Word of God, without shaking confidence in his true Deity, so modern Higher and Lower Criticism make the written Word of God truly human literature, without destroying its inspirational character. Research has not destroyed a single fact upon which Christian faith rests; it has only destroyed the error of conjectures.[48]

Others were less positive in their responses to criticism. John Thomas of Liverpool challenged the criticism of the Pentateuch on its own critical canons[49]. Professor Robertson of Louisville indicated that the problem was not with the critical method itself so much as with the underlying sceptical philosophy that critics like F. C. Baur fed into their studies, which was every bit as prejudicial as the so called prejudices of believing scholars[50], a point taken up by A.H. Strong, who complained that all too many critics lacked the literary sense of being able to appreciate the presence and significance of the spiritual and the supernatural: criticism which was 'animated by the Spirit of Christ and recognises Christ's mastery' was of a wholly different order.[51]

The Intellectual Context of a New Century

E. Y. Mullins, in a clever, clear but demanding, presentation, on 'The Trend of Modern Thought' initially seemed to be categorising recent theology as a sinister drift away from traditional verities. But in the event, he is almost as critical of the traditional:

---

[47] J. T. Marshall, 'Modern Criticism of Old Testament History: the Life of Abraham', *BWA Congress* (1905), p. 132.

[48] Milton G. Evans, 'Modern Criticism in relation to the New Testament', *BWA Congress* (1905), p. 137.

[49] *BWA Congress* (1905), p. 139.

[50] *BWA Congress* (1905), p. 142.

[51] *BWA Congress* (1905), pp. 143-4.

> Much of the newer thought in theology is tentative and unauthoritative because it is simply a protest against the old … Much of the old is also inadequate because it ignores aspects of truth which are essential to a complete Scriptural representation … Both theologies are simplified too much.[52]

Both traditional and modern theology were in danger of being too cerebral. 'Theology, if it is to be adequate, must not be conceived so much as a scheme of thought as an interpretation of a scheme of life.'[53] Whilst critical of a criticism that was the tool of philosophical doubt, Mullins affirmed the positive role that criticism could play.

> Sober, sane and reverent criticism has rendered a mighty service in creating a sense of perspective in the progressive revelation of the Bible, in fostering the method of careful historical exegesis, and in other ways … No man is a true Baptist who is unwilling to accept all the light and truth which criticism may bring.[54]

That said, and admitting some past failings, Mullins seems, in the end, to be rather more sympathetic to the traditional than more recent work with his very clear criticisms of Maurice, Schleiermacher and Ritschl, amongst others, and the enunciation of a traditional view of the doctrine of the last things. In everything, a holy and loving God had to be sovereign over his creatures,[55] though he emphasised the need for doctrinal statements always to be informed by Christian experience. 'Positively stated the best theology of the future will continue to accept the authority of the Scriptures, but it will take as its starting-point, for the interpretation and illumination of scripture, the facts of Christian experience, not in a single aspect but in their totality.'[56] John Raws of Adelaide, Australia, a former colleague of Dr Maclaren, endorsed this emphasis, but took it to a much more extreme point by affirming that conduct rather than creed was seen to be the effective test of commitment, in an age when correct action was more important than correct belief.[57]

In summary, Mullins argued for six axioms which he offered the Congress as 'a statement of the basis at once for a new Baptist apologetic and a platform for universal adoption', which he believed to be 'the predestined goals of man's religious thinking'.

---

[52] E. Y. Mullins, 'The Theological Trend', *BWA Congress* (1905), p. 150.

[53] *BWA Congress* (1905), p. 150.

[54] *BWA Congress* (1905), p. 148.

[55] *BWA Congress* (1905), p. 425.

[56] *BWA Congress* (1905), p. 150.

[57] *BWA Congress* (1905), pp. 152-3.

1. The theological axiom: *The holy and loving God has a right to be sovereign.*
2. The religious axiom: *All men have an equal right to direct access to God.*
3. The ecclesiastical axiom: *All believers have equal privileges in the Church.*
4. The moral axiom: *To be responsible man must be free.*
5. The social axiom: *Love your neighbour as yourself.*
6. The religio-civic axiom: *A free Church in a free State.*[58]

To explore both biblical criticism and modern theology in the context of a 3,000 delegate Congress was far from easy, both from the point of view of the scale of the meeting, and the range of views of those present. But approached within the overall warm confidences of evangelical and evangelistic commitment, such subjects were tackled both without rancour or accusations of sacrilege. Not least was this seen in the nearly universal admiration of Clifford who in his own person combined openness to modern thought with commitment to personal evangelism. Such tolerance said something profound about the ties that bound the Baptist family together.

The Baptist World Alliance is Born

In this context, a new organisation uniting Baptists around the world was born, which inevitably raised the question as who might qualify as 'Baptist' and what common purpose they might undertake in global alliance. Whereas in the seventeenth century different parts of the Baptist family both in Great Britain and the United States of America had issued a series of Confessions, theologically well-argued and replete with full scriptural references, in which their beliefs and defining practices were made abundantly clear, no doctrinal standard was used to approve delegates to the 1905 Congress, or indeed incorporated as part of the subsequent setting up of the new world fellowship. Behind this may lie a difference of practice.

Whereas in Europe the model for trans-local associations of Baptist churches was developed as an extension of the polity of the local church, in America, as made abundantly clear by Professor William H. Brackney in his *Christian Voluntarism in Britain and North America: a bibliography and critical assessment*, the model was that of the voluntary society, as applied to Christian purposes. Philosophically this was encouraged by the definition of

---

[58] *BWA Congress* (1905), pp. 151-2. These ideas formed the basis for his book of the same title originally published n 1908, E. Y. Mullins, *The Axioms of Religion*, (Macon GA: Mercer, 2010).

the church given by John Locke in his *Letter Concerning Toleration,* first published in 1689, as 'a free society of men, joining together of their own accord for the public worship of God in such manner as they believe will be acceptable to the Deity for the salvation of their souls'[59] In the USA, then, whilst state conventions were readily established in the late eighteenth and early nineteenth centuries, when it came to national bodies the newer model of voluntary societies was, in the first half of the nineteenth century, preferred.[60] However the issue of slavery led to discord and conflict over the administration of the Home and Foreign Mission Societies, and in May 1845 the Southern Baptist Convention was founded, in which slave-holding was no bar to service. The new convention, in marked contrast to the previously existing practice, was an ecclesiastical body, with subsidiary boards established for different functions, but always answerable to the governing body of the convention. Whilst after 1845 the societal model was eschewed in the South, Baptist churches in the northern states continued to deploy a range of societies to express their national ambitions until two years after the founding of the Alliance. The Alliance was accordingly born at a time when the Baptist family was still debating the societal and the ecclesiastical ways of organising trans-local relationships.

Representation to the London Congress was secured from the leading Baptist Unions and Conventions in the United Kingdom, Europe, North America, the British Dominions and the churches or mission fields which their missionary societies had established. This process seems to have produced appropriate representation of the mainline denominational groupings, but, in practice, to have excluded those more fundamentalist groups who were often in principle opposed to all trans-local organisation anyhow, which is to indicate that *de facto* they excluded themselves. Accordingly, issues of definition seem to have been tackled in a relaxed manner without prescribing required doctrinal subscription.

Some consideration ought here to be given to why the language of 'Alliance' was used in the title of the Baptists' world body. When that language was adopted, was there, for example, any conscious evocation of the history of the Evangelical Alliance? Associations between Baptists and the leadership of the EA were strong, and the United Kingdom Evangelical Alliance had recently worked with the Baptist Union of Great Britain and Ireland to try and secure greater freedom for the Russian Stundists, with the Alliance agreeing that the Baptist Union should take the lead role in the negotiations with governments. Other possibilities for the adoption of the

---

[59] John Locke, *A Letter on Toleration,* cited in W. H. Brackney, *Christian Voluntarism in Britain and North America, A Bibliography and Critical Assessment* (Westport, CT: Greenwood Press, 1995), p. 11.

[60] J. C. Fletcher, *The Southern Baptist Convention: a Sesquicentennial History* (Nashville, TN: Broadman and Holman, 1994), pp. 37ff.

language of 'Alliance' were 'The Alliance of Reformed Churches throughout the World holding the Presbyterian System' which was founded in 1875. This derivation is however unlikely given that those of the reformed family with which Baptists had most, indeed much, common ground, were the Congregationalists whose global relationships found a home in the International Congregational Council whose first meeting was held in London in 1891. Indeed Ernest Payne claims that shortly before his death Albert Peel stated that it had originally been hoped in 1891 that the Congregational Council would have embraced Baptists.[61] A third source for the word 'Alliance' was the World Alliance of YMCAs, which brought together the several national organisations in a world body in Paris in 1855. Given the carry over from that body of the so-called Paris Basis into the earliest doctrinal statements of the BWA, this is a real possibility.

Whatever the antecedents of the concept of an 'Alliance', the preamble to the Baptist World Alliance, agreed in London in 1905, reads:

> Whereas in the providence of God, the time has come when it seems fitting more fully to manifest the essential oneness in the Lord Jesus Christ as their God and Saviour, of the Churches of the Baptist order and faith throughout the world, and to promote the spirit of fellowship, service and co-operation among them, while recognising the independence of each particular Church, and not assuming the functions of any existing organisation, it is agreed to form a Baptist Alliance, extending over every part of the world.[62]

The language is significant – in establishing the 'essential oneness … of the Churches of the Baptist order and faith' reference is made to 'the Lord Jesus as God and Saviour', a phrase which derives from what is known as 'the Paris Basis', adopted by the International YMCA at their meeting in Paris in 1855. This was subsequently used by the World Student Christian Federation in 1895, and later in 1948 formed the central theological affirmation written into the basis of the World Council of Churches. By 1961 the World Council was persuaded that this wording was insufficient, in so far as it failed to speak of scripture, or to articulate a clear Trinitarian commitment. Accordingly the affirmation was expanded to define the Council as 'a fellowship of churches which confess the Lord Jesus Christ as God and Saviour according to the scriptures , and therefore seek to fulfil

---

[61] E. A. Payne, 'Baptist-Congregational Relationships' *Congregational Quarterly*, 1955, reprinted in *Free Churchmen, Unrepentant and Repentant* (London: Carey Kingsgate Press, 1963), p. 101.

[62] *BWA Congress* (1905), p. 241.

together their common calling to the glory of the one God, Father, Son and Holy Spirit'[63].

The Development of the BWA Constitution

By contrast when the Baptist World Alliance met in Stockholm in 1923, following the disruptions caused by the turmoil of the First World War, a period in which the Alliance had been very active in relief work in continental Europe, the preamble was amended so that the historic Paris formula was contracted simply to identify 'the essential oneness of Baptist people in the Lord Jesus Christ', whilst a new clause was added to the existing statement of purpose, 'to promote the spirit of fellowship, service and co-operation among them', expressing the hope that the Alliance would 'impart inspiration to the brotherhood'.[64] Eschewing precise credal language the alliance worked on an assumed evangelicalism as the tie that bound its member bodies one to another.

The constitution thus remained a pretty skeletal document until after the Second World War. But thereafter a number of attempts were made to fill it out. This process began in Copenhagen in 1947. At the Roll Call certain countries were noticeably absent, whilst others were represented by diaspora members from North America, and there were several delegations of 'Displaced Persons'. Nevertheless at Copenhagen a new section of some seven points was added to the Constitution, amplifying the 'Nature and Functions' of the Alliance', introduced by a very confident assertion of the overall capacity of the Alliance. It read:

> Serving as the nerve-centre and corporate will of Baptists throughout the world, the Alliance shall: [1] have as one of its primary purposes the safeguarding and the maintenance of full religious liberty everywhere, not only for our own constituent churches, but also for all other religious faiths; [2] serve as an agency for propagating Baptist principles and tenets of faith, objectives, and distinctive principles throughout the world; [3] serve as an agency to make surveys throughout the world with a view to furnishing facts to the various Baptist groups and counselling with them in establishing work in new fields when such service is requested; [4] serve as a worldwide agency in making such use of the Radio and Press as may be practicable in preaching the Gospel, propagating Baptist principles, and promoting common tasks of Baptists throughout the world; [5] arrange and conduct preaching missions throughout the world; [6] co-operate with

---

[63] Harold E. Fry (ed.), *A History of the Ecumenical Movement, Vol 2, The Ecumenical Advance, 1948-68*, 3rd edn (Geneva: WCC, 1993), p. 35.

[64] *BWA Congress* (1923), Appendix III, pp. 288-9.

> Baptist groups in instituting and administering relief funds as occasion may require; [7] gather news by means of correspondents in the various Baptist groups and disseminate it by use of bulletins, Baptist and other papers, and Radio; and when feasible by a Baptist world publication. In ministering, in any one or all of these fields of service, the Baptist World Alliance shall limit its activities strictly within the annual budget.[65]

Meeting in Stockholm in 1975, the 'Nature and Functions' section of the Constitution was rewritten as a list of 'Objectives', now some nine in number including paragraphs on fellowship, ecumenical conversations in a paragraph encouraging 'understanding and unity among Baptists and with fellow Christians', the missionary task of the church, and Baptist engagement in world mission [though recognising this was a task already undertaken by a number of national missionary societies], the educational task of promoting Baptist distinctives, the promotion of reconciliation between groups in conflict, and the upholding of fundamental human rights. The world was still a world of need and so the tasks of relief, development and aid remained critical. Publications and other means were to be used to help educate Baptists to undertake their world-wide responsibilities, promoting mutual co-operation through the Alliance's member bodies.[66]

At the fourteenth congress held in Toronto five years later these nine objectives were reduced to eight but more significantly changes were made to the text which at last set the work of the Alliance more expressly within a trinitarian and Biblical framework. In the first place, the introduction to this section now replaced the rather quaint older language of 'Serving as the nerve-centre and corporate will of Baptists throughout the world' with the theologically more appropriate: 'Under the guidance of the Holy Spirit, the objectives of the Baptist World Alliance shall be....'. Secondly, objective 3 now renumbered 2, expands on the nature of the Christian gospel with the words: 'Bear witness to the gospel of Jesus Christ and assist unions and conventions in their divine task of bringing all people to God through Jesus Christ as Saviour and Lord.' And thirdly, not surprisingly for a Baptist organisation, clause four was expanded by additional language which made reference to 'the expression of biblical faith'. The separate paragraph 'to further uphold for all people the claims of fundamental human rights and to further and maintain full religious liberty everywhere, both for our constituent churches and all other religious faiths', was deleted, in favour of adding 'and uphold the claims of fundamental human rights, including full religious liberty' to the paragraph on reconciliation.[67]

---

[65] *BWA Congress* (1947), pp. 163-5.

[66] *BWA Congress* (1975), pp. 263-4, and 292-6.

[67] *BWA Congress* (1980), pp. 283-7.

After three quarters of a century, if the objectives are read as a whole, at last a clear commitment to a trinitarian and Biblical faith is explicitly identified. In practical terms much of the work of deciding on the *bona fide* qualifications of a group applying for membership of the alliance is worked out in the Membership Committee. A minute of the General Council in 1995 reads that the committee agreed 'that in keeping with our general Baptist principles and approach it would not be appropriate to have any specific requirements laid down for applying members but rather to seek what would be distinguishing marks',[68] which the committee seems to have found some difficulty in identifying, though other parts of the Alliance had already clearly identified their understanding of Baptist churchmanship. An example of this can be seen in the document 'Towards a Baptist Identity' a descriptive rather than a prescriptive statement which the Alliance's Baptist Heritage Commission ratified at its meeting in 1989.[69]

Another issue requiring attention was what level of organisation would be appropriate for membership in the world body – regional or national, ecclesial or missional? This was initially handled by offering membership to 'Any general union, convention or association of Baptist Churches'. In 1911 this was extended by adding the words 'or conference of Native churches and missionaries or general Foreign Missionary Society.' The issue that was becoming clear was that an association which was an integral part of a national union or convention in membership with the Alliance should not be allowed separate representation. In more recent years the concern has been with the membership of multiple and competing groups of churches within one nation, but this has proved difficult to handle given the large number of Baptist bodies in the USA in membership with the Alliance. However, the Alliance was clear in its desire not to advantage schism in Baptist life within any given nation; rather it favoured reconciliation between different national groups before application was made for membership.[70]

A further complication emerged as continental organisations emerged alongside the world body. Some like the European Baptist Federation [which later extended its boundaries to include not only the successor states to the former soviet Union in Asia but churches in the Middle East and North Africa] founded in 1950 jealously guarded their independent existence, particularly to be seen in their championing of their right to appoint their own General Secretary, even though that person might also act

---

[68] *1995 Yearbook of the BWA,* p. 77.

[69] W. H. Brackney and R. J. Burke (eds), *Faith, Life and Witness,* [Papers of the BWA Study Commissions, 1986-90] (Birmingham, AL: Samford University Press, 1990), pp. 146-9.

[70] Brakney and Burke, *Faith, Life and Witness*, p. 75, item 18.

as an Associate Secretary of the Baptist World Alliance.[71] Other regional fellowships were much more the creation of the Alliance itself – the North American Baptist Fellowship [1965][72], the Asian [including Australasia] Baptist Federation [1975], the Caribbean Baptist Fellowship [1982], the All-Africa Baptist Fellowship [1982], and the Union of Baptists in Latin America [1983]. These regional organisations were part of the Alliance but not technically members of it – national unions were encouraged to relate directly to the Alliance as well as to secure pastoral care from their regional fellowship.

A major disruption in the life of the Alliance was the withdrawal of the large, influential and well-financed Southern Baptist Convention from membership in 2004[73]. This meant a loss of rather more than one third of the affiliated membership as well as significant financial support. To accommodate state conventions, churches and individuals in the southern states of the USA who wished to maintain an association with the BWA, but not exclusively so, two new categories of membership were approved at the General Council meeting in Seoul in the same year – associate and personal membership. The purpose of both is stated as providing opportunity 'to involve Baptist Churches and organised Baptist groups in the global Baptist ministry of the Baptist World Alliance through prayer, the sharing of resources and the participation in the meetings, congresses and conferences of the Baptist World Alliance.'[74]

Within the fellowship provided by the Alliance, there have developed a significant aid programme [Baptist World Aid], opportunities for promoting the ideals of a missionary church, mechanisms for nurturing member churches both old and new in Baptist history and heritage and in Baptist distinctives. The Alliance has engaged in formal conversations with other Christian World Communions, and has frequently intervened on behalf of member churches undergoing persecution. Where there has been conflict within the family, it has used its best endeavours to reconcile differences. By passing resolutions, Baptists, met in global conference, have addressed issues of social justice and moral direction. However, resolutions are never

---

[71] K. G. Jones, *The European Baptist Federation:* A Case Study in European Baptist Interdependency, 1950-2006 (Milton Keynes: Paternoster, 2009).

[72] The North American Baptist Fellowship had difficulty in establishing a strong separate identity partly because it embraced some very strong and influential member churches, partly because of the unequal strengths of the USA and Canada, and partly because it had responsibility for that territory where the BWA headquarters was located; see special note on p. 327 of R. Pierard (ed.), *Baptists Together in Christ, 1905-2005: A Hundred-year History of the Baptist World Alliance* (Falls Church, VA: Baptist World Alliance 2005).

[73] Pierard, *Baptists Together in Christ,* pp. 295-6.

[74] See *Constitution of the Baptist World Alliance*, Section IV 2/3.

imposed upon member churches, for it remains their responsibility how they choose to act upon such resolutions, the power to persuade lying in the truth and urgency of their content.

Notwithstanding the one major loss of the Southern Baptist convention, reflecting a breach between those who rated a fundamentalist purity, confessionally defined, above a shared Baptist experience within the believers' church tradition, the loose framework of the Baptist World Alliance has served the family well, enabling it to act as an agency of global unity. In this way shared faith has had priority over those matters in which they differ. Whilst some confine participation at the Lord's Table to baptised believers, other open the table to all those who seek to be Christ's disciples. In like manner, some confine membership to those who have been baptised as believers, but others open membership to all who give testimony of their trust in Christ. Some are happy to ordain women, whilst others exclude them from the pastoral office. Most have only one order of ordained ministry; nevertheless there are several churches with Episcopal leadership. In some cases this is a question of language in adopting a title for church leaders readily understood by others; only amongst the Evangelical Baptists Church of Georgia is a three-fold ministry of deacon, presbyter and bishop theologically sustained. Some uphold a traditional Calvinist theology, whilst others have modified this inheritance in various ways, whilst there have always been Baptists who stand within a more obviously Arminian tradition. Embracing both pre- and post-millenialists, there are also differences among Baptists on the nature of eternal judgment and the after-life. Notwithstanding such differences, all are accepted as valued and esteemed family members within the life of the BWA.

8.

A Trinitarian Theology of Ministerial Formation

Anthony Clarke

Introduction

When I began as a ministerial student at Regent's Park College, Paul Fiddes was tutor in doctrine; when I left he was Principal. Now, as Director for Research one of the areas that Paul is still passionately concerned for is the work of preparing women and men for ministry. During that time the syllabus and curriculum have seen radical revisions and the language itself employed in Baptist Colleges and elsewhere has changed and developed, and the recent change by the Baptist Colleges in England and Wales away from the Ecumenical Inspection process to a pattern of peer review has prompted further theological reflection on the nature of ministerial formation. Paul has always had a deep concern for and vision of a Christian view of higher education and all his theological work has been pastorally motivated.[1] So in this essay I attempt to engage with some of the key aspects of Paul's theological vision and building on them to offer a fuller and more explicit exploration of the nature of ministerial formation. In particular I want to pick up three fundamental words / themes, all which are discussed in a number of ways in this volume, but apply them to this particular subject[2]. A full consideration of the theology of ministerial formation will require greater attention paid to other issues, such as the nature of church and the wider understanding of ministry, but this essay seeks to lay some foundations in trinitarian theology.

Participation

Central to Paul Fiddes' theological vision is the concept and experience of participation and in particular expressing Christian experience and

---

[1] See Paul S. Fiddes, *Participating in God: A Pastoral Doctrine of the Trinity* (London: DLT, 2000).

[2] Fiddes himself considers two of the themes to be of strategic significance for Baptists, see *Tracks and Traces: Baptist Identity in Church and Theology* (Carlisle: Paternoster, 2003), ch. 3, pp. 48-64, and the third theme, participation, is the key to his recent writings.

discipleship as participating in the trinitarian life of God. Convinced that the language of imitation or even contemplation is not sufficient theologically, epistemologically, or pastorally,[3] compelling human beings to strive after and copy the impossible model of trinitarian relationships, Fiddes encourages us to explore the gracious way that our lives are drawn into these trinitarian relationships. Thus our lives and human communities do not shape themselves in response to a trinitarian pattern, but are shaped by participation in the very trinitarian pattern itself.

One of the most striking Trinitarian metaphors which Fiddes builds on and develops, and is illustrated in the Matisse picture on the cover of the book, is that of the divine dance. What is particularly creative is the way that Fiddes brings together two distinct patterns of dancing – a circle dance and a progressive dance – to illustrate and develop some intricacies of trinitarian theology, drawing on patristic hints of the trinitarian relations as a dance and the more common description of the world as a harmonious dance with God. Locating himself in the history of trinitarian theology, Fiddes argues very strongly for what are described as 'subsistent relations' in God, that is the persons or hypostases of God are to be identified as the relations themselves rather than as the persons at the end of the relations[4]. Such a view has a long theological history, going back to Augustine, and Fiddes is convinced that this is the best language with which to express the revelation of God as Trinity, and it is within this image that Fiddes' own concept of participation works best. The concept of the subsistent relations and the theological tradition it involves is by no means uncontested[5], but the point of this essay, however, is to develop trinitarian theology in one particular area, and as Fiddes himself suggests, and hopes, that his appeal to the language of participation does not depend on acceptance of the tradition of 'subsistent relations' [6], we will not pursue this particular issue here.

The metaphor of the circle dance, Fiddes argues, encapsulates the best of the Western trinitarian tradition, which lays stress on 'the equality, mutuality and reciprocity of the three persons.'[7] This has certainly been a strong Baptist and Free Church stress. So a previous report to the Council of the Baptist Union of Great Britain, concerned with structural developments

---

[3] See Fiddes, *Participating in God*, pp. 28-30 and 38. Fiddes argues that, in contrast to the strongly objectifying enlightenment approach God is known through an epistemology of participation.

[4] Fiddes, *Participating in God*, pp. 34-46.

[5] Catherine Mowry LaCugna, for example, offers a different reading of the tradition from Aquinas, in *God for Us: The Trinity and Christian Life* (New York: Harper San Francisco, 1991).

[6] Fiddes, *Participating in God*, p. 50.

[7] Fiddes, *Participating in God*, p. 77.

insists that 'in the life and work of the Church we believe Christians must always begin with God' and continues:

> 'Moreover, there is no hierarchy in God, as if the Father rules the Son and both instruct the Spirit. The Persons of the Trinity are co-equal and mutually interdependent one on the other. It is not simply in the distinct Persons but in the nature of their relationship that the Trinity consists.'[8]

The theologian Miroslav Volf, in seeking a position shaped by his Free Church tradition of Biblical interpretation and theological development, insists we must reject the 'pyramidal dominance of the one' and 'the hierarchical bipolarity between the one and the many', and embrace instead 'a polycentric and symmetrical reciprocity of the many'[9], that is the Trinity as a community of free and equal persons. In critical dialogue with Volf and also Jürgen Moltmann, Fiddes himself argues for a trinitarian picture of God, which avoids oppression, dominance and hierarchy, thereby challenging both political and ecclesial monarchianism.[10]Not only are trinitarian relationships marked by mutuality and reciprocity, they are also truly *ecstatic*, that is they are self-transcending, truly open in love to the other so that Father, Son and Spirit live in the constant openness to each other in which true identity is found. Beginning here we may then begin to suggest some initial aspects of ministerial formation.

Formation

Drawing on Fiddes' fundamental insight that we must think in the language of participation not just imitation, the whole concept of ministerial *formation* comes to life. Historically, three words have been engaged in this connection, although their use has not always been clear and straightforward, sometimes being used to refer to one distinct aspect of the process of preparing for ministry but also at other times to the whole of the process.

Ministerial *training* has been a common description of this process of preparation in the twentieth century with training also being used to describe

---

[8] *Transforming Superintendency:* The report of the General Superintendency Review Group presented to the Baptist Union of Great Britain Council, November 1996 (Baptist Union of Great Britain), p. 9.

[9] Miroslav Volf, *After Our Likeness: The Church as the Image of the Trinity* (Grand Rapids, MI: Eerdmans, 1998), p. 217.

[10] Fiddes, *Participating in God*, pp. 62-108. Fiddes criticises Volf and Moltmann for rejecting the idea of 'subsistent relations' because he believes that such a concept does not necessarily lead to monarchical oppression as Volf and Moltmann suggest.

more specifically the development of the skills needed in ministry. The 1960s and 1970s in particular saw a reaction to the perceived heavily academic bias of our Colleges and the more intentional and thorough development of courses in pastoral studies and more practical aspects of ministry. Theological *education* has a long pedigree and has been understood as involving more narrowly the cognitive dimension of learning connected with knowledge and understanding, although this draws on a broader and more foundational epistemology and approach to knowledge, which argues that education engages the whole person in all their dimensions and relationships.[11] This understands the term to derive from the Latin 'educere'[12], to lead or draw out, and is thus centred around the learning of the individual, and all they bring to the process. *Formation* is the most recent term, sometimes understood more narrowly, as concerned with spirituality and character but more recently becoming the most significant attempt to encapsulate the whole process of preparing for ministry.[13]

Fiddes suggests that the whole of Christian discipleship is about being drawn to participate in the trinitarian relations, so as to be shaped and transformed by such participation. Such a concept offers a dynamic picture of what it means to become more 'Christlike' or be formed into the image of Christ, as we are drawn to share in what is like 'a willing response of a son to a father, becoming co-actors and co-narrators with his 'Yes. Amen' to the Father's purpose.'[14] Here is formation that is not simply based on greater human effort but on an openness to the gracious work of God. Formation language is certainly not perfect, but not only is it the emerging paradigm within the wider ecumenical context, it is deeply rooted in a doctrine of God, and thus should be embraced. There will always be passionate discussion as to the priority of different aspects of a curriculum, and the allocation of limited yet precious time, but the invitation is to see the whole curriculum within a formational process of participation.

Formation as Discipleship

The language of participation is rooted in Christian discipleship, and so before it speaks to questions of preparing ordained ministers, it addresses the whole people of God. Formation is a key metaphor for growth in discipleship. In writing of Christian education in general, Jeff Astley

---

[11] See, for example, Jeff Astley, *The Philosophy of Christian Religious Education* (Birmingham, AL: Religious Education Press, 1994), pp. 38-9.

[12] As opposed to the Latin 'educare' meaning to bring up or train.

[13] See *Patterns of Ministry among Baptists:* A Review of *The Register of Covenanted Persons Accredited for Ministry*, A Report of the 'Review of the Register Working Group', presented to BUGB Council in November 2010, p. 11.

[14] Fiddes, *Participating in God*, p. 53.

suggests that 'a person's Christian education, after all, should be primarily orientated to her or his *learning to be Christian*, which is largely a matter of being formed in a Christian character.'[15] In the light of Fiddes' helpful language of participation we would want to nuance this learning to be Christian as being shaped by God's gracious invitation to trinitarian life, but the point remains firm that formation and discipleship are inseparable. This chimes strongly with Baptist understandings of the church in which the ministry and mission of God in Christ is exercised firstly by the whole church and then by some who are called to ministry in a representative way. Again, another recent Baptist document makes these connections between the nature of God, discipleship and ministry.

> 'The foundational ministry in the church is that of the triune God, who has revealed himself to be a Servant God in the history of his people Israel and above all in the life, death and resurrection of Jesus Christ. God freely and humbly submits himself to a path of ministry (ie service) in his purpose to reconcile persons and communities to himself, calling them into the fellowship of his eternal life as Father, Son and Spirit. God's ministry is his chosen way of carrying out his mission, his sending forth (mission) of the Son into the world in the power of the Spirit. Thus 'ministry' in its full sense is all that God seeks to do in, through and amongst his people. We share in his ministry and his mission.'[16]

For Baptists then, ministerial formation is not a particular kind of priestly formation distinct from other Christians, but is located in the formation of the whole people of God as they are drawn to participate in God's life. Rather the vocation to ordained ministry with the responsibility conferred on individuals by God through the church demands Christian formation that is not different in kind but rather Christian formation that is 'intentional and intensive'[17] or 'specialised discipleship'[18], that the few called to ordained

---

[15] Jeff Astley, 'Dimensions of Christian Education' in Jeff Astley, *Learning in the Way: Research and Reflection on Adult Christian Education* (Leominster: Gracewing, 2000), p. 38.

[16] *Forms of Ministry Among Baptists: Towards an Understanding of Spiritual Leadership*. p. 16, which looks back to *The Baptist Doctrine of the Church* in R. Hayden (ed.) *Baptist Union Documents 1948-77* (London: Baptist Historical Society, 1980), pp. 8 and 89.

[17] The phrase was suggested to me by Stephen Finamore, Principal at Bristol Baptist College.

[18] The phrase was suggested by Roger Standing, Principal of Spurgeon's College.

ministry may better enable the on-going formation of the whole people of God.

Formation in Community

Developing his trinitarian picture, Fiddes describes the way that the trinitarian relationships are truly 'ecstatic', that is 'self-transcending in communication with others, especially in the movement of love.'[19]He then relates this to the way human persons exist and are formed in community. Although not explicitly dealing with ministerial formation, Fiddes here addresses two central and related concerns of both experience and language: that entering a process of ministerial formation may lead to the loss of the self and what is unique to the individual, together with the fear that formation is in reality conformity to a particular view of self-hood and ministry. He calls for a 'balance between a proper self-centring, which is not a destructive self-centredness, and formation through our social relationships'[20] and insists that an 'openness to others will not mean conformity to the human other, which would be a loss of one's own will, but conformity to the Christ we meet in and through the other.'[21] These ideas strengthen the way that formation should be understood in an holistic sense in which skills learnt and developed and knowledge acquired is integrated in the whole growth of the individual in community, which happens in this dialectic between self-centring and openness to the other.

There is thus a proper and necessary aspect of what is sometimes described by educationalists as 'formative education'. Indeed all education has a formative element because there is no community or tradition which is neutral and value free. There is a wider community and a tradition in which and through which those preparing for ministry are developing and being shaped. This implies a sense of passing on the church's values, beliefs and practices and individuals being receptive to receive them. Building on our belief that ministerial formation is then one aspect of the wider Christian formation into Christ and Christian character,

> 'as long as such formation does not disable a person's development towards personal autonomy and critical reflection, it seems to me to be a proper – indeed essential – dimension of *any* education that wishes to call itself Christian.'[22]

---

[19] Fiddes, *Participating in God*, p. 22.

[20] Fiddes, *Participating in God*, p. 52.

[21] Fiddes, *Participating in God*, p. 53.

[22] Astley, 'Dimensions of Christian Education', p. 38.

On the one hand we might locate such formation in the gracious invitation of God through which we are drawn to participate in the community of God's trinitarian life. Learning or knowledge is supremely knowledge of God, the foundation of which is being known by God in divine grace. Such an epistemology combining theory and practice and embracing affective knowledge which shapes emotions and virtues is often linked to the concept of 'paideia'[23]. On the other hand such 'formative education' can only be located in a specific community and tradition, for our learning to be a Christian is always mediated in this way, and so we may also assert that there is an explicit formation into the Baptist community with its particular values, beliefs and practices and we would expect those preparing for ministry within Baptist churches to be shaped by their engagement with Baptist history, principles and ecclesiology and by their participation in Baptist worship.[24] There are particular Baptist insights into the nature of the Church, ministry, leadership and mission which are to be positively encouraged and particular Baptist ways of responding to God's gracious invitation in worship. We may further assert then, the details of which will need exploring in greater depth, that there is, and must be, a distinctive Baptist formative education, in the same way as there will be, for example, distinctive Anglican or Methodist formations.

In addition there is also what is described as 'critical education'[25] in which there is reflective analysis and evaluation of the church's self-understanding and tradition in the light of the individual's own experience. This places much more emphasis on the freedom and individuality of the student and an education process which begins with them and draws out from them their understanding. Yet the ability to develop patterns of critical engagement and reflection is neither simply an automatic given nor simply a learnt skill. It is, as John Passmore and Alasdair MacIntyre both suggest something much more deeply embedded in character.[26] As such it is actually part of the process of formation, in which students are encouraged and enabled to develop in this tradition of critical thinking, which might be termed a theological 'habitus', the capacity to think critically and make

---

[23] See, for example, Common Awards Preface, p. 2.

[24] For a sustained argument of worship as the ultimate 'school' of learning and for a clear expression of Anglican formation see Mike Higton, *A Theology of Higher Education* (Oxford: OUP, 2012), ch. 5.

[25] For further discussion of formative and critical education see Astley, *Philosophy of Christian Religious Education*, ch. 5.

[26] See the discussion in Astley, *Philosophy of Christian Religious Education*, pp. 84-6.

judgments.[27] Ministerial formation, which is self-centring but ecstatic in its openness to those who are other, will combine these two aspects together.[28]

One of the challenges is how such formative and critical education is enabled and evaluated. We have argued that that formation intrinsically happens in community – that is in those relationships which are to some degree ecstatic and open – and the hope is that this will happen quite naturally in relationships. Colleges have stressed that inter-student relationships are as important as those between staff and students – and the semi-monastic pattern of Colleges in previous generations when all were young and College-based relied on this. When these work well and develop in their openness and transcendence formation happens a pace. But what of those situations when relationships between a whole group of students struggle, when there is limited openness to the other, or relationships even become destructive and individuals seek their fulfilment at the expense of rather than in cooperation, with others. Further, one of the challenges of those involved in ministerial formation is the 'testing' of the formational aspects of the whole process – teaching and testing for knowledge is much easier, and so can too easily become the default. One of the great challenges for staff in our Colleges is to help create and facilitate the most helpful and appropriate learning environment, in which formation can be encouraged and tested, in a cultural context where consumerist tendencies mitigate against this.

On the basis of a theology of participation and the metaphor of the circle dance we might conclude that the *foundation* of ministerial formation is in the formation of the whole people of God which happens in community, in the negotiation of the self in relation to others.

Returning to our metaphor of the dance, Fiddes suggests that one of the weaknesses of both the western tradition and the image of the circle dance, is that it suggests that God is closed and self-sufficient. Again, Fiddes himself is taking a particular doctrinal position that it is not simply that God *does* open the divine circle to others as a matter of choice but that there can be no

---

[27] Charles M. Wood, 'Theological Enquiry and Theological Education' in Jeff Astley, Leslie Francis and Colin Crowder (eds), *Theological Perspectives on Christian Formation: A Reader on Theology and Christian Education* (Leominster: Gracewing, 1996), p. 342: 'a participation in theological enquiry, ordered to the acquisition of that complex set of intellectual and personal qualities which go to make up what we might still call the theological habitus.'

[28] 'It is clear that theological education can be properly regarded as 'formation' as long as certain long-standing misconceptions concerning the relation of 'formation' and critical enquiry are removed, and as long as it is remembered that formation sought is precisely the formation of the critical aptitude of theological judgment.' Wood, 'Theological Enquiry', p. 351.

dance without human partners being brought in.[29] While this more Eastern pattern of thinking has its own problems, particularly the possibility that the stress on the Father as the sole source of the Godhead can lead to hierarchical and dominating patterns, the picture of the progressive dance whose movements are always purposeful and outward, drawing others in, provides for Fiddes an important counterbalance to the circle dance.

Fundamental to such a trinitarian understanding of God is the sending of the Son and the pouring out of the Spirit, with the temporal 'sendings' corresponding to the eternal generation of the Son and procession of the Spirit, pointing us to a God whose nature is fundamentally characterised by going out to others in mission. God is a missionary God, and 'mission is not primarily an activity of the church but an attribute of God.'[30] During the last fifty years such an understanding of God, categorised by speaking of the *missio Dei*, has become increasingly common, together with the consequential reshaping of our understanding of the mission of the church, which has its origin and very existence in participating in the mission of God. With much of this theology assumed the Baptist document we considered earlier, 'Transforming Superintendency', concludes that 'the God to whom the Bible bears witness is always 'going out' in love to others'.[31] God does not want to be God without us.[32] As churches participate in this self-giving of God which shapes their shared life, mission will be at the heart of ministry, which will enable and model such 'going out in love'. Again we might make explicit connections to ministerial formation.

Formation as Hospitality

First, it emphasises again the priority of grace and the divine initiative in participation. This connects to the fundamental premise behind ministerial formation, that the calling by God of some to this particular office and role within the church is an instance of the same divine initiative, and then also to the experience of ministerial formation itself. We are first sought, included and welcomed by God and on this basis we are changed. This metaphor of hospitality, which has been used quite widely in recent theology, particularly to define the church as a community which makes room for the other and so

---

[29] Fiddes, *Participating in God*, p. 78. The wider issue relating to creation coming from God's choice or God's nature cannot be taken up here.

[30] David Bosch, *Transforming Mission: Paradigm Shifts in the Theology of Mission* (Maryknoll, NY: Orbis, 1991), p. 390, drawing on the work of Moltmann.

[31] 'Transforming Superintendency' p. 9.

[32] See Karl Barth's doctrine of election in *Church Dogmatics* II/2 (Edinburgh: T&T Clark, 1957), pp. 36-75.

is an embodied sign of this process of divine reconciliation[33]may also be applied to ministerial formation[34].

Henri Nouwen, proposing that hospitality is creating a free space where the stranger can enter, writes that 'hospitality is not to change people, but to offer them space where change can take place'[35] that change being intrinsically the work of God, again pointing to the fact that formation is not to be seen as an attempt to conform individuals within a rigid pattern. Such an understanding of hospitality connects together deeply the practice of ministry and the practice of ministerial formation – hospitable ministry that creates space for others formed by hospitable Colleges – based on a deeper connection with the practice of God who welcomes us. Colleges will therefore continue to reflect on the kind of 'space' they are creating, including but certainly not confined to the geographical space, but extending to the spiritual and emotional space. Further, hospitality will always seek to give full attention to the other, expressed in the inter-human relationships within and between staff and students and in the voices heard through placements study and culture. Part of the mix of training and education within the formation of disciples and ministers is to enable the skills and character that is able more fully to give attention to the other, to recognise where a different voice is being heard and to reflect on its significance.

Formation as Missional

Secondly to participate in the progressive dance as disciples is to be 'going out in love to others', thus extending the metaphor of the progressive dance from its trinitarian basis, as Fiddes develops it, to the whole nature of the church. Participating in the currents of divine love churches seek to go out to others and draw them into the divine life.

One of the issues rightly exercising our attention currently is the call to appropriate mission in our contemporary context. One of the unfortunate consequences of some of the current debate is the use of language that can seem to separate out ministry, which is pastoral, and mission, and so those churches deemed to be maintenance based and those involved in pioneering mission – it is as if, to draw on these metaphors, some churches are

---

[33] See, for example, Christine Pohl, *Making Room, Recovering Hospitality as a Christian Tradition,* (Grand Rapids, MI: Eerdmans, 1999) and Luke Bretherton, *Hospitality as Holiness, Christian Witness Amid Moral Diversity,* (Aldershot: Ashgate, 2006).

[34] For the use of the metaphor in theological education see, E. Newman, 'Who's Home Cooking? Hospitality, Christian Identity and Higher Education', *Perspectives in Religious Studies,* 26, no 1, Sept 1999.

[35] Henri Nouwen, *Reaching Out, The Three Movement of the Spiritual Life,* (Glasgow: William Collins, 1976), pp. 68-9.

categorised as only interested in a circle dance and some only in a progressive one. Recognising the strengths and weaknesses of both circle and progressive patterns in trinitarian terms, surely this must also be true for churches and disciples who participate within these trinitarian movements – all pastoral work is seeking to go out in love to others, and all mission seeks to enable individuals to grow in their participation within God.

In terms of the curriculum, while it may be necessary to have sessions or modules or streams that are designated in a way that stresses their more missional or pastoral content – a module for example, on church planting or pastoral care – it is also important that the whole curriculum is understood as both missional and pastoral in an integrative way.

This bringing together of metaphors may help us to reflect further on the categories we currently use for ministry. Since 2001 there has been the distinction between those who are ordained as pastors, youth specialists and evangelists.[36] While it is undoubtedly true that those who are called by God for ministry will be gifted in different ways, the distinction between those called to a pastoral role (pastors) and a missional role (evangelists) is not altogether helpful. The fact that in the Register of Nationally Accredited Ministers published in the Baptist Union Directory of 2012 only 17 are listed as evangelists[37], together with anecdotal evidence that those coming to our Colleges are tending to opt for recognition as pastors for the sake of expediency suggests a certain unhelpfulness. It may be time in both our language and structures to reassert that all sharing in the ministry of Christ, as churches and as ministers, is deeply missional and deeply pastoral.

On the basis of a theology of participation and the metaphor of the progressive dance we might conclude that the *direction* of ministerial formation is always outward looking, so that the call of the church to participate in God's going out in love is echoed in our Colleges, in the going out in hospitality.

Covenant

A second theological area that Fiddes has explored consistently is that of covenant, both in its historical development among Baptists and in the way it opens up dimensions to the doctrine of God, explicitly connecting together a

---

[36] See the Baptist Union Directory 2012 (Didcot: BUGB, 2012), p. 145. The separate issue of those serving in a different way to these three categories is passed over, as the concern here is for those preparing for ordination in one of these categories.

[37] Twenty-eight are listed as Youth Specialists.

trinitarian theology of participation with an ecclesiology of covenant.[38] It is not only churches that make covenants together, but these can be seen as the basis for the life of Associations of a Union and also of a College – South Wales Baptist College for example having a written covenant which the community affirms. It may be that for some 'covenant' is a more theologically sounding alternative to commitment, and it is certainly true that commitment is a significant aspect of ministerial formation. But the concept of covenant, especially as explored by Fiddes, offers greater theological depth than language of commitment on its own.

Formation as Response

In discussing the various biblical covenants, especially the distinction between the Mosaic and Davidic covenants of the Old Testament, Fiddes points out how both, although different, are firmly rooted in the divine initiative and open up ways of response.[39]One of the unique and insightful developments which early Baptists made, he suggests, is the way that they explicitly linked the horizontal, church covenants they wrote with the vertical covenant God had initiated with human beings. Human covenants are not simply statements of commitment, but are a response to and participate in God's divine initiative. This reminds us again that the whole process of ministerial formation is in response to the gracious initiative of God who calls for our response, not just initially in responding to a 'call to ministry' but continually. In the same way that a service of worship can be understood as an on-going dialogue between God and the congregation which God initiates – often represented by beginning a service with a call to worship from Scripture – so ministerial formation can be seen in that same dialogical way. The challenge for those overseeing such formation is to ensure that God's voice in the dialogue is heard both initially and throughout.

One way that this could happen is through the affirmation of a specific covenant that is written by and for a College community, weaving together commitments that are made to each other within the theology of the divine covenant of grace. Such a covenant may find ways of incorporating historic elements, for the horizontal aspect of covenant is not isolated from those who have been before and can be woven into the story of the community in its vertical covenant with God, as well as expressing the vision and commitment of each new re-forming of the community. Such a covenant will want to express, amongst other things, the sense of hospitality offered to

---

[38] Fiddes, *Tracks and* Traces, pp. 78-80. For a further exploration of this theme see my 'The Covenantal Basis of God's Trinitarian Life' in Anthony Clarke (ed.), *Bound for Glory: God, Church and World in Covenant* (Oxford: Whitley, 2002).

[39] Fiddes, *Tracks and Traces*, pp. 74-6.

each other in the light of God's welcome, the desire to go out in love, and the willingness to work at the right kind of self-centring in the midst of open relationships.

Formation as Discovery

The language of covenant may also help us to explore the nature of the commitment this entails. Fiddes suggests that a key aspect of the covenant made between churches is the possibilities it opens up for discovery.[40] While a local congregation sits under the Lordship of Christ and in response to that Lordship assumes responsibility for its life and mission it does not do so independently, but assumes that one of the ways it can discover the mind of Christ and wisdom of God is through covenant relationships with others. Building on what we have suggested about self-hood and hospitality, we might suggest that formation involves the discovery of greater depths to oneself, one's calling and one's understanding of God through committed interaction with others. Reflecting specifically on a vision for higher education Fiddes deepens this further by connecting the covenant of being God's people with the wider covenant God creates with all living things, within God's trinitarian story[41]. On this basis Fiddes argues that theological education – and offers the British Baptist Colleges as examples – should not happen by withdrawing from surrounding culture as if Christians were an alternative society, but should 'live vulnerably on the boundaries'[42] in a whole world where Christ is Lord. What Fiddes seems to be arguing for is that the Christian community should not be separate from the rest of culture – although it will be distinct, and in that sense alternative – but willing to engage from a position of vulnerability.

Formation that was discovery and that lived vulnerably on the boundaries would happen at a number of levels and assumes an openness to the other, expressed in the metaphor of hospitality, working throughout. Core to such a journey of discovery will be staff and fellow ministerial students in a College, who form a distinct community of those journeying together on a life-long process of formation. The openness of staff to such a journey is crucial. Increasingly ministerial formation happens in a church-based context in which 'Ministers-in-training' enter into the practice of ministry in a particular context either as sole pastor or as part of a wider team. Such

---

[40] Fiddes, *Tracks and Traces*, pp. 55-6.

[41] Paul S. Fiddes, 'Christianity, Culture and Education: A Baptist Perspective' in Roger Ward and David P. Gushee (eds), *The Scholarly Vocation and the Baptist Academy: Essays on the Future of Baptist Higher Education* (Macon, GA: Mercer, 2008), pp. 1-25. Fiddes goes on to offer a Christological rationale for this approach as well.

[42] Fiddes, 'Christianity, Culture and Education', p. 18.

placements are not understood as an opportunity simply to put into practice what is learnt in College, but as communities of learning, in which ministry is offered to the church in the same context of life-long learning and formation of the minister as part of the whole people of God.

Fiddes argues, in the context of an understanding of a local church, that such covenant relationships need to be wider still and be open both ecumenically to the whole of the Christian family and beyond to the whole of God's created world. All the Baptist Colleges of England and Wales through more varied student bodies and partnerships with other institutions, offer a broader context in which discovery is possible. All the Colleges in different ways have a commitment to and engage in aspects of ecumenical formation, of which Baptist formation is a part, and are part of wider academic institutions, through which other voices are heard. Again the five Baptist Colleges have developed over recent years partnerships with both BMS World Mission and with specific church communities in other parts of the world so that the openness of formation is not limited geographically to a more local context but there are opportunities for discovery and for hearing some of the voices of the world church. Such wider discovery cannot be seen as an 'optional extra' but, however facilitated, part of the intentional and intensive aspect of ministerial formation. Such breadth, openness and engagement, rather than a purely insular Baptist context, seems to best express the openness of this trinitarian covenant and should be treasured and developed.

On the basis of a theology of covenant we might conclude that the *commitment* of ministerial formation is to life-long discovery within a whole range of intersecting communities.

Vulnerability

A third area which has been at the heart of Fiddes' thinking and in which he has made a particularly significant contribution in international scholarship, is that of reflecting on divine suffering, which is at the heart of his theological thinking and affects so much of what he writes. Elsewhere in this volume Richard Kidd offers the compelling image, drawn from Matisse's work, of Fiddes' book *The Creative Suffering of God*, always in the corner of the study.[43] So the very trinitarian theology he has been arguing for is shaped by an insistence that the 'moment of begetting and creating is thus one of humility, and an opening of the divine life to pain and suffering.'[44] Much of what Fiddes suggests about the nature of God is developed either explicitly or implicitly on the basis of the willing openness of the divine life

---

[43] Paul S. Fiddes, *The Creative Suffering of God* (Oxford: Clarendon, 1988).

[44] Fiddes, *Participating in God*, p. 96.

to suffering. While wanting to affirm this stress myself, it may, as earlier, also be possible to recognise some of the other insights Fiddes offers and the implications that can be drawn out for ministerial formation without the same commitment to divine passibility.

The relationship between God and the world that has been expressed in terms of participation and covenant can also be described in terms of vulnerability. The very particularity of the birth of Jesus expresses God's commitment to creation not only in this unique moment, but also as the climax of God's covenant history with the people of Israel. And this particularity is the 'going out' of God in vulnerability, in which God gives Godself away in love, encountering negativity and death, that which is other and different to God, while remaining true to who God is eternally. These concepts of covenant and willing vulnerability, in which God is genuinely open to the world is not the kind of kenotic theology in which God *becomes* vulnerable on the cross. Rather the very possibility of the cross is based in the eternal covenant and vulnerability within the Trinity between Father, Son and Spirit and is the very basis for God 'going out in love' to the world, and including us in God's trinitarian life.[45] Again we can pursue some implications for ministerial formation.

Formation as Risk-taking

Fiddes affirms the risk at the heart of God in opening up the divine life to others. For many, responding to the call of God to ordained ministry is from the very beginning shaped by taking risks and exercising faith. Change of employment, housing and schools, a drop in income and being launched into an unfamiliar setting are all significant challenges. Perhaps one of the greatest challenges for many is the return to study with the need to write essays, papers and exams which are marked and graded, sometimes replacing a very different employment and situation in life with being a student. This itself can be hard and feel both threatening and de-skilling. In addition those entering College begin an appropriate academic course in theology as a central part of their formation in a College which is integral to or validated by a wider secular university. One of the current key components of ministerial formation in our Baptist Colleges is a university education and a commitment to critical and rigorous study within the wider context of a range of theological views.

---

[45] Robin Greenwood, *Transforming Priesthood: A New Theology of Mission and Ministry* (London: SPCK, 1994), p. 75, suggests: 'There is a growing movement among theologians towards an emphasis less on the unity, transcendence, immovability and independence of God and more on his dynamic, related, even vulnerable aspects.'

Alongside our previous suggestions about hospitality and discovery, and the commitment to formation in community, the risk-taking nature of ministerial formation becomes clear. It can never be something that is considered easy. At Regent's both at interviews and at the very beginning of the course, reference is made back to probably the earliest book on pastoral theology in English, George Herbert's *The Country Parson*, who near the beginning refers to those at University in a preparatory way, 'whose aim and labour must be not only to get knowledge, but to subdue and mortifie all lusts and affections: and not to think, that when they have read the Fathers, or Schoolmen, a Minister is made, and the thing done. The greatest and hardest preparation is within.'[46]

Formation as Kenosis

At the heart of Fiddes' understanding of God is the vulnerability that is expressed both within the divine relationships in which perfect self-giving love is offered and returned and as creation is graciously drawn into these trinitarian relationships in which God offers Godself in love. Formation as disciples and ministers, being drawn into the divine dance, involves being caught up in these same currents of self-giving and so to be increasingly shaped by God's character and nature. Again, it is not the case of a human imitation of God, but rather to be drawn to participate in God's life is a process of gradual change that makes us more Christ-like.

There are, of course, alternatives which do indeed offer other models. In recent years the greater stress on leadership within churches and as a core task of ministry has opened up a whole range of models drawn from within the breath of the Christian Church and from wider society. While too broad and significant a subject in its own right to deal with at any depth here, this essay has argued that the most significant foundations for ministerial formation, and so clearly for ministry too, lie in the trinitarian nature of God. This would certainly question some of the ways in which leadership is cast, and suggests that vulnerability and self-giving become key aspects of ministry and so ministerial formation.

As we have already suggested the process itself not only involves risk-taking but can *impose* a certain vulnerability on those who respond to God's call, placing people in a threatening, if affirming context. But our trinitarian theology describes the *willing* vulnerability of God, in which nothing is imposed on God, but God freely and graciously opens the divine life to the world. Human life will, of course, somewhat differently sit in tension between that which the individual freely chooses and that which is imposed from without, but for the process of ministerial formation to be truly

---

[46] George Herbert, *The Country Parson and Selected Poems* (London: SCM, 1956), p. 13.

formational, it requires participating in this same willing vulnerability, of opening up life to others around. This has significant implications, for example, for the relationships which staff develop and model where the necessary asymmetrical relationship of staff who assess students is challenged by an alternative mutuality, for styles of teaching, that do not hide behind unquestionable expertise but open up a common journey of learning, and for the way that our Baptist Colleges relate together.

Formation as Growth in Virtue

One of the ways that David Cunningham has helpfully developed trinitarian thinking is his stress on both trinitarian virtues and practices. He writes:

> 'I will construe the word [virtue] as naming dispositions that *God has by nature* and in which *we participate by grace*. The 'trinitarian virtues' are characteristics of the triune God that are bestowed upon us, freely, as part of God's work of *producing* the world. As gifts, these virtues are not forced upon us; but we can allow them to form us, and thus allow God to take us up into the divine life.'[47]

Cunningham seeks a middle ground between an understanding of virtue in which human beings are entirely passive and simply receive divine gifts, and the more modern stress on 'values' dominated by the autonomous subject who decides and adopts a moral framework entirely within their own power. Rather, that which is a gift from God bears fruit with human activity, so that aspects of God's character develop into human habits, or as Cunningham suggests, '[m]ore specifically, they are elements of the *triune* character of God, and they are present in our development of specifically *triune* habits. In this way our lives can take on a triune character as well, conforming more closely to the image of God in which we were created.'[48] The trinitarian virtues which Cunningham himself then explores are polyphony, participation and particularity.

This offers a way of drawing together many of these suggestions in this essay into a distinct proposal. There has developed among British Baptists in recent years a greater stress on ministerial competencies. There are various reasons for this, including the debate about the professional nature of ministry and the need for the Union as a whole to have a framework in which to consider and act upon examples of ministerial lack of competence. But the stress on competencies, although not to be discounted, stands somewhat in tension with the understanding of ministerial formation

---

[47] David S. Cunningham, *These Three are One: The Practice of Trinitarian Theology* (Oxford: Blackwell, 1998), p. 123.

[48] Cunningham, *These Three are One*, p. 125.

developed here. What may be better as the foundation for a competence based approach is the development of ministerial virtues, based, as Cunningham proposes, on our understanding of trinitarian virtues, which can then lead to distinct ministerial practices.[49] There has been something of a rediscovery of the language and content of virtue in recent theology, significantly influenced by the work of Alistair MacIntyre, although this has been expressed in other ways. Andrew Mayes, for example, connecting this back to ancient concepts of paideia prefers the language of ministerial qualities[50], and staff at the Scottish Baptist College have been working on drawing together their understanding of ministerial formation around ministerial attributes.

While not intending to be exhaustive, this essay has already pointed to a number of such ministerial virtues, which will in a Baptist understanding of ministry be virtues of discipleship, and which will then be expressed in practices:

- Relationality: participating in God and in the lives of others
- Particularity: having a proper self-centring and self-understanding
- Polyphony: holding together unity and difference
- Vulnerability: being open to the other in love
- Service: giving oneself away in love
- Hospitality: giving attention and welcome to the other

It may be time for those within the Union involved and interested in the developing of ministerial formation and practice to work further on such a list that could be a foundational document for the work of our Colleges.

On the basis of a theology of divine vulnerability we might conclude that the *character* of ministerial formation is one of service, risk-taking and willing vulnerability.

Conclusion

Paul Fiddes has always wanted to write theology for the sake of the church, and one of the greatest contributions he offer is both the insistence upon and

---

[49] There may be some similarity here with the Baptist Union's adoption of *Core Values* which undergird a wide variety of practices in different churches. See *Five Core Values for a Gospel People* (Didcot: BUGB, 1999).

[50] Andrew Mayes, *Spirituality in Ministerial Formation* (Cardiff: University of Wales Press, 2009), p. 82. What is unclear in Mayes' account, as in the draft documents from the Scottish Baptist College, is the relationship between ministerial qualities or attributes and those of the whole people of God.

detailed outworking of a trinitarian doctrine of God. In personal appreciation of what Paul has contributed to ministerial formation this essay has sought to build on his thinking in this area and offer some foundations for our on-going shared practice rooted in a trinitarian understanding of God.

9.

The 'Three-fold Order' in a Radical Protestant Perspective

Nigel Wright

In 1888 the Lambeth Conference of Anglican bishops put forward proposals on the basis of which, it believed, unity among the Churches might be achieved. Three of these, acceptance of the authority of Holy Scripture, agreement in the Apostles' and Nicene Creeds, and the practice of both baptism and the Lord's Supper, would have provided no insuperable obstacles for Baptists in contemplating reunion A fourth provision, however, proved to be particularly contentious and unacceptable. It concerned what is known as 'the historic episcopate', the recognition and acceptance of the oversight of bishops duly and properly ordained within the line of bishops deemed to reach back to the original apostles and so to Christ himself, and otherwise spoken of as Free Churches 'taking episcopacy into their system'. When the so-called 'Lambeth Quadrilateral' was revived in 1920 in a further *Appeal to all Christian People*,[1] the then General Secretary of the Baptist Union, the warmly ecumenical Dr J. H. Shakespeare welcomed it and regarded it as a necessity for the incorporation of the Free Churches into a United Church.[2] In this he was wildly adrift from the denomination he led which was firmly to reject this clause in the Quadrilateral even when, by this time, the language had been revised to read, '[a] ministry acknowledged by every part of the Church as possessing not only the inward call of the Spirit, but also the commission of Christ and the authority of the whole body'[3].

Opposition to episcopacy was strong in that it was held to imply, particularly when it was proposed that Free Church ministers should be re-ordained at the hands of bishops, that non-episcopal churches and their ministers were flawed fundamentally and so lacked 'validity'. It should be noted however that those Baptist representatives who made the response to the Quadrilateral were careful to say that what they rejected was the

---

[1] Henry Bettenson (ed.), *Documents of the Christian Church* (Oxford: OUP, 1967), pp. 327-9.

[2] Peter Shepherd, *The Making of a Modern Denomination: John Howard Shakespeare and the English Baptists 1898-1924* (Carlisle: Paternoster, 2001), p.117.

[3] Bettenson (ed.), *Documents of the Christian Church*, p. 329.

'Diocesan Episcopate' which they did not consider 'to be in accordance with the New Testament law of church government'.[4] Other forms of episcopacy are not excluded by this.

In this article I wish to explore the relationship of Baptists to understandings and expressions of episcopacy and to that pattern of ministry that embraces bishops, presbyters and deacons in the Church's traditional 'three-fold order'.[5] Whereas presbyters and deacons are closely paralleled in Baptist church life, it has passed as the agreed conventional wisdom that Baptists and bishops are incompatible. But such a view depends entirely on a set of prior assumptions about the nature and style of episcopacy. Would it be possible to re-imagine and re-define the episcopal ministry in ways that bring it into line with Baptist convictions about the nature of the church and its ministries? The current volume is an appropriate place to attempt this since it honours a theologian who has reflected more than most on what oversight in the Church must be, and has done so as a Baptist with a keen appreciation of the catholic tradition.[6]

More is at stake in addressing this subject than may at first appear. For the largest proportion of professing Christians, bishops are constitutive of the Church and provide it with its guarantee of legitimacy. Bishops safeguard 'apostolicity'. The Church, according to Ignatius, is where the bishop is.

> All of you follow the bishop, as Jesus Christ followed the Father, and the presbytery as the Apostles; respect the deacons as the ordinance of God. Let no one do anything that pertains to the church apart from the bishop. Let that be considered a valid Eucharist which is under the bishop or one whom he has delegated. Wherever the bishop shall appear, there let the people be; just as wherever Christ Jesus may be,

---

[4] This response was made in the Baptist Union's 'Letter on Reunion', 1889, in reply to the Archbishop of Canterbury. The full text is found in Ernest A. Payne, *The Baptist Union: A Short History* (London: Carey-Kingsgate Press, 1958), Appendix VII, pp. 272-4 (273).

[5] I have entered into this discussion on at least two previous occasions. See Nigel G Wright, 'The Case for Baptist Bishops' in *Challenge to Change: A Radical Agenda for Baptists* (Eastbourne: Kingsway, 1986) and 'The Case for Translocal Ministry', in Stuart Murray (ed.), *Translocal Ministry: Equipping the churches for mission* (Didcot: Baptist Union of Great Britain, 2004). To say I have a 'thing' about it might be too much. It is however an abiding concern.

[6] The Baptist Union report *Forms of Ministry among Baptists: Towards an Understanding of Spiritual Leadership* (Didcot: Baptist Union, 1994) was produced by the Doctrine and Worship Committee of the Union under the moderatorship of Paul Fiddes and can be thought rightly to reflect his own thinking at the time.

> there is the catholic Church. It is not permitted to baptize or hold a love-feast independently of the bishop.[7]

Ignatius set the trajectory. Looking back to the progress of the Christian Church in its first centuries, it is hard not to have sympathy with the early emergence of bishops within the post-apostolic era (Ignatius was writing in AD 107). With the passing of the first Apostles, and at a time when many aspects of Christian belief were in the process of normalising and becoming established, the appeal to look to the bishop for the assured rule of faith was a natural one. Keeping close to the bishop who could be seen to be in some credible line of continuity with the first Apostles, and with their witness to Christ, was the most secure way of holding to authentic Christian teaching against those who promulgated deviant and less than adequate doctrine. The bishop could bring security in the midst of the flux, and this was in the absence not of the scriptures as such, since they circulated widely, but of an agreed canon of the New Testament scriptures and at a time before the landmark events of Nicaea, Constantinople and Chalcedon had defined the most salient of Christian teachings. Bishops understandably represented some kind of guarantee of legitimacy and can certainly be said to have had an essential role to play. There are lessons to learn here to which we shall return. However with the gradual assimilation of the church into the Roman Empire and its legalisation and patronage under Constantine other dynamics were in play.

The Church was on its way to becoming not only an influential presence within the Empire but to inheriting its mantle of power, prestige and *romanitas*. Having decisively entered the realm of power politics, it became inevitable that the Church should wish to buttress its own power and to legitimate the position it now assumed. Bishops were bolstered in their position by the crafting of a validating myth concerning their origin. Now it is claimed that the Apostle Peter became bishop of Rome and handed on his primacy in the Church to his successors as such. It is understandable that Peter comes to be seen by virtue of his closeness to Christ as the authoritative teacher of Christ's way. It is certainly the case that the New Testament portrays him as the leader of the Apostles who had been given a special kind of commission from Christ to 'strengthen your brothers'.[8] In a conceptual leap this authority, the power of the keys, is now believed to be passed on to the bishops of Rome who follow him and who come to be seen as the supreme representatives of Christ for each generation. This is the Roman ideological construct that legitimates the supremacy of the see of

---

[7] Ignatius 'To the Smyrneans', chapter 8, in Henry Bettenson (ed.), *The Early Christian Fathers: A selection from the writings of the Fathers from St. Clement of Rome to St. Athanasius* (Oxford: OUP, 1969), p. 49.

[8] Luke 22:32.

Rome. Historical evidence for this line of continuity is lacking, as even Roman Catholic historians acknowledge,[9] as indeed it is for the later myth of the fabricated 'Donation of Constantine' which fulfils a similar ideological function in bolstering the Pope as the monarch of Rome and supreme power over all other sees.[10] In these ways episcopacy is assimilated to the exercise of monarchical, aristocratic and sacred power which came to characterise the hierarchy of the Roman Church and was then carried over into the Church of England once that Church became separated from its parent.

Given such resonance, the proposition that Free Churches should take episcopacy 'into their system' was, as far as Baptists are concerned, a non-starter. Episcopacy understood in this way is the central construct of an ecclesiology in direct opposition to the most cherished Baptist beliefs. In effect it un-churches those Christian communities that do not stand in the tradition of the historic episcopate. The logic of episcopacy, following this line, is that if the celebration of the eucharist is required to constitute a church, and if a validly ordained priest is necessary for there to be a proper eucharist, and if a valid ordination can only take place under the jurisdiction of a bishop in the historic tradition of bishops and through the laying on of his hands, then there can be no church that possesses full ecclesiality outside the circle of those who recognise the historic episcopate. Where there is no bishop there is no church. A wise and functional connection with the bishop that we saw developing in the early church has thus become in its maturity a form of control and of the denial of ecclesiality to other Christians. In its own way it has become a form of sectarianism in excluding other churches from the circle of the truly ecclesial. It is for this reason that Roman Catholic magisterial documents cannot bring themselves to refer to Free Churches and their kin as anything other than 'ecclesial movements stemming from the Reformation'.

The Baptist conception of church is probably as far away from the above as it is possible to be. Whereas a Baptist might have no desire or cause to despise the value of the tradition and may fervently wish to be in continuity with the historic Church as with its worldwide fellowship, the ecclesiality of a church, that is its true nature as a church, is dependent not on the presence of the bishop but on the presence of Christ in the midst of the congregation. 'For where two or three are gathered in my name, I am there among them.'[11]

---

[9] Eamon Duffy, *Saints and Sinners: A History of the Popes* (New Haven and London: Yale University Press, 1997 and 2001), pp. 286-318. The fact that the construct is not water-tight does not, of course, deprive it of all validity. The episcopal succession remains as near as anything is likely to be to a coherent and ancient system, if that is what one is seeking to prove.

[10] 'The Donation of Constantine', in Bettenson (ed.), *Documents of the Christian Church,* pp. 98-101.

[11] Matt 18:20.

The bishop is not regarded as a necessary guarantee of Christ's presence. The essence of being church therefore consists in being gathered together in the name and in the presence of Christ with the intention of listening to his Word and being his people. The insistence that to this needs to be added the oversight of the historic episcopate neither concurs with their reading of scripture nor corresponds with their living experience, since it is evident that abundance of spiritual life is found in a myriad churches which do not hold to the historic episcopate.[12] Spiritual life is therefore manifestly not linked to the presence of the historic episcopate. Indeed for the Baptist quite the opposite might seem to be the case: spiritual vitality is independent of it. Furthermore, soundness of theology and in the teaching office of the church can scarcely be guaranteed by the episcopate when some of the bishops themselves are believed, rightly or wrongly, to be the most significant threat to it.

Baptists, then, and radical Protestants in general, have good reason against this background to be allergic to any suggestion they should take episcopacy into their system. To them bishops represented an ecclesiology directly in conflict with their own convictions and to accommodate to the episcopal would be to betray what is of the biblical essence of their way of being church. I confess myself entirely sympathetic to this reaction. Moreover, this aversion is compounded once all the trappings of episcopacy are taken into account, the haberdashery, the titles, the deference, the bowings and scrapings. It is no surprise that in contemplating the three-fold order Baptists have, with exceptions as we shall see, wished to reduce it, along with Presbyterians and assorted others, to a two-fold one, presbyters (or elders) and deacons. In fact while rejecting episcopacy Baptists have also insisted that they do in fact possess the historic episcopate, not in the form of a diocesan episcopacy but in that of the oversight of the churches through pastors and teachers, that is to say, in its proper New Testament form.[13] This succession of the Church's teachers from generation to generation is one of the strands of the apostolic tradition but it is located in the presbyterate rather than the episcopate. The suggestion is therefore not that episcopacy is simply to be rejected but that its exercise, which is necessary for the good of the church, is to be conceived differently.

All this is worth affirming, but it also runs the risk of throwing the baby out with the bathwater. Where the Baptist response to the Lambeth Quadrilateral understood its own form of historic episcopate to take place within the local Christian community it is my intention to put forward a different vision of translocal episcopacy which retains the value of a wider-than-local ministry. I consider that the case for translocal ministry among

---

[12] Miroslav Volf makes this point very forcibly in *After our Likeness: The Church as the Image of the Trinity* (Grand Rapids: Eerdmans, 1998), pp. 133-4.

[13] Payne, *The Baptist Union*, pp. 272-4.

Baptists is now widely accepted.[14] My main concern will prove to be the use of the term 'bishop' to describe at least some of these ministries. To approach this topic I aim first of all to follow the changing nature of spiritual oversight and leadership in the unfolding drama of scripture, into the history of the church and then into the present day.

Oversight and Scripture

It should be clear that when we investigate the formal shape and nature of ministry in the Old Testament we are in a substantially different world. The religious needs and services of the people of Israel were provided for by a specific religious caste who were born to the role and so fulfilled their duties in a prescribed and ordered way. Worship in Israel revolved initially around the Tabernacle which was constructed in the time of Israel's wanderings in the wilderness. The Tabernacle was a mobile construct suitable to the nomadic lifestyle of the tribes of Israel and which was tended by the tribe of Levi, one of the tribes of Israel dedicated to the ritual and cultic needs of the Tabernacle and the people. This tribe was separated by divine command given through Moses and supported through the tithes that the people paid. From within the tribe of Levi, Aaron, Moses' brother, and his descendants were chosen as the high priestly family. Priesthood was therefore a construct of inheritance and descent. Under King David the authorised line of descent shifted to the family of Zadok, himself a descendant of Aaron through Eleazar.[15] When the Tabernacle transmuted into the Temple in Jerusalem the role of Levites and priests was further institutionalised and ordered. The role of the priests was to offer sacrifices brought by the people in the prescribed way and also to speak the words of blessing over the Israelites.[16] By these means the presence of God among the people was maintained and the spiritual well-being of the nation maintained. The religious apparatus described in this way should be seen as God's provision to preserve the people in communion with God's own self.

In addition to this structured and formalised provision of religious and cultic services there is a more immediate and charismatic dimension in the rise of the prophets. It is tempting, in true Protestant tradition, to pit the prophetic against the priestly or the word against the institution in ways reminiscent of later conflicts within Christendom. This fancy is overthrown once it is understood that some of the prophets were themselves priests. Yet if the priestly and cultic provisions, providentially given by God for the

---

[14] See for instance the eclectic and affirmative collection of essays edited by Stuart Murray, *Translocal Ministry*.

[15] 1 Chron 6:1-15.

[16] Num 6:22-7.

maintenance of right relations within Israel, catered for the regular and constant needs of the people, the prophets are raised up to address specific abuses of the covenant perpetrated by people, priests or kings, calling them back to faithfulness to God and to the way of righteousness.

A further perspective in the Old Testament concerns the role of the King. Israel practised a form of constitutional monarchy whereby, fully aware of the potential for corruption within the institution of kingship,[17] the duties and rights of kingship were set out, written in a book and 'laid up before the Lord'.[18] Kings were expected to walk righteously before the Lord among a people who were called to be a 'holy nation and a royal priesthood',[19] and to maintain the terms of the covenant, providing government of the people as Shepherd-Kings.

It can be seen then that Israel was provided with a range of ministries designed to identify them as God's own people and to preserve them as such in the vicissitudes of life, not least those for which they themselves were responsible. Yet it is also clear that at each point there are weaknesses. The priesthood was to succumb to corruption; kingship, apart from certain exceptions, never truly thrived, as duly prophesied by Samuel, and the prophets were routinely shunned or ignored. The longing for an anointed one who would be what others proved incapable of being began to stir. Prophets, priests and kings were all installed in office by a literal anointing with oil or an equivalent anointing by the Spirit. It is this expectation of a truly anointed one that Christians see being fulfilled in Jesus of Nazareth.

Christians believe in the God of Israel as this same God is to be interpreted in the light of a Messiah who is both crucified and risen. For them the various trajectories of Israel's religion converge on Christ and are fulfilled and transformed by him. Jesus himself said, 'Do not think that I have come to abolish the law and the prophets; I have come not to abolish to fulfil.'[20]In fulfilling the law and the prophets Jesus does not lessen or negate the moral demand that they make, indeed he intensifies it. But in that he embodies the expectations and hope of Israel's religion in his own person he also transforms the ways in which God's demand upon us is to be perceived. The ministries of prophet, priest and king find their definitive embodiment in Jesus. He is our prophet but more than that, he is the Word spoken by the Father through the Spirit.[21] He is our priest, indeed our high priest and he is the sacrificial offering as well.[22] He is our king, and not only so but the King

---

[17] 1 Sam 8.

[18] 1 Saml 10:25.

[19] Ex 19:6

[20] Matt 5:17.

[21] John 1:1-4.

[22] Heb 9.

of kings and Lord of lords,[23] the Lord of the nations and not of Israel alone. By applying such language to Jesus the New Testament signals that a step change has taken place in Christ that has deep and multiple roots within biblical Judaism and yet has moved beyond it by a process of sublation.[24] Taking up into its doctrine of Christ the images, ideas and expectations of biblical religion so that they are incorporated into a higher and broader vision, it has rendered previous values and practices such as sabbath, temple, land, circumcision, sacrifice, priesthood and kingship optional rather than essential. Christ is all of these things to us and Christian thinking about them now begins with him and is regulated by him. Christ is our Apostle, our Prophet, our Evangelist, our Pastor, our Teacher. Christian thinking about these ministries must now proceed from their origins in him.

We have so far pursued a logic that sees the panoply of Israelite religion as both providential and provisional. God provides ways in which the people of Israel may be sustained, governed and corrected. Yet these are provisional in that they lay down formative patterns which prepare the way for recognising the Christ once he has come and provide the patterns of thought that will convey his benefits to us. The process of sublation extracts from Israel's history that which is to endure into God's unfolding universal purposes, but it leaves the husk in which that enduring truth has been contained and renders it no longer of the essence. As we move into the era of the New Testament and the Church, how does this shape our understandings of ministry?

First of all it proceeds on the assumption that the fundamental task of ministry is to bear witness to the fullness that is in Jesus Christ. For this reason any ideas of priesthood need to be fundamentally qualified. Ministers do not in themselves mediate between God and humans but they do bear witness to the one who does, to the one Mediator between God and humanity.[25] In itself this shifts the balance away from thinking of ministers as priests to seeing them as teachers and pastors. A minister's role is not to be in themselves what someone needs but to serve them by guiding them to the one who is sufficient for all. This does not obliterate any ideas of priesthood but it does relativize them and place them in perspective.

Secondly, given that the community of Christ's regenerate and committed followers is 'in Christ' and both enlivened and activated by the Spirit whom he gives, we are able to understand that all believers are gathered into the life of Christ as prophets, priests and kings. In both Old and New Testaments

---

[23] Rev 17:14.

[24] For the important place of 'sublation' in biblical interpretation see Keith Ward, *What the Bible Really Teaches: A Challenge for Fundamentalists* (London: SPCK, 2004), p. 23.

[25] 1 Tim 2:5.

God's desire is for a holy nation and a royal priesthood.[26] In Christ what he is and gives can find manifestation not only in certain castes, categories or types of believer but through all and any as God the Spirit chooses. 'There is no longer Jew or Greek, there is no longer slave or free, there is no longer male and female'.[27] To affirm the priesthood, prophethood and kingship of all believers is to grant that through the Spirit all believers share in spiritual capacity to do the work of the church. It does not claim that all are right all the time, even less is it an expression of individualism whereby we assert ourselves eccentrically over against each other (I'm as good as you are!). It is about the access of the whole Christian community, acting together, to the wisdom and grace of God and to the capacity to serve each other and God. Nor does it collapse ministries into an amorphous whole thereby denying the distinctive ministries, roles and functions of those God appoints to particular work. Not all are prophets, or apostles or teachers.[28]

Thirdly, and building on what has gone before, although Christ is bodily absent from the world it should not be thought that he is spiritually absent. The Ascension indicates that the earthly ministry has come to an end, that he is now no longer under our human control to be manipulated or managed by us, not even in the Church. Christ is sovereign, free and over all. Christ's promise however was to be in the midst when we gather in his name. He sent his Spirit as 'another Advocate'.[29] He indicated, 'I am with you always, to the end of the age'.[30] Christ is to be found in that community which is called the Body of Christ, which is to do with locatability. Although it should not be understood to be the continuation of the incarnation, the Body of Christ is well understood as the primary place where Christ continues to take form, that is, to be locatable and available to his own people and to the world. Though ascended Christ is actively involved in the life of the Church and its ministries.[31] And to this Body Christ imparts gifts which are themselves dynamic manifestations of his continuing grace in so far as they enable us to be the more firmly rooted in the Christ to whom they witness and in whom fullness is to be found. One Pauline passage summarises these gifts as apostles, prophets, evangelists, pastors and teachers.[32] Each of these can be seen to be, as we have shown, an aspect of the continuing ministry of Christ. That which he alone possesses in fullness is manifested, so to speak, in fragments and slivers through those whom he gives for our upbuilding

---

[26] Ex 19:6; 1 Peter 2:9.

[27] Gal 3:28.

[28] 1 Cor 12:29.

[29] John 14:15-7.

[30] Matt 28:20.

[31] Colin Kruse, *New Testament Foundations for Ministry* (London: Marshall Morgan and Scott, 1983), p. 180.

[32] Eph 4:7-13.

Fourthly, translocal ministries such as are identified in Eph 4 are complemented on the local level by *presbuteroi*, *episkopoi,* and *diakonoi,* elders, overseers and deacons. Presumably when the translocal ministries are active in local contexts they take their place within this three-fold order. These local offices of ministry are plausibly thought to reflect the government of the synagogue. In consolidating their missionary labours Paul and Barnabas appointed elders in the congregations they had founded. The exact nature of their functions is far from fully clear but the titles themselves give some indication. *Presbuteros* suggests an older person (and therefore one who is established and mature) or an official; and continues in English as the word presbyter and even priest. An *episkopos* is an overseer, one who literally 'watches over' a congregation and is the word that transmuted into the later usage 'bishop'. Both *presbuteros* and *episkopos* are used interchangeably in the New Testament. *Diakonos* refers to a 'servant' and is sometimes translated as 'minister'.

Oversight and Historical Development

We have painted a picture therefore of a range of translocal ministries, supremely the apostle, widely recognised across the early church and organically related to them through bonds of friendship and spiritual kinship. Institutional forms are minimal or non-existent. On the local level officers are appointed in congregations either by apostolic authority or inner appointment or both. Towards the end of the New Testament era and into the sub-apostolic period certain challenges become inevitable. What is to happen once the Apostles have passed from the scene? Inevitably a deficit opens up in that no-one can replace them wholly. The first Apostles are unrepeatable (hence the initial 'A') in that they are qualified in their role by having been in the company of Jesus and the other apostles from the baptism of John until the resurrection and being witnesses to that resurrection.[33] It is important to note that there is a limit to this circle. They had a unique authority and so when it came to defining Christian teaching they possessed an incontestable primacy thus giving a criterion in assessing what counts as authentic Christian teaching. It can be understood however that the apostolic task went further than this and included the missionary endeavour of the early church and the formation of new congregations in new cultures. Whereas successors might have proved able to fulfil the latter part of an apostolic ministry they logically could not do the former.

It is at this point that, in my view, an entirely warranted piece of theological innovation takes place in separating out the word *episkopos* to refer to translocal pastoral and missional leaders as bishops. In the absence

[33] Acts 1:21-2.

of validating institutional structures it is also natural that a credible line of continuity from the first Apostles is important as a way of discerning whom to trust and who is best able to safeguard the rule of faith. If we are to imagine that these are steady years of growth in the history of the Church it is also natural to believe that senior Christian leaders who have nurtured churches and led in the transmission of the faith would succeed to these positions organically.

What I describe here is not an ideologically constructed episcopacy fashioned to legitimate the existence of a power structure. Rather it is a warranted organic development in the life of the church that answered to the needs of a growing movement and which filled the gap left by the demise of the first Apostles. Bishops could guide younger leaders and congregations, acting for them as a reference point in doctrine and practice and linking congregations with a high degree of autonomy to each other. It was only later, after the conversion of Constantine, that they progressively hardened into a hierarchy, highly influenced by imperial styles and expectations and functioning as a kind of aristocracy. The rest is history. It is entirely understandable and commendable that radical Protestants should wish to reject this form of episcopacy as a deviation from the true Christian path. My argument is that it is possible to imagine a form of episcopal ministry that differs radically from that which has been known in the episcopocentric traditions and which is adapted to the needs and ecclesiology of radical Protestantism.

Radical Protestants, among whom Baptists take their place, have wished strongly to emphasise the freedom of the local congregation. As a movement in reaction against the centralised power system of the Roman Catholic Church, radical Protestants have understood themselves as proponents of freedom, the freedom of the local congregation, of personal conscience and the right of personal interpretation, and deriving from these concerns, religious liberty within a free society. The model of the 'prince bishop' exercising sacred power over the church and temporal power in the world has been understood as inimical to the freedom in Christ for which we have been set free. But, as we have argued, other models of episcopacy can be imagined and foremost among these is one which conceives of bishops as enhancing the freedom of the congregation rather than restricting it.

Oversight and Contemporary Baptist Churches

Whereas churches with a more catholic orientation follow the dictum that the 'church is where the bishop is', radical Protestants ground the church in the presence of Christ in the midst of a believing congregation. The church is established therefore from below rather than from above. Ministers are regarded as being not of the *esse* of the church but its *bene esse*. On this basis it is possible for a church to be wholly a church even without the ministry of a pastor. The eucharist may rightly be celebrated even under lay presidency since it belongs not to the ministry or priesthood but to the people. Yet none of this is to deny the value of trained and dedicated ministers to enable the church to realise its potential and gifting. So understood, ministers are enablers given to the church for its good and the fulfilment of its mission. This is the logical flow of Eph 4: ministries are bestowed upon the church to enable it to fulfil the work of ministry until the church has come to fullness of maturity and life. Insofar as ministers do not enable this they are failing in their task. What has to be acknowledged with such a philosophy of ministry, correct though it may well be, is that ministers in local congregations are exposed to a variety of pressures among which the burden of loneliness is almost always one. Granted that this may be relieved by learning how to exercise ministry collegially and by drawing on the encouragement of peers, there remains nonetheless a deficit which needs to be filled and to which the role of bishop is able to answer.

It is a matter of observable fact that non-episcopal churches have found it necessary, possibly because of the pressures already mentioned, to create some form of ministry which transcends the local congregation and focuses on meeting needs that neither the local congregation nor local ministers are able to meet for themselves. A generic term for such a dimension is the 'judicatory'. Methodists call them 'superintendents' or 'chairs of district' (and have considered turning these into bishops); the United Reformed Church opts for 'moderators'; new churches call them 'apostles'; Baptists have 'regional ministers', who themselves superseded 'general superintendents'. It should be clear that in their own ways these offices are doing part of the work of a bishop even though denied the title. Stuart Murray points out how in pre- and post-Reformation times radical groups such as Waldensians, Lollards and Anabaptists understood the value of being visited by gifted ministers from outside the local congregation. Waldensians called them 'uncles' (in contrast to 'fathers'); to Lollards they were 'known men'. For Anabaptists they were even called 'apostles' and 'prophets'.[34]

In the United States the United Methodist Church adopted the title of bishop from the earliest days of its missionary work. It is of interest also to note that even Baptists have in some parts of the world begun to adopt the term 'bishop'. This is true, for instance, in Moldova and Latvia. In the latter case the term was chosen under pressure from the Communist regime which found the more bureaucratic or political term 'general secretary' a threat to their own hegemony. In the former Communist state of Georgia Baptists have begun to use the title, and even that of 'Archbishop', not under

---

[34] Stuart Murray, 'Translocal Ministry in Post-Christendom', in Murray (ed.), *Translocal Ministry*, pp. 64-74, (66-9).

Communist pressure but as a form of contextualisation, arguing that the Georgian people have certain conceptions and assumptions about what church is. Some strands of Mennonites in the States, very similar to Baptists in their ecclesiology, have long since used the term. It is also common in the ethnic congregations which now abound in this country, especially in its largest cities, for leading pastors to be accorded the term.

What is significant about this observable phenomenon is what it suggests. As there is a drive born of lived ecclesial reality to put in place a translocal form of ministry for the service of ministers and churches, it implies that the provision Christ continues to make for his Church includes such ministries and that there is an 'underlying pattern of office'[35] in that it demands to be expressed in this way. This is the truth in the traditional recognition of a three-fold ministry, namely that wherever the church exists, there will tend to be a three-fold order of presbyters who bear the burden of care for local congregations, of deacons who will serve them and the church in the practical management and care of congregations, and of bishops who will give translocal leadership in mission, teaching and pastoral care. It is true that some would continue to regard this as a two-fold office of elders and deacons with bishops understood not as a separate order but as an extension or extrusion of the presbyteral office.[36] After all, it involves essentially the same qualities of teaching, oversight and mission and only the sphere of ministry is different – translocal rather than local.[37]

Yet exactly this is what, to my mind, makes a difference. Not all are equipped to offer spiritual oversight and leadership, with all the gaining of trust it involves, to a multiplicity of churches. Besides we should not be beguiled by the word 'office' into imagining tightly defined compartments. Better to ask what (and who) it is that Christ is providing for the well-being of his church. What makes this different from the traditional historic episcopacy is that the centre of congregational authority never ceases to be the local congregation and that bishops in particular can never over-ride the authority of the congregation but must position themselves as resources offering assistance on the basis of choice and invitation. This is not a hierarchy backed by legal and constitutional authority but a service which relies on moral and spiritual authority alone.

Of the need for such a ministry I have no doubt. It is instructive at this point to make reference to a parallel discussion about the nature of oversight within the Church. In ecumenical discussion it is well established that oversight exists in three dimensions, the personal, the collegial and the

---

[35] I attribute the term to Paul Fiddes: *Forms of Ministry*, p. 19.

[36] This corresponds with at least one evangelical version of the episcopate as a 'senior presbyter'. See Tim Bradshaw, *The Olive Branch: An Evangelical Anglican Doctrine of the Church* (Carlisle: Paternoster, 1992), p. 175.

[37] *Forms of Ministry*, p. 20.

corporate.[38] Each of these is necessary. Taking them in reverse order, the corporate is the work of 'watching over one another in love' that is fundamental to a radical Protestant understanding of the congregation. As all are privileged to share in the priesthood of all believers so there is a corresponding responsibility for each other, to care for and assist each other in all ways available to us. The collegial is that recognition that there are those who are set 'over' the congregation to exercise oversight, safeguarding the health of the congregation in teaching and relationships. Collegial oversight is clearly rooted in scripture and is effective and necessary in sharing the burden of congregational leadership. The personal dimension accepts that there are certain forms of oversight that cannot be delivered other than through personal one-to-one engagement, either because there are confidential matters concerned or because effective care requires a more skilled engagement. To whichever tradition of church order one may belong it can be seen that these three dimensions are in play. What differs between traditions is the degree of emphasis given to each dimension. For the episcopal churches the personal assumes a clear prominence in the person of the bishop. For radical Protestants the corporate receives clear emphasis in the focus upon the congregation. But no form need exclude other dimensions.

My contention would be that where there is fellowship there needs of necessity to be oversight. *Koinonia* requires *episcope*. Oversight happens where there is fellowship or covenant.[39] This is clearly seen in the local congregation. *Episkope* works to ensure that *koinonia* remains healthy and is harmonious, and that mutual care is practised to the full. Transferred to the translocal level the same pattern is applied. An association of churches might practise corporate oversight in caring for and supporting each other; collegial care can be extended as those elected to lead and guide the association consider the needs of the churches; personal oversight comes from the 'judicatory', the regional minister or others who are tasked with such care. But the value of the personal dimension needs to be recognised and itself enabled. It also requires sufficient weight to carry conviction and this is achieved both by the personal charisma of the overseer concerned and through the corporate credibility of the churches he or she represents.

Radical Protestants have tended to place their emphasis both on the local church and the practice of corporate oversight with the consequence that they have been slow to affirm the place of personal, translocal oversight such as would in other traditions be fulfilled by bishops. Yet the missiologist Professor Brian Stanley has pointed out how in certain situations, especially in the contexts of overseas mission, a bishop-like ministry emerges. The

---

[38] *Baptism, Eucharist and Ministry,* (Geneva: World Council of Churches, 1982).

[39] Paul Fiddes, *A Leading Question* (Didcot: Baptist Union, 1983), p. 44.

'Form of Agreement', adopted by BMS Serampore missionaries in 1805 concerned itself with the ordination of Indian ministries and agreed they should work:

> 'as much as possible without the interference of the missionary of the district who will constantly superintend their affairs, give them advice in cases of order and discipline, and correct any errors into which they fall; and, who joying and beholding their order, and the stedfastness of their faith in Christ, may direct his efforts continually to the planting of new churches in other places, and to the spread of the gospel in his district, to the utmost of his power' (idioms original).[40]

This is as good a definition of a radical Protestant episcopacy as might be imagined. The assumption that such ministries are no longer necessary in a settled rather than front-line mission context is questioned by this chapter.

If indeed there is an underlying pattern of ministry that will tend to emerge within the sphere of practical church life, it is no surprise to find that, whatever may be the denominational or ecclesial context inhabited, the structure of bishop, presbyter and deacon will tend to emerge, whatever these ministries will be called. One General Baptist Confession of Faith specifically outlines a three-fold order of Ministry:

> (T)here are these three, viz. Bishops or Messengers; and Elders, or Pastors, and Deacons, or Overseers of the poor; and the way appointed by Christ, for the calling of any person fitted and gifted by the holy ghost, unto the office of bishop, or messenger, in the churches is, viz, That he be chosen thereunto by the common suffrage of the church, and solemnly set apart by fasting and prayer, with imposition of hands, by the bishops of the same function, ordinarily, and those bishops so ordained, have the government of those churches that had suffrage in their election, and no other ordinarily.[41]

When in 1916 the 'general superintendency' was established among Baptist churches, it was regarded as a radical departure. But Payne points out that this was not entirely the case. General Baptists in the seventeenth century had already appointed 'messengers' to a similar role.[42] The word

---

[40] Brian Stanley, 'Planting self-governing churches: British Baptist ecclesiology in the missionary context' in *Baptist Quarterly*, 34 (1991-2), p. 381.

[41] Article XXXI in 'The Orthodox Creed' (1678), in W. L. Lumpkin, *Baptist Confessions of Faith* (Valley Forge: Judson Press, 1959), pp. 319-20.

[42] Payne, *Baptist Union*, p. 183. See also John F. V. Nicholson, 'The Office of Messenger among British Baptists in the Seventeenth and Eighteenth Centuries', in *Baptist Quarterly*, 17 (1957-8).

'messenger' was their rendering of 'apostle'.[43] Whereas in episcopocentric churches the ministry of the bishop was paramount and provided the foundation on which new churches might be established, for Baptists and other radical Protestants the local church was grounded on the presence of Christ within the community. Ministers were conceived therefore as arising within the congregation, being validated by the congregation and either appointed to serve within it or sent out from it to serve the wider mission of the church. Ministers are appointed by the calling and acceptance of the local church. Commissioning authority is given from God above, but it is accorded from below. If there are to be bishops within such a pattern it can therefore only be as gifts and calling are recognised, validated and commissioned by a local church or a fellowship of churches acting in concert and, as they would believe, in harmony with God's will. It is to be regretted, as Ian Randall points out, that at the origins of superintendency there was no clear agreement about whether superintendents had episcopal functions. Some resisted the notion on the grounds that they lacked the power of Anglican bishops (quite rightly so) and so could not be called bishops. Others saw that they had moral and spiritual authority and this was the kind that really mattered. Besides, the word 'superintendent' was simply a Latin rendering of the Greek *episkopos*, and furthermore was patterned on the Lutheran Superintendents who served in some regions of Germany whereas their counterparts in other regions were indeed called Bishops.[44]

Within current Baptist church life it is now well-established that local congregations benefit from the ministry of translocal, regional ministers. It would also be widely accepted that such ministries are biblically, historically and theologically as well as practically justifiable. Despite this there would be hesitations about using the title 'bishop'. Perhaps if the noun were turned into a verb and we were to speak of 'bishoping', the hesitation might be less, since the focus would be on the actions of caring for churches and ministers in their missionary calling rather than the holders of the office. The hesitation about the title derives in all probability from the continuing memory of the forms and styles still exhibited by the historic episcopate, as already mentioned. We have argued that episcopacy can be differently conceived in radical Protestant perspective. This done, and in the awareness that the proposition is unlikely to be taken up in the near future but may yield fruit in the longer term, I wish to advocate the use of the term 'bishop' when describing those we currently call regional ministers, or at least the team leaders of the regional ministers in each association.

---

[43] A. C. Underwood gives a succinct summary of Messengers and their commission in *A History of the English Baptists* (London: Baptist Union, 1947) pp. 119-121.

[44] Ian M. Randall, '"A Good Bench of Bishops", Early Baptist Superintendency', in Murray (ed.), *Translocal Ministry*, pp. 33-43, (40-41, 43).

It may be objected that a rose by any other name smells as sweet. What does it matter what they are called as long as people do the job they are appointed to? Whereas it might not matter a great deal, I would contend, it does still matter. It is passing strange that we prefer to call people by bureaucratic rather than ecclesial or biblical titles. 'Superintendent' has strong resonances of other spheres of life. 'General Secretary' is clearly a bureaucratic title that possibly obscures as much as it clarifies in Baptist church life. The point is that titles are necessary in any sphere of life to describe succinctly what people do. A title creates a certain expectation both for the title-holder and for those who may look to them for their assistance, and indeed for those outside the Church. A title has to be lived up to since in itself it is a job description. To name a person 'pastor' requires that person to live and work as just that. It requires others to look to a pastor for pastoral ministry and not for other things, and does so justifiably. I suspect that when looking to appoint someone a bishop within an ecclesial communion, the word requires a person of experience, gravity, intellectual capacity, holiness of life, evangelistic zeal and passion for God. This person has to 'oversee' the community of faith and not just act as a denominational functionary. We want them to be worthy of the trust that is placed in them. The title helps clarify expectation. It is clear that some at least of our forebears in the General Baptists, and a smaller number of the Particulars, had a well-worked out theology of inter- or trans-congregational ministry and that they did not shrink on occasion from calling these servants 'bishops'. Ruth Gouldbourne points out that they could use this language confidently because they were also clear what they did not mean by it. They were working out a new way of believing and acting in accord with their fundamental convictions about the Church.[45]

This is not so much 'taking episcopacy into our system' as though it were presented to us from outside, but allowing episcopacy to arise from within. In these ways, and in contrast to the 'historic episcopate' of the more catholic traditions, which is essentially grounded in a descent of hierarchies,[46] free church principles are maintained. The freedom of the local congregation is not over-ruled or compromised either by elders (presbyters) and deacons serving locally nor by bishops working translocally. It has been a fundamental conviction that spiritual ministry can only properly be exercised where there has been willing reception of it in the first place. Messengers only had authority within churches that had shared in their

---

[45] Ruth Gouldbourne, 'Messengers: Do they have a Message for us?', in Murray (ed.), *Translocal Ministry*, pp. 24-32 (30-31). This chapter also has very pertinent things to say about the criteria for assessing a Baptist form of episcopacy.

[46] It should of course be acknowledged that in many parts of the Anglican Communion and in parts of Orthodoxy, Bishops and Archbishops are elected to office.

election. The responsibility of all and any such ministries is to nurture the freedom of the local congregation to the point of maturity and to facilitate the process whereby it comes to a common mind about its own decisions for the appointment of officers and leaders and for the fulfilment of its mission.

The risen Christ provides for his Church that which it needs to rise to its full stature. The value of translocal ministries is now widely recognised by Baptists, the radical Protestants pre-eminently addressed in this chapter. I do not envisage that the call to rehabilitate the word 'bishop' will be taken up easily or swiftly by this community, and the arguments marshalled against it will be worthy of a careful hearing. I do believe, however, that in growing into the church we wish to be we will in time see the merits of the argument to that effect. As we grow towards the point of allowing episcopal ministries to grow in strength among us, the adoption of a word will in time follow.

10.

The Meaning and Function of 'Dynamic Equivalence' in Ecumenical Dialogues

Myra Blyth

Introduction

Unique amongst contemporary Baptist theologians has been the sustained participation by Prof Paul Fiddes in national and international ecumenical discussions between Baptists and sister denominations and communions. He has taken a leading role for over two decades in the discussions between the BUGB Faith and Unity Executive Committee of the Baptist Union of Great Britain and The Council for Christian Unity of the Church of England[1]. He has in addition served as co-chair of the Continuation Committee of the BWA - Anglican Consultative Council discussions[2] and most recently as co-chair of the BWA - Roman Catholic discussions (BWA/RCC).[3] The huge benefit of his participation is the consistency it has brought to the unity discussions. Through his creative connections and deep theological insights it has been possible in these discussions to build a coherent picture and to avoid the common problem of collective memory loss or sloppy duplication.

This article recognises Paul Fiddes' commitment in ecumenical dialogue to respect and safeguard the integrity of traditions. There is in his approach, realism that progress will not be achieved simply by putting differences behind us as if they don't matter, or by negotiating positions as if truths can be exchanged or traded. He rather seeks to open up a space in which truth will be revealed through mutual learning and prayer. By encountering the

---

[1] *Pushing at the Boundaries of Unity: Anglicans and Baptists in Conversation* (London: Church House Publishing, 2005).

[2] *Conversation Around the World 2000-2005: The Report of the International Conversations between the Anglican Communion and the Baptist World Alliance* (London: Anglican Communion Office, 2005).

[3] *The Word of God in the Life of the Church: A Report of the International Conversations between The Catholic Church and The Baptist World Alliance 2006-2010*, available at

http://www.vatican.va/roman_curia/pontifical_councils/chrstuni/Bapstist%20alliance/rc_pc_chrstuni_doc_20101213_report-2006-2010_en.html.

Spirit in each other and acknowledging God's Spirit at work in the different expressions of church and tradition identities are not lost but enriched. His remarks on the ecumenical calling of the church typify his open and creative approach:

> The form that *episkope* might take in the future is surely only one instance of allowing tracks from the past to converge with traces of God's movement into the future. The ecumenical calling of the church must be a summons to move on, to tread the pilgrim path in ways known and 'to be made known'. God help the church if she gets stuck when she should be walking steadily on, her face turned to the coming kingdom.[4]

This article seeks to analyse Fiddes' distinctive approach to ecumenical dialogue, using the theory of 'dynamic equivalence' as an interpretative key. In translation work dynamic equivalence reflects the fact that the task of the translator is not to translate literally but in a way that is contextually appropriate and equivalent in meaning to the original intention. Fiddes, I shall argue, has sought through successive discussions and through his own writings to find dynamic equivalence in faith and practice between ecumenical partners. This essay analyses themes where this approach to dialogue has been used to good effect. It will focus primarily on the subject of baptism but will also briefly highlight its use in two further areas: patterns of ministry and then church governance and decision making.

The Theory of Dynamic Equivalence

Dynamic equivalence theory was first conceived by the anthropologist Eugene Nida. He revolutionised translating by shifting the focus from the traditional source text-centered theories, which strictly adhere to specific linguistic problems, to the function of translation to make certain that the receptor understands accurately the message carried by the source text.

In the book entitled *The Theory and Practice of Translation,* co-authored with Charles Taber, Nida offers the following explanation of dynamic equivalence:

> The older focus in translating was the form of the message, and translators took particular delight in being able to reproduce stylistic specialties, e.g., rhythms, rhymes, plays on words, chiasmus, parallelism and unusual grammatical structures. The new focus,

---

[4] Paul S. Fiddes, *Tracks and Traces: Baptist Identity in Church and Theology* (Carlisle: Paternoster, 2003), p. 227.

> however, has shifted from the form of the message to the response of the receptor. Therefore what one must determine is the response of the receptor to the translated message. This response must then be compared with the way in which the original receptors presumably reacted to the message when it was given in its original setting.[5]

The concept of receptor response is perhaps the best known of the foundational concepts in Nida's dynamic equivalence theory but also important is his categorising of language according to four functions – Things, Events, Attributes and Relations – and his analysis of language structure using the concept of kernel statements.

Kernel analysis of language has more to do with clauses and sentences than words. Building on kernel statements and symbols Nida developed his system for translating which he described in *Toward a Science of Translating* as 'decoding, transfer, and encoding'[6].

> Instead of attempting to set up transfers from one language to another by working out long series of equivalent formal structures which are presumably adequate to 'translate' from one language into another, it is both scientifically and practically more efficient (1) to reduce the source text to its structurally simplest and most semantically evident kernels, (2) to transfer the meaning from source language to receptor language on a structurally simple level, and (3) to generate the stylistically and semantically equivalent expression in the receptor language.[7]

Using the analogy of dynamic equivalence theory, it can be said that ecumenical dialogues such as Baptist – Catholic or Baptist–Anglican conversations seek to find language that will be understandable across ecclesial cultures and traditions. So, for example, for Baptists the phrase 'fellowship of believers' is a kernel sentence which when analysed and decoded is a message about authority and governance and is foundational to Baptist ecclesiology. This concept needs translating with reasonable accuracy by establishing equivalent points of reference and reproducing in the receptor language the closest natural equivalence of the source-language message. Similarly, in the case of baptism the word is not used in exactly the same way so that a word for word translation is not meaningful. While the

---

[5] Eugene A. Nida and Charles R. Taber, *The Theory and Practice of Translation* (Leiden: E. J. Brill, 1969), p. 1.

[6] Eugene A. Nida, *Toward a Science of Translating: with special reference to principles and procedures involved in Bible translating* (Leiden: E. J. Brill. 1964), p. 146.

[7] Nida, *Toward a Science*, p. 68.

debate has certainly not been resolved, more recently by locating its meaning within the kernel structure of Christian initiation, equivalent meanings have been proposed.

Baptism and the Journey of Initiation

Christian initiation has been a strong dialogue point in discussions on the national level between the Baptist Union of Great Britain and The Church of England[8], and internationally in conversations between The Baptist World Alliance and the Anglican Consultative Council[9] and between The Baptist World Alliance and The Catholic Church[10]. In multilateral dialogues co-ordinated by the WCC Faith and Order Commission the term common baptism continues to be used but in bilateral conversation involving Baptists there has been recognition that the argument put forward by Fiddes offers a hopeful way forward. His argument is that rather than discussing common baptism (which for Baptists is impossible) we can and need to be in dialogue about a common journey of initiation. His argument is as follows: while the path to committed discipleship follows different routes in different traditions there is in the complete journey of initiation a dynamic equivalence across traditions. Baptism is one moment in the journey. For some, baptism takes place at the beginning of the journey, for others it occurs nearer the end.

The case for common initiation within which baptism is a particular moment is developed by Fiddes in his systematic exploration of Baptist identity in church and theology. Fiddes' starting point is the notion found historically in covenant theology and more recently in ecumenical texts such as *Baptism, Eucharist and Ministry* (*BEM*)[11] which understands salvation is a process in which faith is constantly being renewed and deepened. Within the life-long process of salvation Fiddes sees initiation as the journey of Christian beginnings which extends from birth to committed discipleship. He makes the case for understanding baptism not as an isolated event but a distinct moment in this journey of initiation. Baptism occurs at different points in the journey in respective traditions, but always only at one point. This proposal is important on two levels: first, theologically it highlights afresh the importance of process and the danger of reducing conversion and baptism to isolated moments. Second, with regard to ecclesiology, it offers a way forward ecumenically to overcome the classic and violent divide between churches on the question of baptism.

---

[8] *Pushing at the Boundaries*, chapters 4 and 5, pp. 31-74.

[9] *Conversation Around the World 2000-2005*, pp. 45-52, 76-77, 99.

[10] *The Word of God in the Life of the Church*, paragraphs 93-115.

[11] World Council of Churches, *Baptism, Eucharist and Ministry* (Geneva: World Council of Churches, 1982).

The notion of salvation as a life long journey or process is deeply embedded in dissenting thought (immortalised in Bunyan's *The Pilgrim's Progress*). Fiddes suggests that, consistent with covenant theology, 17th century Baptists not only preserved the mystery of grace and freedom but also the sense that salvation was not merely a point but a process or a story. Salvation so understood is not reduced to a conversion moment but an ongoing experience which is revitalised through the life of the church and not least in the acts of baptism and the Lord's Supper.[12]

In the multilateral dialogues on *BEM* it was proposed that churches should seek mutually to recognise whole patterns of initiation and, within those, different forms of baptism as equivalent alternatives.[13] This proposal, notes Fiddes, 'was in recognition that the mere fact that all churches practised some form of baptism would not in itself achieve the mutual recognition of each other's baptism.'[14] More recent Faith and Order discussions on baptism have focused on 'common baptism' which has worked against the appeal to explore a common process of Christian beginnings or a common journey into faith and salvation. The journey motif, however, has been maintained and further developed by Fiddes within bilateral dialogues.

In the chapter titled 'One baptism: a Baptist contribution in the Baptist Union / Church of England report, Fiddes roots his theology of initiation in a dynamic understanding of salvation:

> We need to set baptism in the context of salvation, which the New Testament presents less as a moment than as a journey of life, a 'pilgrim's progress'. Different writings give us three senses or tenses for salvation. Christians 'have been saved' through the once-for –all event of the cross of Jesus (e.g. Ephesians 2.8); we are 'being saved' as we grow day by day in a healing relationship with God and are gradually made more like Christ (e. g. 1 Corinthians 1.18); we 'shall be saved' at the final appearing of Christ in glory (e.g. Romans 5.9-10). We cannot know the mysterious beginnings of our salvation, far back in the secret purposes of God, who begins a work of prevenient grace in drawing human hearts to God's self.[15]

Into this context baptism becomes a decisive point in the whole process of being saved. Baptism is

---

[12] *Pushing at the Boundaries*, p. 41.

[13] See Word Council of Churches, Faith and Order paper 111 (1982) chapter IV paragraph11 on baptismal practice plus commentary 12 on baptismal practice.

[14] Fiddes, *Tracks and Traces*, p. 142.

[15] *Pushing the Boundaries*, p. 41.

> a meeting place provided for us, to which God promises to come in order to meet our faith with divine grace, although we also meet with God in many other times and places in life. While the whole of the Christian life is a saving process of growth into Christ, baptism is a moment within one stage of the journey of salvation, the early phase that we call 'beginnings' or initiation.[16]

The clear benefits of this approach are that different practices are seen as sharing in the one baptism of Jesus Christ. Regardless of their mode of baptising and without any suggestion that infant and believers' baptisms are the same thing the baptism of infants or believers can be celebrated together by churches:

> A concept of common initiation will recognise that different baptismal practices share in some way in the 'one baptism' of Jesus Christ without claiming that different modes of baptism are simply equivalent, or the same thing. It affirms that there is a process or journey of initiation in which baptism may stand either near the beginning or near the end.[17]

In the BWA/RCC report a theology of 'common initiation' is directly discussed and warmly acknowledged by both communions. In the section on baptism the participants agree that 'initiation into Christ and his church is a process wider than the act of baptism itself. We can work towards a mutual recognition of the different forms that initiation takes among us, as an entire 'journey' of faith and grace.'[18] The report draws a strong parallel between the conversation Baptists have recently been having with Anglicans about a process of initiation or a 'journey of Christian beginnings' and the Catechism of the Catholic Church which states 'becoming a Christian has been accomplished by a journey and initiation in several stages'.[19]

The report goes on to elaborate the elements or stages which make up this journey and shows that these elements are common to both traditions, Baptists and Roman Catholics alike.

> For adults who come to faith in both traditions this journey begins with the church's evangelisation, the proclamation of the Gospel that calls a person to faith … belief and acceptance of the Gospel entail several steps or stages along a journey: conversion (which follows in response to the proclamation of the gospel), then water baptism in the

---

[16] *Pushing at the Boundaries*, p. 41.

[17] *Pushing at the Boundaries*, p. 45.

[18] *The Word of God in the Life of the Church*, paragraph 101.

[19] *The Word of God in the Life of the Church*, paragraph 102.

name of the Father Son and Spirit, reception of the gifts of the Spirit with the responsibility to participate in God's mission in the world and a sharing in the Eucharist or the Lord's Supper for the first time. This period of initiation is followed by lifelong discipleship, which has a baptismal pattern of daily dying and rising with Christ.[20]

Having thus articulated a clear and striking agreement, more unequivocally even than in the Baptist Union / Church of England report, the text goes on in a subsequent paragraph to note the place of infant baptism within this same theological framework: 'this journey of initiation can include the baptism of young infants although the sequence of the stages will be different from that which happens with adults.'[21]

Not surprisingly, given the mood and content of the conversation – and yet remarkably given the histories of these two churches – the report concludes that working towards a mutual recognition of common initiation rather than try to make a common affirmation about 'common baptism' is the fruitful way to build relations and future discussions. In other words the concept of dynamic equivalence has served to establish a way forward methodologically on wider areas of discussion.

Two further themes can be briefly highlighted here to illustrate that the tool of dynamic equivalence is being used across a range of conversations.

Patterns of Ministry

In his reflection on ministry in ecumenical dialogues Fiddes has consistently sought to map a Baptist two fold pattern onto the threefold order of Catholic and Anglican structures. He argues not for symmetry but for dynamic equivalence in these patterns. The two fold order of ministry in Baptist ecclesiology and the three fold order in Anglican ecclesiology are presented as distinct but complementary.

His account of the two fold nature of the office of ministry in *Tracks and Traces* is described in ways that builds on New Testament texts and early Baptist confessions: first the office of apostle was to oversee from the perspective of the wider church and second, the office of diakonoi was to undertake a ministry of preaching and pastoral care within the local church alongside the pastor[22].

While this two-fold office of Pastor (or Bishop or Elder) and Deacon has existed since early in the Baptist story, Fiddes is very aware that in the current climate this is not accepted by all as normative for Baptist life, the

[20] *The Word of God in the Life of the Church*, paragraph 102.

[21] *The Word of God in the Life of the Church*, paragraph 102.

[22] Fiddes, *Tracks and Traces*, p. 90.

preference of many being for a more fluid pattern of ministries within local churches and on the trans-local level. Whether a stable two-fold pattern of ministry is desirable is deemed by some as overly prescriptive and viewed by not a few as the slippery road to clericalism. While this complicates engagement in ecumenical discussions, Fiddes has been faithful to the tradition: allowing the dynamic between past and present to inform the discussion.

Patterns of Oversight

Baptist views on authority and oversight are of course very different from the views held in episcopal structures. The difference is clearly acknowledged in dialogues. Fiddes notes how in Baptist ecclesiology power is not delegated or handed down in a chain of command but rather passes 'to and fro' between pastor and people[23]. It is, he observes, the covenant relationship – rather than the person of the Bishop – which is crucial in the Baptist ecclesial structures: by churches covenanting together unity is safeguarded between the local and the wider body and at the same time covenant theology also acknowledges that the local church, when it gathers under the rule of Christ, is not a segment of the church universal but complete in itself.

At the same time as highlighting the differences in the way authority is understood and handled Fiddes still adopts the method of dynamic equivalence by suggesting that patterns of oversight in local Baptist churches are both personal and communal as well as collegial, where a local setting has a team of ministers/elders and on the trans-local level where church members and ministers meet in association. [24] The mutual and fluid relationship in congregational decision making structures between local church, association and national assembly leads him to conclude that there is a dynamic equivalence to the decision making structures found within Free Church and episcopal churches.

In the world conversations between Anglicans and Baptists the concluding section posed questions for both communions which seek to deepen understanding and appreciation for the integrity behind the different oversight patterns and structures:

> Can Anglicans and Baptists discern the same reality of *episkope* (pastoral oversight and responsibility) in each other's churches, despite differences in church structures? In particular, can Anglicans

---

[23] Fiddes, *Tracks and Traces*, pp. 221-223.

[24] Fiddes, *Tracks and Traces*, pp. 221-223.

> find the reality of *episkope* in Baptist churches even though there is no bishop in the Anglican understanding of this office?[25]

In the dialogue between Catholics and Baptists a three-fold pattern of oversight was mutually affirmed as

> episcope is exercised in personal, collegial and communal ways in the church. These ways are not exclusive to one another but bound together in a network of dynamic relationships which together make up overall episcope in the church.[26]

The contrasting ways in which these forms of oversight are expressed are seen as differences in emphasis or accent rather than kind:

> For Baptists the New Testament *episkopos* is primarily the pastor in the local congregation, while for Catholics it is the Bishop who shepherds a community of many parishes. Baptists and Catholics emphasise the exercise of episcope in different ways ... Catholics tend to think of individual oversight first and so give greater accent to its personal character, as embodied in the ministry of bishops ... Baptist by contrast emphasize its exercise in communal ways.[27]

Conclusion

The hard reality is that ecumenical dialogues often lack systematic follow up even though popular material for local group reflection is available. The underlying obstacle for Baptists is that the reports emerging from these dialogues attract little interest and receive little attention. There are many reasons for this but perhaps the overriding challenge is the perception amongst many Baptists that these discussions place high value on questions relating to tradition and ecclesiology: themes that seem far removed from the missional questions which shape their thinking. For this reason, amongst others, the immediate impact of ecumenical dialogues is muted but I believe that these dialogues will stand the test of time and they will feed future generations with a depth of insight that is not sufficiently treasured in the present. Perhaps through some creative 'translation work' within the Baptist Union, the achievements of these dialogues will be appreciated better by a mission receptor culture and this will result in a rich and more holistic appreciation of both the nature and mission of the church.

---

[25] *Conversation Around the World 2000-2005*, p. 79.

[26] *The Word of God in the Life of the Church*, paragraph 173.

[27] *The Word of God in the Life of the Church*, paragraph 194.

What then has been achieved by applying the concept of dynamic equivalence to ecumenical dialogues? There are two substantial benefits. First this approach has successfully nurtured a spirit of ecumenical generosity. It has produced a desire for better mutual understanding and for deeper respect across once bitter historical divides. Second this method opens up fertile new ground for mutual critical theological reflection. The examples cited in this article show how the concept of dynamic equivalence represents the single most important theological tool for developing Baptist dialogue with ecumenical partners in the last 30 years. For this, Baptists worldwide and their dialogue partners owe a huge debt to Professor Paul Fiddes.

11.

Attuned to God

John Weaver

Introductory Remarks

It is a pleasure and a privilege to contribute to this book, a tribute to Paul Fiddes' deeply held concern for the Church and its mission and ministry. I am indebted to Paul's teaching and writing as a student at Regent's Park College (1978-1981), and through his continuing friendship over the last thirty-two years. Paul was always interested in the experiences and issues raised within pastoral ministry and encouraged me to reflect on the questions that these aspects of ministry raised for our understanding of God: how God acted in the world; and what we might learn about God's desire for human lives.

After ten years of such theological reflection Paul encouraged me to apply for the post of tutor in Pastoral Studies at Regent's. Through my role as tutor I continued to explore theological reflection with Paul as a mentor - always ready with a probing question and insightful observation in areas of practical theology.

Whilst at Regent's Paul encouraged me to explore the dialogue between science and theology, again with theological reflection at its heart: how does theology address the questions that modern science is posing about the origin and evolution of the cosmos and human life; and what do we learn about the nature of God and God's purposes in creation from such discoveries. These twin tracks of pastoral/practical theology and the dialogue between science and faith have shaped my own academic career over the last twenty-five years, for which I am indebted to the encouragement and inspiration that I have received from Paul.

In this contribution to his festschrift I will engage with his work in the area of pastoral/practical theology, particularly: *Participation in God*[1] and 'Ancient and Modern Wisdom: The Intersection of Clinical and Theological Understanding of Health'[2].

---

[1] Paul S. Fiddes, *Participating in God: A Pastoral Doctrine of the Trinity* (London: DLT, 2000).

[2] Paul S. Fiddes, 'Ancient and Modern Wisdom: The Intersection of Clinical and Theological Understanding of Health' in Stephen Finamore & John Weaver (eds),

Walking with God

As Christian disciples part of our growth comes through reflecting on our lives and circumstances in the light of the Gospel we believe. The things that happen to us, around us, within us, register at different levels. The complex interaction of mind, emotion and spirituality, the impact of the encounter on me, is determined by how attentive I am to my own inner life and to the life of others around me.

We can question our emotions and feelings. The connection between understanding what we experience now and what we have already experienced is a given of human life. Why I am angry with someone is partially answered by the history of the relationship, the incidents that are significant, the other circumstances of my life, and the impact of other relationships on this relationship. Each experience is coloured by its context in my life, each relationship feels the impact of commitments to others who have different roles in our lives. We need to understand this and know ourselves at each moment during our lives.

Beyond feelings it is useful to consider our thought processes. What did I think about? What questions were raised by the thought process – what did I think about what I felt; how did I feel about what I thought? Identifying feeling, clarifying thought, and disentangling feeling from thought, is part of that instinctive desire to make sense of, to understand, and to discover meaning in what happens to us and around us.

All of these experiences are shaped by what we believe about God, and we move on to ask theological questions such as: Where was God in these events? Does faith in Christ have any relevance in these encounters in other people's lives? What is appropriate pastoral ministry in these situations? What does it mean to be Christ in this place and time? Are there clues here that give glimpses or hints of the Spirit's life-giving, life-enriching, life-transforming energy?

It is clear that godly wisdom is necessary in unravelling the complexities of this world and our life experiences within it. Paul Fiddes has helpfully explored our participation in God and opened up our understanding of Christian discipleship through an exploration of the Trinity and pastoral practice.[3] For Fiddes our participation in the life of God affects the way we do theology, we are not observers but are involved in the energy and patterns of the divine life.

Eugene Peterson offers a complementary view as he challenges us to consider the way in which we experience creation. Each new day presents us with a world we did not make. We perceive it in every sight, sound, smell;

Wisdom, Science and the Scriptures; Essays in Honour of Ernest Lucas (Oxford: Regent's Park, 2012).

[3] Fiddes, *Participating in God.*

around, above, below, inside, outside; every experience. It is, he observes, the sheer 'is-ness' of colour, shape, sound, texture.[4] Jesus is the key to our understanding of creation as illustrated in Hebrews 11:3; John 1:1-14; Colossians 1:15-20. Recognising that creation is God's creation we submit to what God will do, has done, and is doing.

> We are not spectators of creation but participants in it. We are participants first of all by simply being born, but then we realise that our births all take place in the defining context of Jesus' birth. The Christian life is the practice of living in what God has done and is doing.[5]

In Jesus God is a participant in creation, totally committed and personally present (Hebrews 4:14-16; John 1:14; 3:16). When we ask how we live and move and have our being in God, Fiddes' image of dance helps us to move away from rational doctrines to a participation in movement, which I would express as being in the Spirit. Such participation has freedom to respond and is the outworking of God, who in love allows us to be.

We will need to explore our understanding of spirituality in this respect as we consider such participation. Elizabeth MacKinlay describes spirituality as 'that which lies at the core of each person's being, an essential dimension that brings meaning to life' and Deborah Dunn suggests that:

> Spirituality means not just one compartment of life, but the deepest dimension of all life. The spiritual is the ultimate ground of all our questions, hope, fears, and loves ... It concerns our struggles with loss; questions of self-worth and fear of reaching out to make new friendships.[6]

I find the definition proposed by William Stringfellow in *The Politics of Spirituality* to be most helpful:

> Whatever else may be affirmed about a spirituality which has a biblical precedent and style, spiritual maturity or spiritual fulfilment necessarily involves the whole person – body, mind and soul, place, relationships – in connection with the whole of creation throughout the era of time. Biblical spirituality encompasses the whole person in the

---

[4] Eugene H. Peterson, *Christ Plays in Ten Thousand Places. A Conversation in Spiritual Theology* (London: Hodder & Stoughton, 2005), p. 51.

[5] Peterson, *Christ Plays in Ten Thousand Places*, p. 54.

[6] Albert Jewell, *Ageing, Spirituality and Well-being* (London: Jessica Kingsley, 2004), pp. 14-16, where Jewell refers to essays by these authors that appear later in the book.

> totality of existence in the world, not some fragment or scrap or incident of a person.[7]

It is this definition that best sums up the spirituality that I believe is encompassed by the celebration of the Eucharist or Lord's Supper. Here we explore our relationship with God through Christ, our relationship with each other in the presence of the Holy Spirit, and our relationship with the world where, as Fiddes discusses, we share in the perichoresis (mutual indwelling) of the triune God.[8]

However, God always seeks to encourage us in his desire for our life, and I agree with Fiddes that the whole world is a place to encounter God. It is in the universe that we see God's creativity continuously at work. We have a sacramental universe that displays God's grace, love and faithfulness, and which in this sense can be described as expressing the body of the Trinitarian God,[9] as Christ expresses what it is to be truly human. My own work in exploring the dialogue between science and faith develops this theme.[10] Fiddes offers a useful summation of this argument:

> we should envisage sacraments drawing us deeper into the heart of the interweaving flow of relationships in God. The key is participation, so that God is always open to make room for the world, while remaining an event of relationship in God's own self. God has a body, in so far as finite bodies are in God, and so movements of love and justice in God are expressed through bodies.[11]

This suggestion echoes what I have said elsewhere[12] about our participation in Christ, his death and resurrection life for the world, through the Eucharist. Through such participation the church and its individual members become both a sign and a sacrament of the Gospel, that is, Christ's body for the world. While the image of God's participation in the world is important for us to hold, we should not lose sight of God's transcendence as creator, sustainer, and the one through whom the universe will reach its final

---

[7] William Stringfellow, *The Politics of Spirituality* (Philadelphia: Westminster Press, 1984), p. 22, quoted in Alister McGrath, *Christian Spirituality. An Introduction* (Oxford: Blackwell, 1999), p. 4.

[8] Fiddes, *Participating in God*, pp. 89, 281.

[9] Fiddes, *Participating in God*, p. 299.

[10] John Weaver, *Christianity and Science. SCM Core Text* (London: SCM, 2010).

[11] Fiddes, *Participating in God*, p. 300.

[12] John Weaver, *Outside-In: Theological Reflections on Life* (Oxford: Regent's Park College, 2006), pp. 30-2.

consummation. As a way of expressing our discipleship, I agree with Fiddes' understanding of what it means to participate in God:

> we should feel through their [our neighbours] reaction the real pain of facing the particular. This is the kind of cost to be carried by those who are willing to be 'living sacraments'. The sacramental life is one that is open to the presence of God, and can open a door for others into the eternal movements of love and justice that are there ahead of us, and before us, and embracing us. This openness can be felt like the invitation to a dance, but sometimes like the raw edges of a wound.[13]

In all of these feelings, thoughts and questions we can feel confused and impotent, and we recognise the need of God's wisdom.

Knowing God's wisdom:

In my own work on the environment[14] and genetically modified crops[15] I have been helped greatly by the engagement with wisdom explored by Celia Deane-Drummond[16] and by Paul Fiddes.[17] For example, with Deane-Drummond we can conclude that the church is ambivalent toward various aspects of genetic engineering and the current environmental crisis, although the WCC in its statements and publications is more aware of the global issues and the effects on the poorer nations of the world. Deane-Drummond encourages us to move the argument forward through a discussion of 'wisdom' in the Bible, noting that belief in God as creator is taken as read and that faith and reason are indistinguishable from each other. Thus observation of the natural world is not about seeking evidence for God's existence, but rather emphasizes the celebration of God's creativity. Wisdom's place in creation is outlined in Proverbs 8.22-31.[18]

We note the place of humility in regard to creation and the sense in which human beings do not have an autonomous mandate to rule, as we find in God's declarations to Job in Job 38-41. Wisdom is portrayed in three ways: human, social and cosmic. Human wisdom is aware of its limitations; social wisdom deals with societies, nations and issues of justice. Deane-Drummond

---

[13] Fiddes, *Participating in God*, p. 302.

[14] Weaver, *Christianity and Science*, pp. 183-218.

[15] John Weaver, 'The Ethics and Theology of GM Crops', paper presented to the Redcliffe Conference on GM Crops, March 2013, Redcliffe College Gloucester; available on the website of the John Ray Initiative: www.jri.org.uk.

[16] Celia Deane-Drummond, *Biology and Theology Today* (London: SCM, 2001).

[17] Fiddes, 'Ancient and Modern Wisdom', pp. 75-97.

[18] Deane-Drummond, *Biology and Theology*, p. 88.

notes that 'a broad approach that takes into account *both* the *goodness* of creation and the particular human social and environmental *consequences* of human action is in continuity with the biblical Wisdom tradition.' In addition she notes that 'the cosmic scope of Wisdom refers to the emphasis on the human and natural environment considered as a whole rather than in any dualistic sense.'[19]

Paul Fiddes[20] hones these ideas as he observes that in the Bible we find two kinds of wisdom: observable factual wisdom based on experience and the senses; and in addition there is Lady Wisdom who invites us to discover deeper truths – the wisdom of God. These are seen in the book of Job, where we find in chapter 28 factual observations about the world, earth, rocks and minerals. But this is not all the truth there is to know as we discover at the end of the book of Job (38-40), where God leads Job on a walk through creation. Here we learn that to understand the nature of God, the world and the nature of suffering, Job needs to be in tune with God.

Fiddes notes that in the last two decades there has been an increasing volume of voices in healthcare circles about the need for 'wisdom' in medicine. Usually, what is meant by 'wisdom' here is the clinical judgement of the practitioner, shaped by his or her experience over the years, and this is often contrasted with 'evidence-based medicine.' Evidence-based medicine relies on guidelines supplied by databases of evidence culled from tests and from observed outcomes over a wide range of the population, and the guidelines for good practice may well be formulated and disseminated by a government agency, notably in the UK by NICE ('National Institute for Health and Clinical Excellence'). So there has been a vigorous debate in which 'wisdom' has been asserted over against mere 'evidence'.

To illustrate the exercise of wisdom in medicine Fiddes gives the example of a doctor who diagnosed a case of meningococcal meningitis through a second-hand report over the telephone. Through his personal knowledge of the family, and his own experience of many thousand stories of illness, the use by the mother of 'behaving strangely' to describe her son's condition rang warning bells. But Fiddes cautions that:

> The example is not *typical* of instances where the clinical judgement of the doctor is critical, since an initial diagnosis is made here on the basis of a second-hand report. The place for wisdom to be exercised is usually the clinical encounter, a dialogue between doctor and patient in which two life-worlds and stories are opened to each other and interpretation happens.[21]

---

[19] Deane-Drummond, *Biology and Theology*, p. 9.

[20] Fiddes, 'Ancient and Modern Wisdom'.

[21] Fiddes, 'Ancient and Modern Wisdom' p. 77.

There is evidence which comes through an examination of the patient, but there are also further elements of self-awareness and sensitivity to the other person. These three aspects can in fact, Fiddes suggests, be reduced to two overall. The first is the wisdom of careful observation, and the second is a wisdom of attunement to what the philosopher Hans-Georg Gadamer, when reflecting on the nature of health, calls 'the rhythm of life'.[22] In the example that Fiddes quotes there is an element of wisdom beyond statistical probabilities, involving factors of empathy and attunement, both to the doctor's own attitudes and capacities and to the patient's fears, hopes and expectations.

The Bible presents us with two aspects of wisdom: observing and knowing. On the one hand, wisdom comes from observation, from the careful collecting of evidence; it is a technical skill requiring discipline and humility, or the 'fear of the Lord'. On the other hand, wisdom has a personal, relational quality, symbolized by the figure of Lady Wisdom; wisdom is learning to be attuned to creation and to its Creator, vibrating with its rhythms of life, living in sympathy with others. In this theological dimension, the wise live in a world where they are always receiving the offer to participate in God's own wisdom, seeing the world as God sees it. Technical and relational wisdom thus belong together, each assisting the other.

In his book *Why Evolution is True*[23], geneticist Jerry Coyne has produced an honest and forthright account of the evidence for evolution, and while those with differing views are criticized for their lack of scientific understanding, they are not attacked in the inflammatory tones that are the manner of some other non-Christian scientists. Coyne ends his book with a humble statement characteristic of the whole text: 'Deriving your spirituality from science also means accepting an attendant sense of humility before the universe and the likelihood that we'll never have all the answers.'[24] We need the wisdom that God offers to us as we seek to participate in the life of God and of creation.

Fiddes observes that wisdom in the Bible is both subject and object at the same time, crossing the boundaries between the human consciousness and the world. The Hebrew Bible uses *hokmah* (wisdom) to mean on the one hand *faculty of mind*, a skill of approach gained through experience, and on the other *an area of knowledge,* a body of instruction. This

---

[22] Hans-Georg Gadamer, *Über die Verborgenheit der Gesundheit* (Frankfurt: Suhrkamp Verlag, 1993), p. 145, quoted in Fiddes, 'Ancient and Modern Wisdom', pp. 89-90.

[23] Jerry A. Coyne, *Why Evolution is True* (Oxford: Oxford University Press, 2009).

[24] Coyne, *Why Evolution is True*, p. 252.

wisdom can be something yet to be discovered through observation, exploration and experiment of the world as an object of study.[25]

But from a Judaeo-Christian perspective we cannot fully understand the objective world without an empathetic appreciation of all that it implies and reveals about the Creator. Fiddes maintains that 'wisdom requires empathy with the other, whether persons or the natural realm .... the figure of Lady Wisdom who offers a relationship with herself'[26] is God's way of enabling such an understanding. It is here that Lady Wisdom, as a symbol of participation, becomes essential to human perception, through which we may find the empathy needed to understand the created world. Fiddes concludes that:

> In this context talk about God becomes appropriate. God who 'sees all' is supremely wise,[27] and to use this descriptor means that – like human wise people – God is always committed to the signs of the material world; indeed, God is deeply immersed in them and in the time and history in which they exist.

And further, he observes that the figure of Lady Wisdom in the Hebrew Bible

> points to a certain complexity within God, together with ideas of the Word and the Spirit of God. However, the witness she makes to a participatory form of life and being comes to fullness in the later church doctrine of the Trinity.[28]

At this point it will be helpful to give further attention to Wisdom in the book of Proverbs.

Wisdom in the Book of Proverbs:

Ernest Lucas believes that the book of Proverbs is about Old Testament spirituality.[29] He quotes Alister McGrath's definition:

---

[25] Fiddes, *Ancient and Modern Wisdom*, pp. 86-7.

[26] Fiddes, *Ancient and Modern Wisdom*, p. 87.

[27] Proverbs 5:21; 15:11.

[28] Fiddes, *Ancient and Modern Wisdom*, p. 87.

[29] Ernest Lucas, 'The Spirituality of Proverbs' in *Proverbs, Two Horizons OT Commentary*, (Grand Rapids, MI: Eerdmans, 2014), forthcoming and used with permission of the author.

> Christian spirituality concerns the quest for a fulfilled and authentic Christian existence, involving the bringing together of the fundamental ideas of Christianity and the whole experience of living on the basis of and within the scope of the Christian faith.[30]

Lucas believes that the book of Proverbs is all about how to cope with the demands of everyday real life. 'The fear of the Lord', which is paralleled by 'the knowledge of God', is the motivation toward moral and ethical behaviour and implies a personal relationship with God. Wisdom in the book of Proverbs is presented by Lucas as

> the epitome of goodness and godliness, [which] clearly provides the balance to the adulteress of Proverbs 7, who accosts a youth stealthily by night with deceitful words. Wisdom, in contrast, appears in broad daylight in public places, addressing everyone in words that are right, true, just, faultless, free of wickedness and perversity (Prov 8:6-9).

and that in Proverbs 8:1-21 lies the assertion

> that Wisdom is to be found in the public places of our culture, places of recreation, commerce, the law and government. Even in a fallen world God's 'common grace' is still at work.[31]

Lucas maintains that according to Prov 14:26 a personal relationship with God brings confidence and trust in Yahweh (cf. 29:25). It also gives hope for the future (23:17-18), and a fulfilled life (19:23; 22:4).[32] The fear of the Lord is seen to be the precondition for gaining wisdom, whereby human beings recognise their place in the world as those totally dependent on the God who created them and sustains their lives.

The wisdom of the creator comes from being in a right relationship with God. The purpose of the book of Proverbs is set out in Prov 1:2-7, identifying virtues and wisdom, and reaching a climax in 'the fear of the Lord' (1:7). Lucas comments that the

> sages were concerned about changing people into better people, and by the way they lived such people would change the world into a better place. This is particularly so because the moral virtues which are highlighted in v. 3b are ones that are essential for the maintenance of

---

[30] Alister E. McGrath, *Christian Spirituality, an Introduction* (Oxford: Blackwell, 1999), p. 2.

[31] Ernest Lucas, 'The sacred in the secular' in *Encounter with God Thursday 1st August 2013*, Milton Keynes: Scripture Union, 2013, p. 39.

[32] Lucas, 'The Spirituality of Proverbs'.

> proper governance of community. In fact they are communal virtues that are key ones in Israel's understanding of the nature of covenant community.[33]

We see that the virtues of justice, righteousness and equity are makers of the path of wisdom, which leads to a harmonious and healthy community, which Lucas believes should be the focus of discipleship as Christian character formation.

There is no division between the sacred and the secular in the spirituality presented in the book of Proverbs; there is one world of experience, where all knowledge and understanding is to be found, as it is all within the presence of God. So Proverbs seeks to produce integrated people. Lucas comments that 'a person's inward commitment and their outward behaviour should be an integrated whole.' Lucas observes that the book of Proverbs ends with an example of someone who displays the integrated spirituality of the book: this is the poem of the 'valiant woman' (31:10-31).[34]

Taking as one example the environment and the natural world, we can ask: how far should we be allowed to become co-creators with God in engineering crops and animals for our own benefit? How far should we take transgenic experimentation? How do we distinguish one research project from another in terms of its likely risk and benefit for humanity and the earth? A theology of Wisdom serves to unite themes of creation and redemption by identifying Christ the Redeemer and the divine Logos with Sophia, the Wisdom of God involved in the creation of the world.'[35]

Key to the argument that Deane-Drummond rehearses is the wisdom to recognize the presence of God in the new technologies. There are key questions to which we need answers: are we achieving God's purposes? Do we know what God intends? Are we excluding God from our discussions?[36] We have the scientific understanding and the technological expertise, but how do we judge what is right? As Fiddes suggests, and Lucas implies, the answer is to be found through being attuned to God's wisdom.

We are raising ethical issues of what is good in the economy, politics and production of food, and of human reproduction. Deane-Drummond concludes that it would be naïve to suggest that we can go back to an agrarian culture or a pre-industrial understanding of medicine in ignorance of modern technology.[37] However, with her we can suggest that too great a focus on human achievement and human freedom obscures other theological principles, such as the mandate to care for the world or to protect the sanctity

[33] Lucas, 'The Spirituality of Proverbs'.

[34] Lucas, 'The Spirituality of Proverbs'.

[35] Deane-Drummond, *Biology and Theology*, pp. 94-5.

[36] Deane-Drummond, *Biology and Theology*, pp. 98-9.

[37] Deane-Drummond, *Biology and Theology*, p. 111.

of human life. Technological manipulation of living things may not be good stewardship, and may lead us to miss our need for justice in the face of global inequality and poverty. We need a wisdom that goes beyond the technique.

The support or rejection by theologians of genetic technologies depends on their presumptions about anthropology. An optimistic anthropology sees humans as co-creators and agents of evolution. A pessimistic anthropology sees human sinfulness usurping God's place as creator. With Deane-Drummond we can conclude that 'Wisdom, on the one hand, affirms the special dignity of the human race, but the idea of Wisdom as agent of creation of the world shows that it is also cosmic in scope. Wisdom should, however, encourage caution on the part of humans rather than impulsive action.'[38]

The book of Proverbs recommends walking with Lady Wisdom through the world in the company of others. In the Christian context of the doctrine of the Trinity, we are encouraged to find rhythms of giving and receiving in love, relations which are wider and deeper than ourselves in which we can participate. This last perspective does not mean expecting a supernatural intervention, but seeking to cooperate with a gentle but effective flow of life which does not overwhelm or replace human action but which has a gift-like quality ('grace' is the theological word) which continually sustains natural processes and promotes human flourishing.[39] Here is our guide, learning to listen to God and walk with God in God's garden - a return to the initial relationships of creation: even paradise regained. It is for us to be in tune with God's promises and purposes.

Reason, Truth and Wisdom:

In consequence of what we have said thus far, it will be useful to explore where reason and truth relate to godly wisdom. Brian Haymes[40] considers the place of beliefs alongside the evidence of science. He notes that in the view of what has been termed The New Atheism[41] all forms of religious belief are seen to be dangerous and irrational. As such, Christian believers

---

[38] Deane-Drummond, *Biology and Theology*, p. 117.

[39] Fiddes, 'Ancient and Modern Wisdom' p. 91.

[40] Brian Haymes, 'The Way of Practical Modesty' in Finamore and Weaver, *Wisdom, Science and the Scriptures*, p. 99.

[41] The term is used of the writings of, among others, Richard Dawkins, Daniel Dennett, Sam Harris and Christopher Hitchens. I shall not be engaging with their work in detail in this short essay, although I hold that their challenge is very significant and that there is no doubt but that their work reflects a growing and widespread mood.

are self-deceived and do not know what they are talking about in worship, prayer and preaching, because there is nothing or no one to know beyond the empirical world explored by science.

Haymes maintains that 'God' may not be open to study in the way the universe invites our questions and exploration but that does not mean that all talk of knowing God is delusional. Religious believers do not hold their beliefs in the way scientists hold to convictions about their hypotheses; which is to say that religion is not science and that appeals for evidence may not always be appropriate. But that does not mean that holding religious beliefs is irrational or delusional. 'Knowing' amounts to more that proving by empirical demonstration. It can entail acquaintance, direct experience, possibly intuition and certainly practice.[42]

Science can never give an exhaustive account of the nature of the reality we experience. It is a reductive approach to knowledge to suggest that we know only what we can empirically prove to be the case. That this has been the highly productive and successful approach of science we may readily thank God. But such an approach does not account for all human experience. It has limited explanatory power. This is helpfully summed up by agnostic cosmologist, Paul Davies who is

> convinced that human understanding of nature through science, rational reasoning and mathematics points to a much deeper connection between life, mind and cosmos than emerges from the crude lottery of multiverse cosmology combined with the weak anthropic principle ... Somehow, the universe has engineered its own self-awareness.[43]

Davies believes that life and mind are etched deeply into the fabric of the cosmos, 'perhaps through a shadowy, half-glimpsed life principle,' and furthermore he concedes that this is a form of religious conviction.

Davies like Coyne[44] is aware of aspects of the universe and life that are beyond scientific reason. The knowing of persons is different from that of scientific proof and Haymes maintains that:

> This world is where deep personal relationships of love are enjoyed, where there are moments of wonder, even awe. This happens to us because we are persons and because this world has surprising depth without which we would be less than the humanity we share. If we think of God in personal terms then we might still have faith in his

---

[42] Haymes, 'The Way of Practical Modesty', p. 106.

[43] Paul Davies, *The Goldilocks Enigma. Why is the Universe just right for Life?* (London: Penguin Books, 2007) pp. 261-3.

[44] Coyne, *Evolution is True*.

> hidden, quiet, persuasive presence, expressing God's own freedom and honouring ours.[45]

The world of persons, while open to scientific study and testing, is not exhausted by such work.

It is in this one world, the world of persons, that many Christian speak of experiences of God; the experience of moral claim, sometimes of an absolute quality we cannot lay upon ourselves; of being addressed by an 'other' who calls for respect and honour; of contentment and joy before beauty and wonder. It is remarkable how widespread such experiences are and how varied. Haymes goes on to quote David Bentley Hart, who maintains that:

> A rational life is one that integrates knowledge into a larger choreography of virtue, imagination, patience, prudence, humility and restraint. Reason is not only knowledge, but knowledge perfected in wisdom.[46]

With Pontius Pilate we are left to ask: 'What is truth?' (John 18:38). Truth is a key word in the Gospel according to John. The prologue to the Gospel (John 1:1-18) and Col 1:15-20 express the relationship between Christ and creation. The Apostle John presents Jesus as the Wisdom of God (the Logos, the Word) in the creation of the universe. John tells us that Law comes through Moses, but the truth – reality, wisdom – comes through Jesus. Before his crucifixion Jesus tells his disciples that he is the way, the truth, and the life, and that no one comes to the Father except through him. In effect he is saying that truth – the reality of God and God's world – is discovered through a relationship with Jesus, walking through life in his company. He goes on to promise another Counsellor, the Spirit of Wisdom and Truth, who will be present with the disciples after Jesus has returned to God.

We can discover a great deal through scientific observation and research, experiment and testing, and through our five senses (sight, hearing, smell, taste and touch), but there is still a sixth sense. There is the knowledge that comes from being attuned to God's wisdom – walking with God in God's world; living with Jesus; knowing the presence of the Holy Spirit – leading us into all truth, and understanding the reality and meaning of God's world.

---

[45] Haymes, 'The Way of Practical Modesty', p. 110.

[46] David Bentley Hart, *Atheist Delusions: The Christian Revolution and Its Fashionable Enemies* (London: Yale University Press, 2009), p. 236, quoted in Haymes, 'The Way of Practical Modesty', p. 111.

Considering Wisdom: A Conclusion

Our ultimate value is to be found in God; to be loved, accepted, forgiven and made new in Christ; drawn into an eternal relationship with God, which death cannot break. James Woodward stresses our uniqueness:

> This uniqueness that is me is what I have been, is what I have to offer to my Creator, who knows me infinitely better than I know myself, and who graciously welcomes me home, not in spite of what I have been, but because of what I am.[47]

Richard Rohr through an exploration of growth into the second naïveté of Ricoeur, concludes that if we have forgiven our-self for being imperfect and falling, we can also forgive just about everybody else. If we have not discovered that we are forgiven in Christ, then we are likely to pass on our sadness, absurdity, judgment, and futility to others. Rohr observes that

> This is the tragic path of the many elderly people who have not become actual elders, probably because they were never eldered or mentored themselves. Such people seem to have missed out on the joy and clarity of the first simplicity, perhaps avoided the interim complexity [of wrestling with God's universal and unconditional love and acceptance of others], and finally lost the great freedom and magnanimity of the second simplicity as well.[48]

We see that wisdom is not what you know about; it is what you know, deep inside you, the essence of your inner life. Wisdom is the art of holding together the old and the new, of balancing the known with the unknown, the pain and the joy; it is a way of linking the whole of our life together in a needful integrity. Growing in wisdom, patience and a contentment to move more and more from 'doing' into that equally rewarding and much more important stage, the state of 'being' – so that we may discern what matters and what doesn't. It will mean detachment and learning to let go, and it may indeed mean replacing a life of independence with one of increasing dependence on others. We cannot prepare ourselves for birth, but we can prepare for death.[49]

---

[47] James Woodward, *Valuing Age. Pastoral Ministry with Older People* (London: SPCK, 2008), p. 195.

[48] Richard Rohr, *Falling Upward. A Spirituality of the Two Halves of Life* (London: SPCK, 2012), pp. 114-5.

[49] Woodward, *Valuing Age*, p. 192.

Through a paper I produced for the Baptist Union of Great Britain on retirement[50] I have examined wisdom that is discovered in older age. Wisdom is different from knowledge – different in content, process, outcome and purpose because it is grounded in everyday life. Woodward comments that 'wisdom can be a kind of 'ordinary theology' as it is accessible to all as they reflect on their life in the light of faith and God'.[51] Wisdom is put into a broader perspective and is related to the quality of life, wholeness, health and living a good life. It is this wisdom, which Fiddes helps us to recognise, which comes from being attuned to, and participating in, God.

Woodward believes that older age, if nothing else, will provide an opportune time to explore the undiscovered self. He stresses that

> We should not underestimate the spiritual and existential search for meaning that age can bring. The following questions: Who have I been? Who am I now? Who will I be? What will become of me? are very significant. These questions will no doubt generate a range of reflections resulting in meanings and interpretations that have a significant influence on the health and well-being of the older person. Life review, story-telling and story-sharing can offer a real potential for facilitating a definition of the self and exploring this in the light of the concept of 'successful ageing'.[52]

I want to challenge us all to embark on this search and not to wait until we are older. We are on a spiritual journey which will include our physical, mental, emotional and relational being, but will also include our wonder at the created universe of which we are a part. All lead to a deeper sense of our understanding of our life and of God – our spirituality. Our spirituality will include our love and concern for all other people, recognising their uniqueness and significance to us and to God, and realising that in the Cross we see the love, value and purpose that God has for every living being. We recognise that life has meaning and purpose and we discover more of who God is in our experience of God.

In the preface to Ignatius' Spiritual Exercises[53], Gerard Hughes notes that Ignatius himself suggests that everything on earth is created to help us to praise and serve God. 'Everything' includes failing strength of body and mind, disappointment, disillusion, failure, guilt, feelings of helplessness and hopelessness. Hughes notes that the Psalmist says: 'Be still and know that I

---

[50] John Weaver, 'A Theology of Retirement for Ministers', 2013, available on the Baptist Union of Great Britain website: www.baptist.org.uk.

[51] Woodward, *Valuing Age*, p. 141.

[52] Woodward, *Valuing Age*, p. 204.

[53] Spiritual Exercises of St. Ignatius of Loyola (Leominster: Gracewing, 2004).

am God'. 'In old age, nature helps us to be more still, and in the stillness we can better listen to God, our teacher.'[54] It is a matter of prayerfully focusing on the nature of God and bringing all our experiences before God in the assurance of God's love for us. In this we ask God to help us to recognise God's action within each experience.

Rohr maintains that we all desire to find 'home', a place where we feel secure and at peace. He suggests that 'home' is another word for the Spirit that we are, our True Self in God. *The self-same moment that we find God in ourselves, we also find ourselves in God*, and this is the full homecoming, according to Teresa of Avila.[55] Rohr helpfully maintains that the end is planted in us at the beginning and it gnaws away at us until we get there freely and consciously. The Holy Spirit is our inner compass. This is our hope. True spirituality is the co-operation between God and the soul. (Rom 8:28).

It is being attuned to the Wisdom of God.

---

[54] Gerard Hughes, 'Is there a Spirituality for the Elderly? An Ignatian Approach' in Jewell, *Spirituality and Ageing*, p. 17.

[55] Rohr, *Falling Upward*, p. 91.

12.

Play, the Origins of Culture and the Formation of a Christian Mind

Nicholas Wood

Introduction

In 2001 Regent's Park College published the ninth volume in its series of Study Guides under the editorship of the then Principal, Professor Paul Fiddes. Entitled *Faith in the Centre: Christianity and Culture*, it was a collection of papers based on lectures given under the auspices of the Oxford Centre for Christianity and Culture over the first five years or so of its existence (1994-2000), beginning with the inaugural lecture of my predecessor as Centre Director, Dr Alan Kreider, and concluding with a chapter from myself, who took up the role in the millennial year 2000. It scarcely seems possible that in 2014, we are marking twenty years since the foundation of what was initially called the Centre for the Study of Christianity and Culture, and which has since evolved into the Oxford Centre for Christianity and Culture or simply 'OCCC'.

In the introduction to that volume Paul Fiddes, whose brainchild OCCC essentially was, sets the development of the Centre in relation to the core mission of Regent's Park College, education and formation, but also in dialogue with Harry Blamires' discussion of the 'Christian Mind'[1]. Blamires laments the lack of both a 'community of discourse' and of intelligent Christians willing to think through the issues thrown up by the dominant thought world of our day. Interestingly, in the same year as the Study Guide appeared, Blamires himself published a follow-up book, tellingly entitled 'The Post-Christian Mind',[2] acknowledging the changing landscape, and very different context, for Christian formation some forty years after his initial work. In this further study Blamires deliberately adopted a perspective beginning not with the faith community but with the world beyond the church, which already, over a decade ago, Blamires perceived as hostile, with an 'insidious assault' on Christianity by a militant secularist humanism.

---

[1] Paul S. Fiddes (ed.) *Faith in the Centre* (Oxford / Macon, GA: Regent's Park College/Smyth & Helwys, 2001), p. 1; see Harry Blamires, *The Christian Mind* (London: SPCK, 1963).

[2] Harry Blamires, *The Post-Christian Mind* (London: SPCK, 2001).

This charge has been levelled repeatedly in recent years by both Christian and conservative commentators. The rise of so-called 'militant atheism' has certainly been a notable feature of cultural life in the last decade or more, although how far such vocal attacks on religion, especially its place in public life, impact wider thinking is not yet clear. However, OCCC has never been defensive in its relation of faith and culture. We do not feel the need to be apologetic in either its more technical or its more popular usage. Our mission, as Paul Fiddes suggested in that opening discussion, is the creation of a 'field of discourse' set within our context as a Baptist foundation within the University of Oxford, relating to both Church and Academy, and seeking to engage imaginatively with both constituencies. In other words, within OCCC, we aim to continue positively the discussion in which the Church has been occupied from its earliest days, perhaps most famously encapsulated in Tertullian's famous question, 'What has Athens to do with Jerusalem?'

Now of course it must be acknowledged that Tertullian posed the question in an apologetic context, in his volume 'Against Heretics'. It is worth considering the quotation in a fuller version:

> What indeed has Athens to do with Jerusalem? What concord is there between the Academy and the Church? What between heretics and Christians? Our instruction comes from the porch of Solomon, who had himself taught that the Lord should be sought in simplicity of heart (Wisdom 1:1). Away with all attempts to produce a mottled Christianity of Stoic, Platonic, and dialectic composition! We want no curious disputation after possessing Christ Jesus, no inquisition after enjoying the gospel! With our faith, we desire no further belief.[3]

Now I suspect that few of us would be attracted by any variety of 'mottled Christianity'! But equally we might be more cautious than Tertullian in asserting that the wisdom which issued from 'the porch of Solomon' was unengaged with, or uninfluenced by, extra-biblical culture: simplicity of heart does not rule out complexity of mind; nor does it necessarily negate the significance of cultural context. Tertullian poses his rhetorical questions within a dualistic paradigm in which 'Athens' symbolises the Academy and Heretics, whilst 'Jerusalem' represents Christianity and the Church. We might point out the irony that this very dualism owes rather more to Greek philosophy than it does to Biblical understanding. But of course Tertullian's context predates the Augustinian synthesis of classical and Judeao-Christian thought, which subsequently led to the flourishing of 'Christian Civilisation', albeit in the context of the ambiguous legacy of post-Constantinian church life. Whatever we make of the politics, for a thousand

[3] Tertullian, *Prescription against Heretics*, 7.

years and more, culturally Athens and Jerusalem, in both Church and Academy, coexisted relatively harmoniously and arguably in a very fruitful dialogue.

Early in the 21st century we now stand at the other end of the chronological tunnel, surveying the rise and fall of Christian Civilisation from the perspective of, what some at least would see as, its final demise. But perhaps we find ourselves in a not dissimilar place to Tertullian: pondering the relationship between Christianity and culture in a world where a faith perspective takes the form of a 'minority report'. The challenge for us is to develop credible and intelligent Christian thought in this post-Christian context, and to consider what space may be left, within our predominantly scientific-materialistic worldview, for Christianity and indeed other religious traditions too. The danger might be that we find ourselves in a similar position to those nineteenth century scholars who attempted to make room for faith within the prevailing scientific paradigms of their day, but found the 'gaps' for God increasingly squeezed. We need to avoid developing a similar approach in relation to culture as a previous generation did with regard to science.

In this paper I will aim to explore not so much the place of faith as the origins of culture itself. This analysis of culture has arisen out of some research on the experience and idea of 'play', which I have been undertaking in conversation with one of our Visiting Centre Fellows, Helen Woolley, Reader in Landscape Architecture and Society in the University of Sheffield. In a previous discussion of the experience of play in human life, [4] I suggested that play raises some interesting anthropological and indeed theological questions about the fundamental character of both human and divine nature. The key question is this: is play simply a distraction from the serious business of being or becoming a human person, or is it in fact of the very essence of that quest? In this paper I will suggest that our experience of play, both in childhood and as adults, reveals some significant features of culture in which we might discover space both for humanity and for the divine.

I will briefly review the study of play in the fields of developmental psychology, evolutionary biology, and socio-cultural studies. Based on these key analyses of the human experience this paper will argue that play (which includes drama, music, games and sport) is vital to life, and may even be understood as in some way constitutive of the human person and human culture. Although many people associate play mainly with children, arguably it is characteristic of adults too: in fact, as the German philosopher Friedrich

---

[4] Nicholas Wood *Playing with God?* The McCandless Lecture, Georgetown College, Kentucky (2008).

Nietzsche put it, 'In a real man (sic) a child is hidden – and wants to play'[5]. But why do any of us want to play? I will argue that in the inventiveness of play, space is created for culture and civilisation to emerge. We might see this as parallel to the way in which the divine play of creation brings to birth the universe itself, with all its possibilities and ambiguities (Prov 8:22-31). Thus, in exploring the relationship of play to culture, we may discover the space in which both the human and the divine may truly be found and where faith and culture may happily co-exist.

1. Defining Play

Play is a complex and ambiguous phenomenon which requires a multidisciplinary approach in order to analyse and understand its place in human experience, and indeed in the wider animal kingdom. Yet like many other common human phenomena, such as art or religion, strict definitions of play remain elusive. A leading play theorist, Brian Sutton-Smith, observes that, 'We all play occasionally, and we all know what play feels like. But when it comes to making theoretical statements about what play is, we fall into silliness.'[6] He goes on to suggest that definitions tend to fall into one of three categories: a) experiential – definitions constructed from the perspective of the player; b) intrinsic – which analyse the function/s of play by reference to its inherent motivations; c) extrinsic – which analyse the function/s of play with reference to wider culture.[7]

Probably the most important discussion of play in the wider cultural context during the last century was that of the Dutch scholar Johan Huizinga in his influential 1938 work, 'Homo Ludens: A Study of the Play Element in Culture'.[8] This was written in the shadow of the looming Nazi threat in Europe, and in response to the experience of industrial-scale conflict during the Great War of 1914-18. He makes the bold claim that 'civilization arises and unfolds in and as play.' For Huizinga play is *significant*: it is a signifier, it *means something*; it is not simply a biological or psychological function, however important they might be.[9] Therefore, he argues:

---

[5] Friedrich Nietzsche, *Thus Spoke Zarathustra*, trns. Walter Kaufmann (Harmondsworth: Penguin, 1978) part I, speech 18, 'On Little Old and Young Women'.

[6] Brian Sutton-Smith, *The Ambiguity of Play* (Cambridge, MA: Harvard UP, 1997), p. 1.

[7] Sutton-Smith, *Ambiguity of Play*, pp. 16-17.

[8] Johan Huizinga, *Homo Ludens: a study of the play element in culture* (Boston, MA: Beacon Press, 1955 [1938]).

[9] Huizinga, *Homo Ludens*, p. 1.

> Play only becomes possible, thinkable and understandable when an influx of *mind* breaks down the absolute determinism of the cosmos. The very existence of play continually confirms the supra-logical nature of the human situation. Animals play, so they must be more than merely mechanical things. We play and know that we play, so we must be more than merely rational beings, for play is irrational.[10]

This sense of the irrationality, the superfluity or even the apparent 'wastefulness' of play is central to a number of discussions about the role of play in the evolutionary process of species and for the psychological development of individuals. The zoologist Patrick Bateson comments that, 'In all its manifestations play is characterised by its apparent lack of serious purpose or immediate goal. Play is the antithesis of the adult "work", in which behaviour has an obvious, and usually short-term, goal.'[11] There is recognition of the intrinsic benefits of play, but there is also resistance in many theorists to its instrumentalization. There seems to be an intuitive understanding that if play is simply reduced to physical or psychological functions, something essential is being lost. Robert Johnston notes that when play becomes 'purposive' it loses many of the benefits of play as an intrinsic activity; but when enjoying play for its intrinsic value, one discovers that, 'paradoxically … play has external value'[12]. In other words play is indeed good for us, but if that is the only reason we engage in it, it loses the essential enjoyment which belongs to play. In other words it is no longer play but work. More importantly, it is not fun! So what in the end is play? According to Huizinga play is:

> … a free activity standing quite consciously outside 'ordinary' life as being 'not serious', but at the same time absorbing the player intensely and utterly. It is an activity connected with no material interest and no profit can be gained by it. It proceeds within its own proper boundaries of time and space according to fixed rules and in an orderly manner. It promotes the formation of social groupings which tend to surround themselves with secrecy and to stress their difference from the common world by disguise or other means.[13]

---

[10] Huizinga, *Home Ludens*, pp. 3-4.

[11] Patrick Bateson, 'The Role of Play in the Evolution of Great Apes and Humans' in Anthony D. Pellegrini & Peter K. Smith (eds), *The Nature of Play: Great Apes and Humans* (New York / London: The Guildford Press, 2005), p. 14.

[12] Robert Johnston, *The Christian at Play* (Grand Rapids, MI: Eerdmans, Grand Rapids, 1983), p. 44.

[13] Huizinga, *Home Ludens*, p. 13.

This definition focuses a number of important issues about the nature of play, especially the question as to how far it is a 'firmly bounded' experience, proceeding always in a fixed and orderly manner, and to what extent play is a more impromptu phenomenon. Certainly some forms of play operate within a fixed space, in a given time-frame and create clear rules; this form of play is usually denoted by the language of 'games'. But play can also be spontaneous, imaginative and impulsive; this type of play is frequently characterised as 'free play', and can be experienced and perceived as subversive of order. Play can be both a rule-maker and a rule-breaker: we speak both of 'playing *by* the rules', and 'playing *with* the rules'.

Such ambiguity is well illustrated by the association of the word 'play' with both music and drama where 'performance' is also ambiguous. It can refer to the recital of a pre-existing piece of music or to the production of an extant play; this is analogous to play as 'game' or 'playing *by* the rules'. But both music and drama may take the more extemporary form of improvisation, in which case they are analogous to 'free play' or 'playing *with* the rules'.

This association of play with the creative arts also underlines several further significant factors. First, in much of the literature there is a close relationship between play and creativity; so for example, a leading theorist of play, D. W. Winnicott, comments that, '... in playing, and perhaps only in playing, the child or adult is free to be creative'.[14] Secondly, as Winnicott indicates, play is not an activity restricted to children and young people, but in various forms recurs across the generations, involving children, young people and adults, albeit in different ways. Thirdly, we might note that play is also found across cultures, and arguably too across species. There is a developing literature about non-human play, especially in relation to other primates,[15] although we should note Robert Fagen's observation that 'play occurs in only a small minority of the Earth's million or more species ... Mammals and birds, and perhaps a few fishes and reptiles are the only kinds of animals known to play.'[16]

[14] D. W. Winnicott, *Playing and Reality* (London / New York: Routledge Classics, 2005 [1971]), p. 71.

[15] See for example the discussions in Pellegrini & Smith (eds), *The Nature of Play*.

[16] Robert Fagen 'Animal Play' in Anthony Pellegrini (ed.), *The Future of Play Theory* (Albany, NY: NY University Press, 1995), p. 24.

2. Play in the Human and Natural Sciences

Developmental Psychology

Because of the close association between play and children, there has inevitably been much interest in play by many developmental psychologists and it features in the work of such influential theorists as Jean Piaget (1896-1980)[17] and Lev Vygotsky (1896-1934). Play was central to the work of D. W Winnicott (1896-1971), a paediatrician who went on to become an influential psychoanalyst, much of whose work centres on the role of what he termed 'transitional objects'. These are objects which facilitate the developing relationship between the infant and the mother-figure, and so in Winnicott's theory they are crucial in understanding the psychological development which enables engagement between the worlds of inner and outer reality. Such transitional objects and phenomena may include the thumb which is sucked or a soft toy or piece of cloth. Vygotsky also recognised the importance of objects in children's play and suggested that their gradual disappearance during adolescence and after reflects the internalisation of such objects through the development of the imagination.[18] This is perhaps implicit in Winnicott's use of the terminology of 'transition' for such objects. But does this imply that play itself is also only a temporary or juvenile phenomenon?

Winnicott is especially interested not simply in the construction of these twin worlds of inner and outer reality but in the relationship between the two. This relationship constitutes a third dimension of 'experiencing' that involves *both* the inner and outer realities. The transitional object is that which contributes to the development of this process: 'I am concerned with the first possession, and with the intermediate area between the subjective and that which is objectively perceived'.[19] In due time such phenomena and objects come to be understood as symbolic, which indicates an ability to distinguish between fact and fantasy, and the ability to accept both difference and similarity. Melanie Klein (1882-1960) (with whom Winnicott trained in psychoanalysis, but from whom he parted company), had earlier posited the notion of an 'internal object' as a mental construct, but Winnicott comments: 'The transitional object is never under magical control like the

---

[17] See for example Jean Piaget, *Play, Dreams and Imitation in Childhood* (London: Heinemann, 1951[1945]).

[18] Lev Vygotsky 'Play and its role in the Mental Development of the Child' (2002 [1933]), Psychology and Marxism Internet Archive http://www.marxists.org, accessed 27.02.2012.

[19] Winnicott, *Playing and Reality*, p. 4.

internal object, nor is it outside control as the real mother is'[20]. Rather, the significant point is that:

> ... the task of reality-acceptance is never completed ... no human being is free from the strain of relating inner and outer reality, and that relief from this strain is provided by an intermediate area of experience which is not challenged (arts, religion, etc.). This intermediate area is in direct continuity with the play area of the small child who is 'lost' in play.[21]

So we see that for Winnicott playing is neither 'inside' (within my control) nor 'outside' (beyond my control) but in the space between the 'self' and the 'not-self'. This 'potential space' originates as that between the baby and the mother but subsequently develops as the area in which play and other cultural life subsists. He argues that, 'there is a direct development from transitional phenomena to playing, and from playing to shared playing, and from this to cultural experiences.'[22] He sums up his argument like this:

> The place where cultural experience is located is the *potential space* between the individual and the environment (originally the object). The same can be said of playing. Cultural experience begins with creative living first manifested in play.[23]

Thus in psychological terms, separation of the 'me' from the 'not-me' can be 'avoided by the filling in of the potential space with creative playing, with the use of symbols, and with all that eventually adds up to a cultural life.'[24] What Winnicott is arguing is not so much cause and effect, that is, that childhood play should be understood as the *root cause* of adult cultural life, but rather for the recognition that play and culture *occupy similar space* and operate within the same sphere of human experience. This suggests that the association between the language of play and that of drama and music is entirely appropriate. Arguably this analysis confirms, from a psychological perspective, Huizinga's historical-cultural analysis of the significance of play as foundational for civilisation or culture.

---

[20] Winnicott, *Playing and Reality*, p. 13.
[21] Winnicott, *Playing and Reality*, p. 18.
[22] Winnicott, *Playing and Reality*, p. 69.
[23] Winnicott, *Playing and Reality*, p. 135.
[24] Winnicott, *Playing and Reality*, p. 147.

Evolutionary Biology

We turn now from psychology to biology. In a comprehensive review of the significance of play in modern thought, both philosophical and scientific,[25] Mihai Spariosu notes that, *for the sciences*, play became a serious topic of study only in the second half of the nineteenth century with the development of the evolutionary approaches pioneered by Spencer and Darwin. Since then play has been an increasingly significant theme in various scientific disciplines and indeed Spariosu suggests that, 'an increasingly playful attitude in science has gone hand in hand with an increasing interest in studying play.'[26] In his discussion of *philosophical* accounts of play, Spariosu draws attention to the tendency to analyse play in terms of either its rational or irrational qualities. But he notes that:

> 'In most contemporary scientific theory … play and the creative imagination remain separated from violent power and firmly bound to orderly rule-determined process; they remain faithful servants of the rational mentality.'[27]

In two influential studies 'The Play of Animals' (1896) and 'The Play of Man' (1899), Karl Groos (1861-1946) argued that play is closely related to 'evolution and natural selection: through play animals and men (sic) practice the necessary skills for survival in the struggle for life'[28]. Groos believed that this functional approach should inform the approach of modern people to children's play: responsible adults should encourage 'good', that is, disciplined and reasonable forms of play, and discourage the 'bad' forms, which tend towards indiscipline and self-indulgence. This has led to a generally favourable, but somewhat instrumental, assessment of the role of play in human development with a 'tendency to see (rational) play as a positive evolutionary factor … discernible throughout the human sciences'[29]. This is play as rule-maker, rather than rule-breaker.

The anthropologist Gregory Bateson (1904-1980) was influential in the development of meta-communication theories in which play is distinguished from other behaviours by a series of signals given by the participants, and which links play with cognitive development and especially with a 'capacity

---

25 Mihai Spariosu, *Dionysus Reborn: Play and the Aesthetic Dimension in Modern Philosophical and Scientific Thought* (New York: Cornell UP, 1989).

26 Spariosu, *Dionysus Reborn*, p. 165.

27 Spariosu, *Dionysus Reborn*, p. 168.

28 Spariosu, *Dionysus Reborn*, p. 173.

29 Spariosu, *Dionysus Reborn*, p. 190.

for abstraction'.[30] More recent studies confirm that play is developmentally significant both for the species and for individuals with some evidence to support the contention that, 'cognition and social intelligence … develop in special social relationships' which are fostered by the experience of play. Rather more controversially, it has been further argued that 'these socially-derived cognitive strategies become the basis for later logical-mathematical cognition', which in turn may be related to the development of more sophisticated levels of cognition, depending on the complexity of the social context.[31] It is often asserted that symbolic or pretend play is especially significant here: 'young children … learn best by interacting in pretend-play situations … because of its emotional and flexibility dimensions.' Such play allows 'children to be many things they cannot be in reality. Consequently, they enact many different roles; these different roles are, in turn, important in children's cognitive development.'[32]

Spariosu suggests that although biologists 'rarely take the ludic phenomenon (i.e. play) itself as their object of study, many of them have increasingly used play concepts as tools in understanding evolution by natural selection'[33]. He cites as evidence Richard Dawkins' discussion of game theory which deliberately adopts a 'playful style'[34]. Two prominent biologists who directly addressed the phenomenon of play are Professor Robert Fagen and Sir Patrick Bateson FRS (b.1938, not to be confused with his distant relation Gregory).

Based on evidence from Ethology, comparative psychology and Darwinian evolutionary theory, Fagen develops a taxonomy of animal play in ascending order of complexity, from Grade 1 (non-interactive, single actions) to Grade 5 (social play, involving special intimacy or cognitive interaction). He relates this to play's structure, development, motivation and biological consequences.[35] This tends to support his assertion that 'playtime in animals is real and has special significance'[36], which in turn allows further connections to be made:

> Evidence that play sessions are real makes questions about their temporal structure possible and indeed inevitable. And this line of

---

[30] Spariosu, *Dionysus Reborn* p. 199; see Gregory Bateson, *Steps to an Ecology of Mind* (Chicago: University of Chicago Press, 1972).

[31] J. Deegan & A. Pellegrini, 'Play and Linking Trajectories for Social Origins of Cognition' in R. Bogue & M. Spariosu (eds) *The Play of Self* (NY: State University, 1994), pp.120-122.

[32] Deegan & Pellegrini, ,Play and Linking', p.126.

[33] Spariosu, *Dionysus Reborn*, p. 205.

[34] Spariosu, *Dionysus Reborn*, p. 213.

[35] Fagen, 'Animal Play', pp. 32-35.

[36] Fagen, 'Animal Play', p. 33.

> enquiry further extends in directions that link play and games to story and myth. Here is a gateway to other times and spaces, to the universals in myth and fairytale ...[37]

Such evidence suggests that play is biologically important as well as motivated and fun. Indeed play is engaged in despite its occasional risks, which might at first glance be seen as a counter-indicator to its evolutionary usefulness. What is the use of play if it is so dangerous that it threatens the survival of the individual or the species? Nevertheless, a generally affirmative assessment of play persists and is usually related to a posited adaptive significance for play.

Fagen also draws attention to the analysis of play as 'performance' which is too often neglected by biologists and others. In other words we should not always focus on the assumed *cognitive* benefits of play, but rather, with Sutton-Smith, also analyse play in terms of performance, rhetoric and metaphor, and indeed fun! But, also like Sutton-Smith, we should guard against the 'idealization' and romanticization of animal play, recognising that it also has a darker side such as bullying.[38] Yet, we might reasonably conclude from a biological/scientific perspective that:

> Play evolved through a series of phases involving development of physical capacity and skill, development of close positive dyadic social relationships, assessment of well-being, and ... integrative aspects of individual personality ... [such] as self-confidence, emotional resilience and a sense of fun.[39]

Tellingly, Fagen goes on to argue: 'Without these gifts, we are most certainly lost, as powers, potentialities and dark alignments have always known quite well. Is it any surprise that such forces, whatever names we may give them, may seek to suppress play by more or less heavy-handed means?'[40] Throughout human history, totalitarian regimes have always sought to suppress or censor creative aspects of culture which, perhaps correctly, they perceive to be subversive of the order which they seek to impose. We might then agree that an adequate account of play must allow for its biological and its aesthetic dimensions (to which we might add perhaps the spiritual), the comic as well as the tragic. But the question remains: is it 'just for kids'?

Patrick Bateson argues that play is not limited to, but is especially characteristic of, the activity of juvenile animals and young children: 'play

---

[37] Fagen, 'Animal Play', p. 32.

[38] Fagen, 'Animal Play', pp. 38-39.

[39] Fagen, 'Animal Play', pp. 39-40.

[40] Fagen, 'Animal Play', p. 40.

… is typically something that children and young animals do. Adults play too, of course, but generally have less time for it and less inclination.'[41] He suggests that play may be seen in biological terms as 'developmental scaffolding' that enables the young animal to develop and which naturally 'falls away' once the animal matures. In particular he is sympathetic to the argument that play is especially significant in negotiating risk and suggests that, 'play allows young animals to simulate, in a relatively safe context, potentially dangerous situations that will arise in their adult lives. They learn from their mistakes but safely.'[42] Yet Bateson concludes that, 'play is an effective mechanism for facilitating innovation and encouraging creativity.'[43]

Contemporary biologists are increasingly uncomfortable with the rather utilitarian accounts of earlier scholars and are tending to emphasise the sheer gratuity of the evolutionary process, which Gordon Rattray Taylor has described as less 'a struggle to survive, it looks more like one glorious romp'.[44] We might then see the phenomenon of play as one manifestation of this sheer exuberance of nature and an expression of the joy and fun of living. Such biological perspectives accord well with Winnicott's psychological studies. However, we should also note that the notion of play potentially poses a significant challenge to those forms of scientific investigation which operate within narrowly defined forms of rationality.

3. Play in the Socio-Cultural Disciplines

Hans-Georg Gadamer disputes modern scientific inductive reason as the sole means to truth and offers instead a hermeneutical approach. According to Monica Vilhauer, 'the concept of "play" is the key to understanding the real alternative to modern scientific conceptions of knowledge, method and truth that Gadamer wants to articulate'[45]. It is to such socio-cultural analyses of play as potential 'rule-breaker' that we now turn. Gadamer's pioneering work stands in a tradition shaped by Kant and subsequently developed by Schiller, Nietzsche and Heidegger.

Spariosu suggests that Kant, 'consistently subordinates imagination to reason, art to philosophy and science, and play to morality and

[41] Bateson, 'The Role of Play', p. 14,

[42] Bateson, 'The Role of Play', p. 17.

[43] Bateson, 'The Role of Play', p.18.

[44] Gordon R. Taylor, *The Great Evolution Mystery* (Londo : Secker & Warburg, 1983), p. 195; Spariosu, *Dionysus Reborn*, p. 238.

[45] Monica Vilhauer, *Gadamer's Ethics of Play: Hermeneutics and the Other* (Lanham, MD: Lexington Books, 2010), p. 25.

seriousness'.[46] Schiller, by contrast, 'raises Art to the same level as Science' and therefore, 'Art can carry out the task of Reason precisely because of its double nature as semblance and reality, play and seriousness, entertainment and reality'[47]. Indeed Schiller goes on to claim that, 'man (sic) only plays when he is in the fullest sense of the word a human being, and *he is only fully a human being when he plays*'.[48] Similarly Heidegger, in his later work, emphasises the notion of wager or risk that we have already seen under discussion in biological terms. He seems to affirm Schiller's view of the *existential* character of play in his assertion that: 'the dispensation of Being is a child at play.'[49] Spariosu concludes that, 'by transferring power from beings to Being itself,' Heidegger consolidates Nietzsche's 'return to the prerational, archaic notion of power as *Welstspiel* – a violent, arbitrary, and ecstatic play of forces in which man is both player and plaything'.[50]

Gadamer likewise emphasises the absorbing quality of play which contains a number of paradoxical aspects. Thus play is both fun, or 'not serious', yet at the same time also possesses its own innate, and even 'sacred seriousness'.[51] Indeed it is this serious commitment to the play experience which 'makes the play wholly play'.[52] It is here that the risk identified by Heidegger is located, in that through the commitment to the experience of play we are, as it were, 'possessed' by the essence of play itself which transcends the player. Of course many types of play, especially games and sport, are designed to allow the players to encounter risk in various forms. There are freedoms within the experience over which the player has limited control, there are elements of chance, or one risks the potentially superior skill of an opponent. For Gadamer, 'the attraction of the game, which it exercises on the player, lies in this risk. The player enjoys a freedom of decision, which is at the same time endangered and irrevocably limited', and therefore he concludes, 'all playing is a being-played' and that, 'whoever "tries" is in fact the one who is tried'.[53]

Through the experience of play in its many and varied forms, play gives expression to its own essence or 'spirit', and yet also allows the player to

---

[46] Spariosu, *Dionysus Reborn*, p. 39.

[47] Spariosu, *Dionysus Reborn*, p. 58.

[48] Friedrich Schiller, *On the Aesthetic Education of Man, in a Series of Letters,* ed. & trans. E. M. Wilkinson & L. A. Willoughby, (Oxford: OUP, 1967), pp. XV, 9; see Spariosu, *Dionysus Reborn*, p. 59.

[49] Martin Heidegger, *The Principle of Reason*, trans. R. Lilly, (Bloomington: University of Indiana Press,1991), p. 189; see Spariosu, *Dionysus Reborn*, p. 120.

[50] Spariosu, *Dionysus Reborn*, p. 124.

[51] Hans-Georg Gadamer, *Truth and Method* trans. G. Barden and J. Cumming, (London: Sheed & Ward, 1975), p. 91.

[52] Gadamer, *Truth and Method*, p. 92.

[53] Gadamer, *Truth and Method,* p. 95.

achieve at least some degree of self-presentation or expression. Play's 'mode of being is self-representation. But self-representation is a universal aspect of the being of nature.' At the same time, by, 'playing the game' players are also playing *themselves* out and thus also achieving a degree of self-representation. Thus in and through play human beings both lose and find themselves at one and the same time.[54]

Drew Hyland is critical of such approaches since he argues that for thinkers such as Heidegger and Gadamer play is fundamentally 'irrational', having neither origin (*arche*) nor purpose (*telos*). In such approaches this irrationality is generally seen as a virtue and represents the freedom and spontaneity of play. While this may be adequate for some forms of play, perhaps child's play, Hyland is not persuaded that this is a sufficient account, for example of sports. Equally, is this enough to justify its characterisation as 'irrational', or does that betray too narrow a conception of 'rationality'?[55] Hyland, in describing what he calls 'the stance of play', offers instead some clarifications (not definitions) of the notion and experience of play which he suggests possesses the elements of: responsive openness, finitude, value and fun. While these are not exhaustive of the qualities of play they are 'central'. Clearly each of them may also be present in non-play experiences, but:

> part of the very value of play is that certain issues and themes, present but often hidden, in everyday life are highlighted in play and brought to the position of centrality which they should perhaps have for us always.[56]

Despite his criticism of the continental philosophers, Hyland's own approach does not seem too far from what Gadamer and others are trying to articulate. He seems to believe that in their account it is only the essence of play which comes to self-expression. But as we have seen, the player too, at least to some degree, finds self-actualisation. This is anecdotally expressed by many participants, for example whether in sports or music or drama, that they find themselves to be 'more fully alive'. For Hyland this is best expressed as a search for fulfilment, which acknowledges the common human experience of incompleteness, perhaps most fully expressed in the erotic aspects of human life. The most obvious example of our human incompleteness is the need for sexual union, through which we may attain fulfilment. In returning to consider the Platonic origins of play discussions, Hyland takes up the themes of Plato's *Symposium* and argues that:

---

[54] Gadamer, *Truth and Method*, p. 97.

[55] Drew A. Hyland, *The Question of Play* (Lanham, MD: University Press of America, 1984), p. 81.

[56] Hyland, *The Question of Play*, pp. 72-3.

> The play experience, an experience of that unified immersion in which our involvement is total, is thus an experience which cuts through the superficial duality of our bodily and physical expressions to their unity in our natures as erotic.[57]

Such love-play reveals yet another paradoxical dimension of play: 'eros individualizes us in our monadic nature, but it individualizes us *as relational*'.[58] Play creates relationship and nurtures community, but also fosters the individual journey of self-discovery: 'an affirmation of precariousness and finitude does not exclude but celebrates play as at the pinnacle of human possibilities. In play, too, we know ourselves, we are ourselves'.[59]

Conclusion

In the light of this discussion it becomes apparent that the varied, rich and complex phenomenon of play has something very significant to offer to our understanding of human nature and development, or formation. Although certain forms of play are particularly characteristic of children, in various ways, whether in sport, games, drama, music or art, play remains important to adults too, as the space where we can be creative and in which culture can develop. In conclusion I want to underline some areas for further reflection.

Play is a common phenomenon across cultures and to some extent across certain animal species; although clearly in different cultures it may take different forms and may be given widely differing valuations. Throughout history some cultures have focused on an ethic of work and self-discipline, and some of these seem innately suspicious of the perceived 'frivolous' and 'wasteful' aspects of play. This reflects an ongoing conversation between competing ideals focused alternatively on 'rationality' and 'irrationality'. However, the ambiguity of play as both 'rule-maker' and rule-breaker', and the importance of some forms of play, such as professional sport, in which competition and self-discipline are highly valued, suggests that play need not be seen only as a frivolous pastime to be abandoned early by those with serious ambition. Indeed, its very ambiguity suggests the vital role which play provides, both in the development of systems and rules as intrinsic and necessary for the emergence of all civilisation, but also in play's function as a guardian against oppression and totalitarianism in all its forms, from the playground bully to the tyrannical dictator. Play helps us both to create the rules necessary for living in community, but also enables us to challenge the

---

57 Hyland, *The Question of Play*, p. 142.

58 Hyland, *The Question of Play*, p. 143.

59 Hyland, *The Question of Play*, p. 151.

rules when they become self-serving and oppressive. Indeed human experience suggests that play is vital in challenging the forces of rationality when they become over-powerful, for all too often in history it is the players, the artists, the musicians and the dramatists who have themselves proved the most resilient to the dark powers, and who have also provided the spiritual and creative energy by which such forces may be subverted and overcome.

Such insights underline the important role of play in the opening up of 'space', and the vital significance of its intrinsic values of freedom and creativity. As we have already noted, Winnicot can assert that, 'in playing, and perhaps only in playing, the child or adult is free to be creative'.[60] Likewise modern philosophers such as Schiller and Heidegger view play as fundamental not only to human being, but to Being *in itself*. There is a close link here in these existential analyses between freedom and creativity and the notion of risk or wager, which entails both freedom and creative imagination. Such thinkers argue that it is through embracing freedom and creativity that identity is formed and our being comes to fuller expression, albeit we may discover that sometimes the player is also the plaything!

This reminds us that another important aspect of play is in coming to terms with the reality of the 'other', both in psychological and in social terms. We might argue by extension, from a theological perspective, that part of such encounters may be a meeting with the transcendent 'Other'. As we grow and develop and negotiate our identity and come to terms with the realities of our existence, play helps us in the continuing task of relating what Winnicot characterises as 'inner and outer reality', and he suggests that in this way play occupies a similar space to the arts and to religion. Likewise biologists agree that imaginative play in particular helps cognitive development and builds capacity for abstraction as well as emotional intelligence and social interaction. It is in such space that communication, language and therefore civilisation itself begins to emerge.

But this is also the space in which the realm of religious faith takes shape. If we are inclined to agree with Winnicot that 'cultural experience begins with creative living first manifested in play',[61] we might argue that we find here also the origins of religious faith. In the freedom and creativity of play, we discover, as Huizinga argues, the roots of civilization, which in turn both reflects and creates the worldviews of peoples and cultures. Our fundamental apprehensions of the world are located in such experiences and encounters. Play is deeply rooted in our human experience and is a significant way of engagement with the created order. In the Judaeo-Christian tradition play is also a sign of a new order, the coming kingdom when, in a creation restored

---

[60] See note 13 above.

[61] See note 22 above.

to God's original intention, the universe will resound to the happy sounds of fun, laughter and play.[62]

Play helps us to discover who we are through adventure and imagination; it helps us create relationships as we negotiate the intricacies and changing rules of children's games; it helps us to push the boundaries and explore our limits as we take risks on the climbing frame or the white water raft; it expresses our own skills and creativity as we perform music, act in dramas, compete in sporting events; it helps us celebrate the gift of life in festival and feasting. It is a dimension of life in which the sheer energy and exuberance of living can find expression, where we do things not because we have to, but just because we can. In other words, play is fun! But it is not *only* fun. I agree with those who suggest that in play important aspects of human character are revealed which might otherwise remain hidden. It helps us to achieve a proper balance in life, refocusing our values, allowing us to become absorbed or lost in activity simply for the joy of the play itself, and not for any external reason.

In other words, play is crucial to the processes of human formation and central to the creation of religious identity: 'the formation of a Christian (or indeed a Jewish, Muslim, Hindu or Buddhist) mind'. For the theistic believer all this might suggest that play is close to the heart of God too, that somehow play might even be characteristic of God, central to who and how God is. This is what the Wisdom tradition of the Hebrew Scriptures hints at,[63] and it certainly seems to be a feature of Jesus' own enjoyment of 'life in all its fullness'.[64] For Christian faith the life, death and resurrection of Jesus is the definitive expression of both humanity and divinity, and the Gospels present Jesus as a person who is fun to be with, full of life and laughter, inviting all who will to experience the playfulness at the very heart of all things. We often read Jesus' emphasis on children and childlikeness with reference to simplicity and trust, but might it not also be about the ability to play, to have fun, to be adventurous in exploring new areas of experience, and unselfconsciously to delight in all that life has to offer – to share in that freedom and openness which is characteristic of play?

Play is free, complete in itself, done for the pleasure of the activity, bounded by its own space and time, and characterised by a sense of

---

[62] In Isaiah 11 the messianic age is evoked in wonderful imagery of peace and harmony including the child playing safely over the vipers nest (Is 11:8). Safe play for little children is thus characteristic of the kingdom. Similarly, when Zechariah imagines the restoration of Jerusalem, it is the voices of children happily playing which provide the soundtrack to the pictures (Zech.8:5). This is perhaps reflected in some accounts of Jesus' arrival in Jerusalem on Palm Sunday accompanied by the happy voices of children (Matt. 21:16).

[63] e.g. Prov 8:22-31.

[64] John 10:10.

adventure, freedom and delight; creating relationships where other players, and even playthings, are treated as personal. In this we may see characteristics of the Creator God, and through playing with others in autonomy and pleasure, we may catch a fresh vision of the God who also delights in the free play of creation. Huizinga concludes: 'The human mind can only disengage itself from the magic circle of play by turning towards the ultimate.'[65] Perhaps rather we may conclude that it is *through* play that we finally discover something more of what, or perhaps even Who, that Ultimate might be.

[65] Huizinga, *Homo Ludens*, p. 212.

13.

Following God's Call and Bringing Good News and Glimpses of Hope in Ferentari

Oti Bunaciu

I met Professor Paul Fiddes for the first time 31 years ago, in 1983 on a visit to Oxford, which I took together with my father, Ioan Bunaciu. He was invited to do some reading in the College library by Barry White who was at the time the Principal of Regent's Park College. Among my memories from that visit is being invited for tea and coffee in Paul Fiddes' apartment in Angus block. I was fortunate enough to have Paul Fiddes as my tutor for Patristic studies and for engaging with Karl Barth as the special theologian in my programme and I am sure that I shared with other students the experience of becoming acutely aware of the weaknesses of my argument when asked to read my essay and, most importantly, the hopeful encouragement that next time my work could be better.

Through his theological work Paul Fiddes serves the Baptist community by contributing to a Baptist theology that reflects the life and faith of Baptist churches worldwide. His commitment to the wider Christian community is also seen by his engagement in many dialogues between Baptists and other churches and in the fact that he always claims that theology is common to all Christians although it may be done from a confessional perspective.

A significant contribution of Fiddes that I must mention is his enthusiastic support of Romanian Baptist theological education. Regent's Park College has invested for many years in training and supporting the training of many of the teachers and leaders of the Bucharest Baptist Theological Institute and of the Facultatea de Teologie Baptista in the University of Bucharest. Fiddes' long term and ongoing engagement in support of theological education in Romania was recognized in 2004 by the University of Bucharest, which honoured him with a *Doctor Honoris Causa* degree, making him a member of this academic community. His recent involvement in helping start *The Centre for Faith and Culture*, a research centre of the Facultatea de Teologie Baptista is a significant step towards developing theological research among Baptist theologians in Romania.

This current essay attempts to reflect and think through the implications of the involvement of a local church in Bucharest[1] in the needs of the local community. This is the church in which I grew up and which I currently serve as a minister together with Sorin Badragan, a colleague who has also benefited from Regent's Park College's effort to support young Romanian theologians. As a young minister in 1992 I helped start, under the name of Project Ruth, a charitable work among poor people mostly from a Roma background. This continues to grow and expand under Fundatia Providenta a charity related to Providence Baptist Church. In various stages of the development of Project Ruth, Paul Fiddes was involved in helping promote the cause and recently in preaching for the 10-year anniversary of the Gypsy Smith School in 2013. Students and other staff from Regent's Park College have also been involved in visiting and supporting the ministry. Some Regent's Park College graduates have been supporters of its ministry from its inception and another graduate, Andrew Brockbank, was its Executive Director for more than ten years.

In the last few years the issue of the Roma people has featured high on the agenda of European social issues and more recently it has become part of the political debate as well. With the opening of the borders for the new European Union members, free movement has allowed Roma groups to migrate to western countries in search for better economic opportunities. The Roma population is perceived as finding it difficult to integrate easily in other cultures and their own culture has proven to be very resilient when encountering other contexts. Therefore the Roma are increasingly being considered as a problem population by many countries in Western Europe. On several occasions, well published in the media, they were sent back by force to their countries of origin, mainly to Romania and Bulgaria. This has had an effect on the Roma people as such who saw their basic rights to free movement within the European Union curtailed but also on their relationship with the majority populations in their countries. Since they are citizens of those countries they are now perceived as ruining the reputation of the other, non-Roma citizens. This has led to renewed racist attitudes from a population who now dislikes or even hates them more than before. Both national governments and the European Union have attempted to tackle the situation and have tried to develop some general strategy for the situation of Roma in Europe. This has not proved to be a very successful approach as each situation appears to be very different and specific to each context and therefore attempts to develop a general solution seem to miss the needs of the specific context.

---

[1] Providence Baptist Church in the Ferentari, Str. Talazului 16, Bucharest, Romania.

The Roma in the General Context of Europe and Romania

It is generally believed that the Roma people have come to Europe from the area of India and Pakistan around 800 or 900 years ago. Because of their skin colour[2] and extended family type of social structure existing populations treated them with suspicion. During their entire history the Roma suffered from persecution and from racism from the majority populations; the map below shows minority Roma populations in Eastern Europe.

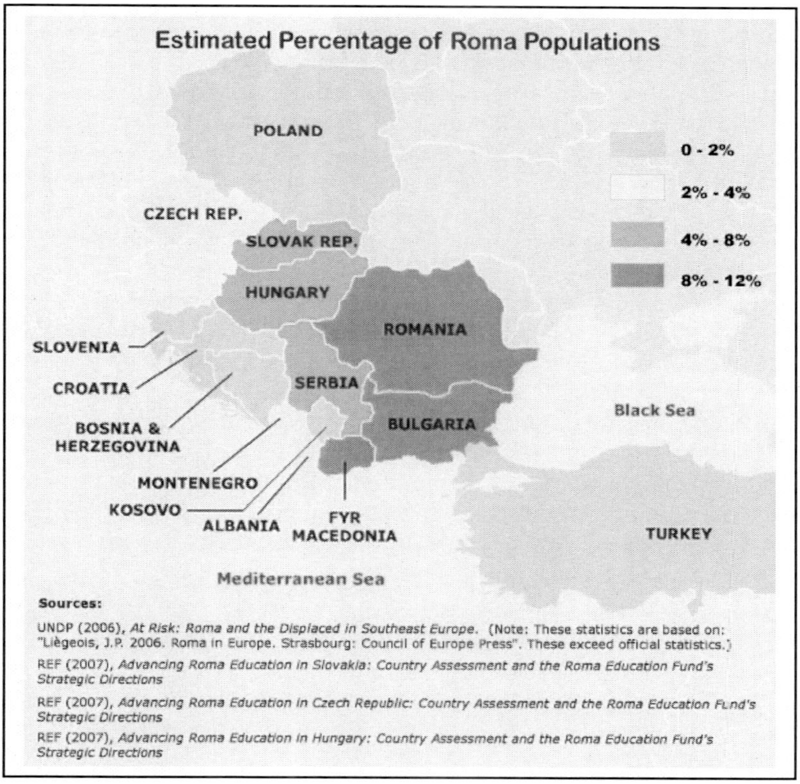

The first known attestation of Roma in Romania is in a document from 1385 where a local king, Dan I of Wallachia included a group of Roma slaves in a

---

[2] Some suggest that the name 'Gypsy' comes from a suspicion that they originally came from Egypt.

donation made to the Monastery of Tismana[3]. These Roma slaves developed various skills and their various groups are named after these crafts[4]. There is usually not much cooperation between these groups and their language is based on old Sanskrit with new words and pronunciation adopted from the local population. Due to the fact that the crafts they used to support themselves are not in demand in modern economies, most Roma people find themselves looking for unskilled work in agriculture, construction or street cleaning.

Although the Roma live in all the European Union, the countries which host larger numbers are Romania and Bulgaria. Evaluating the size of the Roma population has been notoriously difficult because of their isolation and also because of the stigma that acknowledging their ethnic origin carries, which leads to many not declaring their Roma identity. A 2009 study[5] from Spain estimates the total Roma population of seven European countries as being 2,795,233. These countries are: Greece: 125,000; Portugal: 33,338; Czech Republic: 230,000; Slovakia: 320,000; Romania: 1,050,000; Bulgaria: 370,908; Spain: 665,987; making the total of Roma in Europe to be 2,795,233. Other studies claim that around 9 to 10 million Roma live in European countries making them one of the larger groups (see the Council of Europe graph below).

Roma communities living in rural areas can have a homogeneous social structure in which case the structure is clan like with a social leader who has a lot of authority. Sometimes a council of elders is also part of the leadership of such a community. In such settings the Roma will wear traditional clothes and follow their own traditions. In urban settings these communities tend to be less homogeneous and Roma people find themselves at the fringe of the local population and also of the traditional Roma. In such settings they have abandoned traditional dress but they still retain some of their traditions. One

---

[3] Education, Audiovisual and Culture Executive Agency, *Romaninet - A Multimedia Romani Course for Promoting Linguistic Diversity and Improving Social Dialogue: Report on Roma People* (2012), Instituto de Enseñanza Secundaria Ribeira do Louro (Spain), Asesoramiento, Tecnología e Investigación S.L. (Spain), Fundación Secretariado Gitano (Spain), "ETHNOTOLERANCE" (Bulgary), Secretariado Diocesano de Lisboa da Obra Pastoral dos Ciganos (Portugal), Grup Scolar Industrial Victor Jinga (Romania), SC CONCEPT CONSULTING SRL (România), University of Manchester (United Kingdom),

[4] In Romania, for example, one the largest numbers of Roma people belong to the 'caldarari' group who used to make and repair metal pots. Another large group is 'ursari' who used to be entertainers (dancing bears sometimes) and the 'caramidari' who made bricks, or 'lingurari' who made spoons.

[5] Fundacion Secretariado Gitano (ed.) *Health and the Roma Community, Analysis of the Situation in Europe, Bulgaria, Czech Republic, Greece, Portugal, Romania, Slovakia, Spain*, (Madrid: A.D.I., 2009).

tradition that remains controversial is the custom to marry girls in arranged marriages quite early, often at 13 or 14 although legislation allows for marriage only to take place after 16 with parents' approval.

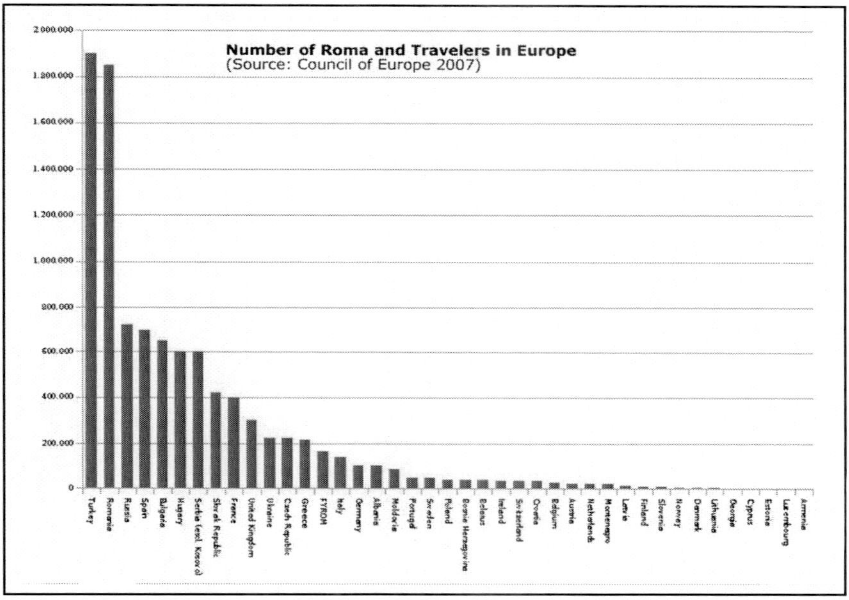

In terms of religion Roma in Romania tend to adopt the majority religion (Orthodox) although they often develop syncretistic beliefs where superstition plays a great role. Often activities like fortune telling are presented as being part of a Christian way and take place under the guidance of God. In the last twenty years many Roma have converted to Evangelical beliefs, most of them being attracted to Baptist or Pentecostal groups, the latter being more attractive due to the more open style of worship.

Hearing a Call as a Vision to Respond to the Need

Statistics regarding the conditions of Roma people in Romania are quite grim. According to studies, more than 30% of the population suffer from extreme poverty and 30 % suffer from severe poverty. Over 70% of the Roma population in the city of Bucharest does not have access to medical care in spite of the existence of a National Health Care in Romania. In terms of infrastructure over 50% of Roma population does not have the benefit of minimal infrastructure (drinking water, electricity, etc.)

According to a UNICEF study for 2011-2012[6], 29.2% of Roma pupils experienced hunger at school during last month because they did not have food at home while only 10% of non-Roma pupils experienced the same. The main income for 25.5 % of the Roma families that had pupils came from child allowance compared with only 11.1% for non-Roma families and for 32.4% of Roma pupils their families came from social subvention compared with 5.7% for non-Roma families. Around 5.5% of the Roma pupils feel ashamed to go to school with the clothes they have compared with 1.3% of the non-Roma pupils and 29.1% of the parents of Roma pupils have no school or just primary education in comparison with only 3.4% of the non-Roma families.

Providence Baptist church in Bucharest is located in the southern part of the capital city, which has about 2 million inhabitants[7]. The fifth district of the city has 271,575 inhabitants and the area where the church is located (Ferentari) has 90,000. Ferentari is considered one of the poorest areas of the city with some of the highest incidence of crime, which many attribute (rightly or wrongly) to a large presence of Roma people. Providence Baptist Church has about 300 members with 200 in regular attendance and was established almost 90 years ago as the 2nd Baptist church in Bucharest. Although the church is located in an area with many Roma people these do not attend the church. Only three or four Roma families who have abandoned Roma traditions and have adopted 'Romanian ways' have become members. In the area there are several other Orthodox churches and a few Evangelical churches as well. Interestingly enough official statistics (official data from the Romanian National Institute of Statistics, 2011 census[8]) found, for reasons mentioned previously, only 23,973 Roma in Bucharest and only 6,990 Roma in the entire fifth district.

The initiative to start Project Ruth came as a result of a challenge brought by a missionary from the US who was a member of our church at the time and who asked why Roma people did not seem to attend the church. It started with inviting Roma children who were roaming the streets to play in the churchyard and attend our Sunday school classes. Soon a day centre was organized which was attended by fifteen to twenty children at first but when some food was served the numbers grew quickly to seventy-five to ninety children. The church did not have many facilities at the time since under communism expansion of church work including buildings was almost impossible to achieve. The day centre operated in the basement of the

---

[6] *Early School Attrition – the Causes and Effects*, accessed at http://romaeducationfund.ro/download/The%20School%20Dropout%20and%20Early-School%20Attrition%20among%20Roma%20Children.pdf

[7] According to the 2011 census there were 1,883,425 inhabitants in Bucharest (http://www.recensamantromania.ro/rezultate-2/).

[8] http://www.recensamantromania.ro/rezultate-2/

church, which was also where the youth group met. It was the young people who named the work as Project Ruth because Ruth was accepted as a foreigner among the people of God. The activity started with volunteers but soon the level of work demanded a full-time person and in about six months from the start of the work, Project Ruth employed its first worker and it operated daily for four hours.

Engaging with the Need to Offer Better Chances and Hope

It was quickly noticed that most of the children were illiterate although they were above the age of schooling and there were free state schools in the area. Because of the existing law, which excluded from school those who were two years older than the age of schooling, many of the children had lost their chance to go to school. Nutrition was an obvious problem, as the children would fight to get a sandwich with cheese or honey or even a piece of bread. We also noticed that hygiene was a serious problem as 80% of the children had head lice and some had scabies. There were also some health issues mainly due to poor oral hygiene but also none of them had glasses even if they needed them.

Twenty years later the work has developed under Fundatia Providenta which now employs twenty-eight people in several types of activities which attempt to help the Roma community. It also helps run a similar project on a smaller scale in the village of Rascaieti, in the Republic of Moldova. Much of the work of Project Ruth is done with the help of volunteers mostly from abroad but also from Romania. Funding is an ongoing challenge and besides regular sponsorship finance comes from individuals, churches, other NGO's and more recently from grants accessed from companies interested in supporting charitable work.

The main activities of Project Ruth reflect the needs of the community and currently these include:

- *Education*: The Ruth School is an accredited school in the Romanian educational system (accreditation in 1994 and 1999) with 220 children in grades 1 to 8 plus a preparatory class in which over 2400 pupils have been educated since 1992.
- *Food*: Project Ruth provides a daily meal for all the children with the intention to address basic needs of good nutrition and therefore they include hot meals, fruit and vegetables.
- *Hygiene and Health:* Hygiene and health is an important focus for Project Ruth and is led by a family doctor and a nurse who organise hygiene programmes and provide medical services for children coming from families that are not insured (dental care is provided with help from volunteer dentists).

- *Humanitarian assistance:* Project Ruth tries to find partners to help support children and their families cope with their situation better with an emphasis on winter clothing and shoes as the conditions in Romania are harsh in the winter.
- *Leadership training:* Project Ruth has tried to become involved in Roma communities through churches by providing leadership training especially in the Gypsy Smith School which trains about twenty-five people in a two year long training programme.
- *Counselling and job training for women:* Because women are often in an inferior social situation and are frequently abused Project Ruth has started the Naomi Centre which runs a counselling programme for women and as part of helping women the Centre also runs a sewing club where women can learn how to sew with the help of a qualified sewing teacher.
- *Community development*: In an effort to develop good relationships with the Roma communities various programmes are developed to build trust and avert suspicion and lack of interest by involving parents in information exchanges and in discussion issues of general interest like drug use, trafficking and unemployment.
- *Advocacy and Resource Centre*: As the ministry developed other issues have become evident and Project Ruth is involved in advocacy and also in developing a resource centre in which the experience gained is made available to those working in similar communities.
- *Witness*: Although the main work of Project Ruth is to help the Roma community the ministry has provided important opportunities to become a witness of the Kingdom of God and since most Romanians are not inclined to help the Roma community the work has attracted the attention of specialists in education and social work, media, politicians and businesses interested in helping.

Leaving the Old to Facilitate the Coming of the New

In what was his last, unfinished, essay, 'Starting Out, Turning Round, Confessing' in 1968, Karl Barth talked about the church. He says that in the first instance the movement of the church must be a starting out. 'Starting out takes place when something already there has grown old and must be left behind, when the night is past, when something new replaces it and a new day dawns'. Our church did not feel quite like that but close. Barth also says that 'starting out' takes place in a crisis:

> A resolute farewell is then said to what is familiar, what is close at hand, what has its own advantages, as in the form of the well-known fleshpots of Egypt. And there is a resolute turning instead to what is distant, to what is affirmed in hope, to what has disadvantages, to what is still largely unknown in its glorious form. When the church sets out, it has made a choice, a decision.[9]

My question was how do churches make such decisions or do they ever make them? What motivates a church to move towards such a decision? Barth himself gives an answer:

> The true and authentic starting out of the church is first and supremely an acceptance of the future and only then and for that reason a denial of the past. Mere weariness or criticism or distaste or scorn or protest in relation to what has been thus far, to what would now be called the establishment, has nothing whatever to do with the church's great movement of starting out. When Moses killed and buried that wicked man that was not by a long way Israel's liberation from imprisonment. In both confessions today we often hear a justifiable but empty negation – empty because it is not filled with affirmation of the better future. An empty negation will always have a more or less disagreeable and melancholy sound. When the church genuinely negates what has been thus far, it will be a clear negation, but one that is also friendly and cheerful. It follows, then, that the church's true and authentic starting out takes place only when it sees the new as promise and therefore as future, as clear and definite promise and future … The exodus from Egypt began when Moses came down from the mount of God and away from the burning bush, where he had heard God's Word, and was thus able to tell the people and Pharaoh something about where they were going.[10]

Churches, like society, in post communist Romania needed a radical change and although some transformation took place there were so many elements of continuity that remained. Churches have reacted pragmatically to the new situations, that is, by responding to concrete needs. Soon it became evident that pragmatic responses from church communities will have to find some grounding in theology as churches always seek to understand and justify what they are doing from a perspective of their understanding of Scripture integrated in the call to spread the Gospel and to serve the world. The challenge for the church is to move beyond responding

---

[9] Karl Barth, 'Starting Out, Turning Round, Confessing' in *Final Testimonies* (Grand Rapids, MI: Eerdmans, 1977), p. 29.

[10] Barth, 'Starting Out', p. 29.

to a crisis (something otherwise necessary) but to hear what God is calling the church to do so that it can be what God calls the church to be. In a sense for the Romanian churches the dilemma that they were facing was whether the churches and the people of God should accept the old situation as the God given one or whether they should strive for a change and also aspire to be involved in it.

An appropriate theological understanding of the relationship between the church and the world should start from an adequate understanding of God and of how God engages with and works in the world. One of the biblical themes that can constitute a natural basis for theological reflection is that of the covenant. Walter Brueggemann points to the fact that even if covenant may not be an overarching and unique theme of the Bible, it is nevertheless an important one as 'the central affirmations of covenant stand against and subvert the dominant forms, patterns and presuppositions of our culture and of cultural Christianity.'[11] The God of the Scriptures differs from any other gods in that it resists human attempts to understand him in the terms of those gods because covenant shows God engaged in a 'faithful interrelatedness' and 'steadfast solidarity'. God does not remain self-sufficient in heaven but gives up of his power in order to embrace human beings as his covenant partner, opening in this way the opportunity for new hope and a new beginning. This new beginning is what becomes possible amongst humans because of God's covenant and this is community as Jeremiah notes: 'Behold, the days are coming, says the LORD, when I will make a new covenant with the house of Israel and the house of Judah.'[12] The coming into being of this earthly community is not proclaimed on the basis of a sociological understanding of the world, because that would not be possible, but because of God's new move to covenant himself to us and to this community which is not therefore just a voluntary organization. This community, Brueggemann thinks, although it is centred in the covenant extends to the world because it is called to be a witness, a mediator or a partner to the others bringing therefore the hope that they have discovered, 'and that, perhaps is the most important and the most subversive thing the church can now do: to refuse to give up on the world and its promised transformation.'[13] Therefore the idea of covenant presents to us a different idea of God with the implication that it also shows us a different understanding of social life and social practice in which peace and justice are two fundamental concerns.

In discussing the meaning of covenant in Baptist ecclesiology Paul Fiddes points out that a Baptist understanding is not identical with that of the

---

[11] Walter Brueggemann, *A Social Reading of the Old Testament*, (Minneapolis, MN: Augsburg Fortress, 1994), p. 43.

[12] Jeremiah 31:31 (RSV).

[13] Brueggemann, *A Social Reading*, p. 51.

tradition of Calvin and introduces Karl Barth's understanding of electing grace as a more dynamic understanding of this doctrine.[14] For Barth, the covenant of grace is first of all part of the relationships between the Father, Son and Holy Spirit in the Trinity as God determines that he is God for us. Although Fiddes points out that Barth avoids speaking of an intra-Trinitarian covenant when such an understanding of this is considered in conjunction with an understanding of the election of Jesus Christ as the representative of all humanity, this gives covenant a deeper meaning than just a 'strategic alliance'. 'Thus our mission to the world shares in the mission of the Father who eternally 'sends forth' the Son.'[15] It is this kind of theological understanding, I believe, that facilitates an engagement of the church with the world, which is beyond a pragmatic (and much needed) reaction to a local reality. As Fiddes points out, the voluntarist, empirical and pragmatic spirit of Baptist churches (he has in mind their coming together in associations) should not be understood just as being 'merely task orientated but a means of exploring the purpose of God in his world'[16].

An adequate understanding of the meaning of covenant can ground the church's existence in the world as a community called and sent at the same time. I believe that another insight from Paul Fiddes' theological thinking, that of participation, can help understand how the church can better think of being a community that is not just imitating the triune life but participating in it[17]. He discusses four tensions related to individual persons' participation in community and how considering them from the perspective of engaging in God would change our understanding.

First when we think of the triune God who sends the Son eternally into the world we are drawn into modelling a community by participating in the movement of sending. 'There is an identification not of substance but of act and event and therefore by being engaged in God's relational life we can discover what roles the community requires, how it needs us to 'represent' the signs of the Christ in order to be a community open to the needs of all.'[18] Secondly, the question of the integrity of the self and openness towards others leads us to the need to understand how we can be open to the other not by conforming to the other but to the Christ we meet through the other. Fiddes sees this possibility when participating in God because this 'means that there is the ever-present opportunity to be aligned with a movement of communication beyond ourselves which is pure love, and which is also a

---

[14] Paul Fiddes, *Tracks and Traces, Baptist Identity in Church and Theology*, (Carlisle: Paternoster Press, 2003), p. 35.

[15] Fiddes, *Tracks and Traces*, p. 37.

[16] Fiddes, *Tracks and Traces*, p. 45.

[17] Paul Fiddes, *Participating in God, A Pastoral Doctrine of the Trinity*, (London: DLT, 2000), p. 50.

[18] Fiddes, *Participating in God*, pp. 51, 52.

movement of the will.'[19] This is like the response of a son to a father when he says yes because he agrees with the father's purpose. There is a room therefore for real choice of the individual person. A third theme is that of dependence and independence where participation in God can be seen in terms of an interdependence which is made possible because God in an act of self-limitation opens up the divine communion to enable others to participate in it. Fiddes sees this also as a temporal movement in which the Spirit opens up opportunities in the future making in this way relationships part of God's journey towards new creation. Lastly he comments on the tension between diversity and unity and thinks that participating in God means 'to participate in the otherness of the personal relations in God, which are united at the same moment in a communion of love, will and purpose.'[20] This also means that engaging in the relationships in God enables us to the possibility of experiencing fellowship in a more intimate way than we would otherwise do when faced with the challenge of the stranger and the radically different.

In the last chapter of his study of participation Fiddes writes about incarnation and sacramental life which he understands also as a way to participate in God. In Baptist life this is illustrated by baptism where believers are included in the body of Christ and in communion as the fellowship of the body of Christ but also in the church meeting where the body of Christ comes together to find the mind of Christ. We can attempt to understand what this means from the perspective of the divine love seen as God acting to achieve his goal of dealing with the sin of the world in Jesus Christ. The fact is that God decided to do this in the particularity of one human being limiting itself to this identification in the movement of love in God, which overwhelms the entire universe. 'Thus at all moments in the story of the universe we lean on the movement from the particular to the universal, as we participate in God. There is always a particular 'yes' in which human daughters and sons make their 'yes' to the creative love of God.'[21] We understand that we need to pay attention to people as they are and not by generalizing about their situation. The hope we can bring to others comes when we see them as images of God and are willing to give them the value God does. This comes often at a cost for those who are willing to live as "living sacraments".

[19] Fiddes, *Participating in God*, p. 53.

[20] Fiddes, *Participating in God*, p. 54.

[21] Fiddes, *Participating in God*, p. 301.

Conclusion

Providence Baptist Church as a local Baptist Church has been involved for over twenty-one years in a ministry for needy people in the area (Roma community). This has been an important journey for the church, as it has had to learn that the Good News includes getting involved with our neighbour and often this may not be someone acceptable in the very community where the church is located. Therefore, beyond the pragmatic response the first big challenge was to accept a calling to serve a community that seems difficult to engage with.

In the process of engaging with the needs of this community Project Ruth has found that beyond the search for immediate solutions an equally important part is trying to understand what the causes of those needs are. A theological understanding of what the church was doing becomes more and more important as the involvement grows. Understanding its involvement with the help of such ideas as covenant and participation helps bring a Christian perspective to the pragmatic engagement with need.

The journey of Project Ruth is an exciting one for Providence Baptist Church, which has learned that it is as much about changing itself as it is about changing the world around it. By doing this Providence Baptist Church hopes to become a visible sign of the Kingdom of God in Romania because of listening to the call of God to serve a community in need.

14.

An Appreciation and an Interpretative Suggestion for Reading the Fiddes Corpus

Timothy Bradshaw

It is a great pleasure to be invited, as an Anglican colleague and friend, to contribute to this set of Baptist essays in honour of Professor Paul Fiddes. He took the great risk of appointing me to teach Christian Doctrine to students of Regent's Park College, even ministerial students, truly an act of faith on his part and illustrative of his wide ecumenical sympathies. His truly catholic sensitivities even extend to attempting to understand my obsession with cricket. Not a sports enthusiast himself, he nobly turned up to a lecture I gave three years ago on 'Sport and the Rhythm of Creation', arguing that Peter Berger's 'signals of transcendence' might be a way of giving the mad irrationality of sport a minor place in the great scheme of things. Paul not only sat through it, but joined in discussion, asking about the feeling of a batsman completing a cover drive, in truly empathetic generosity of spirit! We worked together in Baptist-Anglican Conversations culminating with the publication *Pushing at the Boundaries of Unity* in 2005. We must also recall he has served for many years as Free Church observer on General Synod, creatively suffering its morass of bureaucracy, an heroic task indeed, once noted pictorially on the front page of the *Church Times*. He has also served on many other ecumenical commissions for the Baptists, notably co-chair of the Baptist Roman Catholic Commission, which is quoted tellingly by Brian Haymes in his essay, and explored at some length by Myra Blyth. Now Professor Fiddes has pushed the boundaries further out to engage with fundamentalist Islam in the *Common Word* Project. His setting up the Centre for Christianity and Culture in college again shows his width of concerns, as well as the Centre for Baptist Heritage and History.

It is also worth stressing the massive effort he has given to the Oxford Theology Faculty, now the Faculty of Theology and Religion, over several decades, including serving as its chairman. As a teacher of undergraduates he has contributed tremendously, but it is the effort he has given as a post graduate supervisor and examiner that I would like particularly to highlight, going way beyond the call of duty in helping the Faculty provide supervision to a list of students that must run into the hundreds. His willingness to examine seems boundless as was the willingness of the Faculty to send him theses to read during those lazy weeks of the summer vacation!

Professor Fiddes, as Rex Mason has commented in his warm introduction, has both literary and theological foci of expertise, including both systematic and biblical scholarship, and now we must add, after his Bampton Lectures, a specialism in post-modern French philosophy, shared with our colleague Dr Pamela Anderson to whom his Bamptons are dedicated. While he has this very wide palette of paints and colours to deploy in his writing, he seeks to combine them, to remain coherent and *theological* however far into Derridean territory he may be operating. This set of essays written by his fellow Baptists succeeds in picking out the major theological themes found in the Fiddes corpus and making splendid points of application from these.

An Appreciation of the Essayists' Engagement with Fiddes' Theology

Professor John Briggs gives a very apt horizon for the symposium with his consideration of the forming of the Baptist World Alliance as a way of being Baptist in a denomination famous for its strong identity as local, congregationalist and independent in type. Serving on the Baptist Anglican conversations Professor Fiddes was always stressing that the radically independent congregationalist doctrine stressed today was really a development of the nineteenth century and its individualism, and looking to the earliest Baptist movement we see a concern for congregations to affiliate and make covenant in a wider way of being Christian. He has clearly taken that message to very many conferences, boards and commissions in his ecumenical role for the Baptists. Professor Briggs' account of the BWA notes the diversity of the communion today and its ability to hold together more and less conservative groupings, a 'being as communion' ecclesial model, doing justice to the diversity of church polity as well as commonality and mutuality. Professor Briggs has hit precisely the right note for this volume in terms of ecclesiastical history.

Brian Haymes' essay ponders the usefulness of shared written formulas of faith, their divisiveness and unifying effect, and the vital importance of a shared life together in the Church even if at the expense of vaguer formularies and *de fide* beliefs which demand obedience. Haymes cites the covenant principle and practice of Baptists as central, rooted and grounded in the Trinity, as agreed by the Roman Catholics in conversation with the Baptists. Fiddes commends a participatory way of thinking, sketching and reflecting the reality in which we find ourselves and the immanent divine movements running through everything. Pinning down the life of God in conceptual propositions is more than difficult, and the revelation of the divine life in Jesus might be said to be enough as a guide to the way, the truth and the life of the Church. The rest are attempts, offerings by theologians, which will stand or fall in the test of time and the Spirit. This seems to be how Fiddes understands doctrine and wisdom as a tapestry of text and praxis, not just an ideal, as a commitment to personal participation and self-giving, not simply theoretical agreement. 'Blest be the tie that binds', a hymn cited by both Haymes and Ellis, as they long for the actual fellowship in Christ of Christian disciples in the world of blood, toil, tears and sweat. Church, covenant and interweaving Trinitarian life register this living praxis.

Anthony Clarke and Richard Kidd ponder this Trinitarian movement in human historical life, the former in the task of helping ministers shape themselves in preparation for ordained ministry, the latter in the realm of the artistic movement and life. Both take up the theme of participatory dance, as in the Matisse picture on the cover of *Participating in God,* emphasizing the circle and yet the open nature of the circle. A dynamic centredness and an expanding life of church and humanity, inhabited by the divine Spirit, seems to be visually evoked by this Matisse under Fiddes' interpretative hand. This also brings out perhaps his greatest gift, taking up a theological master concept and developing it to his own ends. Hence Barth's doctrine of God's election of himself in the Son incarnate for us as both elect and reject, is taken and reworked to forge a doctrine of covenant, overspilling for and into creation and church and the whole world. Again Barth's famous 'Way of the Son into the Far Country' is fashioned into 'The Journey of Forgiveness', into the realm of threat and hostility. But Fiddes, taking up the theme of the self-giving, covenant sustaining, divine Son who undertakes costly empathetic immersion in hostile humanity, develops it in a different direction. He insists that humans addressed by this empathetic forgiveness must accept it so as to allow complete at-one-ment.

This is the point at which Tom Smail objects on the grounds that the act of the Son at Calvary is only his, not to be completed by us.[1] But can we interpret Fiddes as more faithful to Barth, if the 'yes' of the rebellious human is in fact said by the elect Jesus for us and so we are being taken into the subjective 'Amen' of Jesus to the Father, in our 'yes'? This suggestion may conflict with the authentic Baptist stress on the decision of the disciple individually to believe and be baptised, but Alexander Schmemann tells us that 'From the Orthodox point of view, the essential question about faith in its relationship to the sacrament is: *whose* faith? And the equally essential answer to this question is: it is Christ's faith, given to us, becoming our faith and our desire.'[2]

Fiddes faithfully represents the Radical Reformation tradition here, insisting that the disciple's individual 'yes' is crucial and indeed integral to

---

[1] Tom Smail *Once and for All: A Confession of the Cross* (London: DLT, 1998), ch. 4.

[2] Alexander Schmemann, *Of Water and the Spirit: A Liturgical Study of Baptism* (New York: St Vladimir's Seminary Press, 2000), p. 67.

'atonement'. The covenant of election covers us in so far as it evokes the 'Yes' of Christ to the Father and its shattering effect on our shell of hard-hearted rejection of God. The sacrifice of Jesus does not, for Fiddes, ultimately destroy sin, as for Barth, but it breaks down our hardness of heart, individual by individual, producing repentance – as Abelard taught – assisted by grace. Fiddes is very keen to avoid the notion that salvation is done 'above our head', to provide a 'ticket' which we can pick up free of charge. But Christ has the role of exalting humanity, as well as his priestly role of annihilating sin with his holy love. We can share in this new life not by a Pelagian, autonomous, free, heroic act, but by grace, by the paradox of grace enabling our 'yes'. Limited atonement, limited by the number of yes votes, is not what Fiddes aims for, but the 'Promised End' remains open everlastingly until the final stray sheep returns to the fold, with echoes of Origen. Then we could say that judgement had been enacted by God in each and every creature's life as the Spirit transforms them and opens them up to divine patterns and possibilities. Judgement for Fiddes can never be detached from individual persons in relation to each other and in the eddies and currents of the divine, and is primarily the self-transformatory outcome of self-judgement provoked by the journey of forgiveness. As Kreitzer and Rooke point out, the Baptist imperative of walking together with God, journeying in God's journey, is a very apt metaphor for Fiddes' pastoral theology.

Stephen Finnamore and Ruth Gouldbourne engage with sacramental theology and bring us to another major interest and expertise of the work of Paul Fiddes, that of language, text and sign. Gouldbourne takes up the theme of eucharistic 'memorialism' and Zwingli's theological probing of the medieval idea of the real presence in the Eucharist. She makes the point that a 'mere' memorialist doctrine does tend to a mentalism, a 'calling to mind' by each of us, with the emphasis on our response to God's grace. This in fact does resonate with Fiddes' atonement theology wherein our response is critical to closing the gap between God and ourselves, one by one, prompted by the Calvary story, and so here a classic Radical Reformation note is struck. And indeed arguably this note goes much further back, for example to Origen's doctrine that the Cross evoked faith to re-connect with the Logos and begin the journey back to our source and origin, ending our alienation.

Gouldbourne wishes to go on to stress divine grace at the Lord's Supper, rightly pointing out that we are often at the end of our resources, beyond summoning up an act of faith at all, and we just need the gift of grace in bread and wine, as receivers. The common life of the church in the body of Christ, in the Spirit, adoring the Father in praise, again a Trinitarian dance, is needed for a common sign language, for words to signify the ungraspable. The Anglican Roman Catholic Dialogue in ARCIC I spoke of the movement of the eucharistic memorial: 'There is therefore one historical, unrepeatable sacrifice, offered once for all by Christ and accepted by the Father. In the celebration of the memorial, Christ in the Holy Spirit unites his people with himself in a sacramental way so that the Church enters into the movement of his self-offering.'[3]

I wonder if this movement of self-offering might be close to Fiddes' atonement theology of our saying yes to divine grace in forgiving love, enacted in Christ, at the eucharistic dynamic of anamnesis, the past event becoming afresh present salvation? But Fiddes does not, I think, teach that Jesus Christ has already made this act of penitential 'Amen' to the – forgiving – judgement of God, as do McLeod Campbell and Moberly, *for us* as that might be construed as done 'over our heads', and yet it would not be incompatible given his stress on mutual participation as well as individual reception.

Stephen Finamore takes us to Spurgeon's eucharistic teaching and hymnody in order to emphasise the presence of the risen crucified Christ as the focus of the Lord's Supper, so moving away from 'mere' memorialism. Zwingli's examination of the idea of the body of Christ is placed beside Jenson's theology of space and time, and Aquinas' subtle conceptuality of sacramental presence, drawn on also by John Colwell. Christ crucified and risen is somehow present sacramentally in a special way, in the Body of Christ, as they share in the great thanksgiving in bread and wine, an embodiedness so emphasised by Fiddes throughout his theology.

In fact there is no God-free zone in Fiddes' universe. *Participating in God* might be equally well entitled 'God participating in us', in all our relationships: the divine movements of love and response are in, with, and under our relationships, actions, and desires. The empathetic activity of God is continually 'creatively suffering' in the universe, from the very first. Indeed we may ask if God has ever been without his creatures, if the movement of expressive being has not always been linked to the creaturely reality in Origenistic fashion, or in the panentheism of John Macquarrie and his dialectical theism. Finnamore's essay stimulates us to ponder the place of the 'risen Christ' in this family of theology: does that reality assume a transcendent ontology, a correspondence theory of being and truth, which does not fit with panentheism, save in Bultmann's wholly subjective interpretation of Jesus' rising in our hearts as we commit to the Gospel kerygma, or a way of significatory meaning as being? This theology is freighted on the cross and our response, with a Trinitarian background nexus holding all things together, 'letting be' to use Macquarrie's terms, in movements of Being.

Myra Blyth's suggestive contribution on ecumenism probes the theme of process or journey as the common reality being felt for by Baptists, Roman Catholics and Anglicans in their timing of baptism, confirmation, and first

---

[3] Anglican Roman Catholic International Commission, *The Final Report: Windsor, September 1981*, (CTS/SPCK: London, 1982), p. 20.

communion: the sacramental path embodies the journey of salvation. Dr Blyth's method of 'dynamic equivalence' equates well with Fiddes' stress on empathy with others, and also perhaps the depth of dialectical probing in the interests of finding new syntheses.

Professor Oti Bunaciu maintains the global perspective from his own Rumanian situation and deep pastoral concern for the Roma. He draws on statistics in order to help fashion his pastoral theological analysis of their plight, as well as a Trinitarian theology of outreach. This matches interestingly with Fiddes' emphasis on ethnography as important for ecclesiology in conjunction with theology, a double sided approach to gain as strong a grip as possible on the actual embodied problems of people: the embodiedness needs proper examination from 'outside' as well as from 'inside' revealed theological truth.

The divine permeation of all life, beings by Being or 'Letting be', in a more perichoretic mode than in Macquarrie, is behind the aspects of Fiddes' theology addressed by Nicholas Wood and John Weaver. Wood's splendid summons to consider play as an important anthropological and theological dimension of reality, with creation as a glorious romp, strikes a note of joy over against the post holocaust *Angst* so dominant in theology. This could be linked to the Matisse dance, and to the movements of the divine perichoretic being holding together, while opening up, the universe in a theatrical extravaganza, a divine samba suffusing our play and relationships; but it has to be said that the predominant tone of Fiddes' theological programme overall is one of wrestling with the pain of the universe, wrestling by God as he indwells his creation and bestows space and freedom. But if the cross reveals God's experience, why not the resurrection if that is an ontological reality – or why not the perichoresis of willow on leather, or the perfectly pitched, spun, googly?!

The phenomenon of play connects to divine Wisdom biblically, through Proverbs 8 and the play of Princess Wisdom rejoicing at the dawn of creation, and in the teaching of Jesus on the free rejoicing of Wisdom who is justified by her deeds in the world (Matt 11). John Weaver's essay ponders the Wisdom of the Universe, uniting our inner self to what is outside of ourselves in a common Spirit suffusing the universe, or indeed a Logos spermatikos, ontologically grounding our being with ultimate Being, supremely revealed in Jesus. The romanticism of Wordsworth and Coleridge seem echoed in the call of God in and through nature, resonating with the inner Spirit, in Weaver's theology of Wisdom, with a neo-platonic echo of a desire to return home, to the God suffusing all things, for a being to know full participation in 'Letting Be', and find peace at the core of our being.

Concluding Interpretative Suggestion – Hegel as a Useful Historical Guide

Paul Fiddes has written on a very diverse range of subjects, from systematic theology, to literature, to ecclesiology, to French Post Modern philosophy and the ancient Wisdom Tradition. Our essayists above have brought out core themes of his thought, notably a Trinitarian ontology of being in movement, the great ocean of Wisdom supporting covenant and participation, mutual indwelling and immersion. It may be that having a half an eye open to the great German philosopher theologian Hegel could be something of an aid to understanding the wide-ranging corpus of Fiddes' writing. This would hardly be surprising biographically, after all Professor Fiddes did study for a year under Jüngel and Moltmann, great German theologians whose thought is suffused in Hegelian concepts, notably 'God's being in becoming', 'God as the mystery of the world', and 'The Crucified God'. Fiddes in Oxford would have sat under John Macquarrie in lectures, also a theologian of the 'Hegel, Marx, Bloch' family.

The Divine Experience of Negativity

The obvious early and structural concept of Hegel found in Fiddes' theology, as well as in other modern theologians, is that of the divine journey into the finite. Breaking with the Platonic 'upstairs-downstairs' model of God and world, Hegel historicises the divine activity, *Geist* proceeds into finitude and *as* finitude, a pathway of self-discovery as 'the other'. In the totality of this process or progress, God reveals himself to himself, experiences what is entirely new, and develops in objectifying himself to himself. The process is complete when it understands itself. The dogma of the Trinity gives this truth in religious form, and dialectical reasoning, incessant questioning and counter-questioning, leads us to this philosophically and historically. We know ourselves as the phenomenon of the unhappy consciousness, the sense of feeling alienated from the world and the good, the experience of 'non-being', finally overcome as we understand that our individuality is rooted in the universal Spirit and finds freedom in surrendering to this Spirit, realising that the unhappy consciousness was a necessary phase in self-understanding, prompting us to 'die to live', to give ourselves to this process of reconciliation, being taken up into the Absolute, truth itself.

For Hegel the Christian revelation of incarnation and reconciliation teaches precisely this truth. The Trinitarian movement is the truth of this pathway of consciousness. The Son is posited, generated, eternally distinguishing God from God as the self-objectification of God in finitude. The Son is the world of finitude in distinction from the infinite yet identical with it. The differentiated other struggles to return and achieve reconciliation, uniting the finite with the infinite in reconciliation, meaning that the Spirit knows itself as one with the Eternal. The whole history of the universe is subsumed in the life of God, *union in distinction* being the conceptual dynamo of movement running through all things which all interfuse in the whole.

Fiddes' well-known theology of the divine journey of costly forgiveness, a journey travelled since the start of the finite creation, is one of creative suffering, revealed and brought to a head at the Cross by Jesus' suffering, an event which was real for God, bringing new experience of negativity to the divine, taking the divine to the depths of human agony – and overcoming that. Jesus is fully a man and also the finitude of the Son whose death, in Hegel's teaching, expresses:

> an awareness that the human, the finite, the fragile, the weak, the negative, are themselves a moment of the divine, that they are within God himself, that finitude, negativity, otherness are not outside of God, and do not, as otherness, hinder unity with God. Otherness, the negative, is known to be a moment of the divine nature itself. This involves the highest idea of spirit. In this way what is external and negative is converted into the internal.[4]

In Christ's death God suffers and forgives us, overcoming the pain of the negative, realising the depths of human misery, and seeking to prompt the human unhappy consciousness to embrace and surrender to the divine reconciling approach, to reunite the finite with the infinite source of life. In Fiddes' words:

> Thus here to a degree which has happened nowhere else, God is drawn into human flesh and stands where humankind stands. In this past event the God who was and is always willing to forgive gains through the cross that experience of the human heart that gives a new way into our hearts. A change in God (in the sense of a new experience) thus makes change in us. We experience God as the one who empathises with us, and so we are enabled to face up both to judgement and to acceptance. The conditioning of God by the world creates a new condition for human response and opens up the future.'[5]

Fascinatingly Fiddes immediately cites Barth as a theologian who also realises that divine freedom is even free to be conditioned and so be truly free, and this is also a motif anticipated by Hegel. God's freedom to be self-

---

[4] G. W. F. Hegel, *Lectures on the Philosophy of Religion Vol 3*, edited by Peter C. Hodgson, (Berkley: University of California Press [1827] 1998), p. 326.

[5] Paul S. Fiddes, *Participating in God: A Pastoral Doctrine of the Trinity* (London: DLT, 200), p. 207.

conditioned, and our true freedom as immersion in the other, is a rich theme in Hegel, some say his key motif: we discover ourselves as free in our self-consciousness as we truly know ourselves to be at one with the other in love. This insight is seen in other major theologians, notably Pannenberg, who draw on the treasury of Hegel in their own way.

The power of God is to persuade and incite hard-hearted humans by divine empathetic exploring and, indeed, divine experiencing and discovering, prompting us to forgive others and so expiate our sins by this transformation, provoked or evoked by God's self-presentation, revelation, as suffering, creative love.[6] Jesus is God in human form, his forgiving love at Calvary is God's love to us, and that transforms us; this is the expiation of our wrongs, a process of sanctification.[7] The divine Spirit discovers itself, gains a radically new experience of itself as the alienated other, in this journey of human experience, and at the same time the repentant finite human spirit finds itself at one with the divine, no longer alien and unhappy of consciousness. This is the Trinitarian movement of God the Son incarnationally moving into the bonds of the human, negating the negative of sin and death, evoking our response of dying to self and rising to new life, at one with God, our spirit with the divine Spirit. This is Hegel's view of resurrection, a risen new life for us, rather than a risen Christ in the midst of the Church, and this is also a credible interpretation of Fiddes' theology of the resurrection, akin to that of J. A. T. Robinson[8] rather than Bultmann's individualistic interpretation. Fiddes asks about the dangers of remythologising of Christ's resurrection victory over non-being:

> While the resurrection body of Christ is not simply exhausted into the Church without remainder, the followers of Jesus may be said in a sense to be his 'Body', so that the risen Jesus leads a life of deeper participation in others than was possible in others than was possible during his earthly life.[9]

The cross, the negation of death and alienation, is the climax of this Trinitarian incarnational movement reconciling the world to God and revealing this transforming truth and love. God, whose becoming is a history of movement into otherness and self-differentiation, takes up the difference of our otherness to bring us lovingly to return. The history of the death of Christ reveals God's being as becoming. This revelation is the truth to be

---

[6] See Fiddes, *Participating in God*, p. 207.

[7] See Hegel, *Lectures on Philosophy of Religion*, p. 337.

[8] J. A. T. Robinson, *The Body: A Study in Pauline Theology* (London: SCM, 1952).

[9] Fiddes, *Participating in God*, p. 246; see also Paul S. Fiddes, *The Creative Suffering of God* (Oxford: Clarendon Press, 1988).

accepted for reconciliation with the Spirit and overcoming alienation. The fact of this divine reconciling movement is true for all humanity, for church and society. Hegel's view of the movement of the Son into the negativity of human suffering and rejection does chime in well with that of Fiddes' trinitarianism and theology of at-one-ment, of return, of the liberation into freedom through the shattering event of the Cross, or rather the impact of its narrative on us sinners as it comes to us through the preaching of the Church, and this reality of God's movement impacts on the particularities of human relationships generally, as the Matisse dance image indicates.

The cross is then theologically a movement of the divine Trinity, in the Son into particularity, into the negation of God, into death, which is overcome or negated by the enduring love of the Father for the Son, through the experience, in the Spirit. Death is put to death and new life arises. Fiddes, like Hegel, rejects a judicial or moralistic view of redemption, it is a movement freely undertaken by God to release and open up our unhappy self-consciousness into true freedom and unity with the Spirit. This is the creative long-suffering of the persuasive God.

At this point we should consult Fiddes himself on Hegel, in particular his criticism that Hegel's metaphysics of the Spirit generating 'the other' in its movement fails to produce a sufficiently alien 'other', since it springs from the divine and is a necessary movement rather than being rooted in divine freedom.[10] Fiddes stresses in this passage that his theology of God and the world focuses on divine desire, not necessity, although of course not quixotic desire, for the desire is revealed in this narrative leading to Calvary and not another different choice. For Hegel freedom and necessity are not total opposites, indeed we would not know of one without the other; there needs to be the tension in concept and in reality. God's very being is dynamic, vitality, and knows of movement and response. As to the point about the depth of alienation into which the Son moves, Fiddes ends his fine passage appreciatively: 'Hegel just stops short of saying that God faces the most alienating experience in the cross of Jesus *because* he has been drawn most deeply there into humanity through human response and obedience to him, but it is a natural conclusion from what he does say.'[11]

Fiddes' theological stress is on the suffering of God, his journey into the pain of alienation and chaos, and he finds Hegel lacking in this incarnational pain, notwithstanding it is that of a man's consciousness in all its agony in a Roman crucifixion. This is a theology of a history of God, the economic Trinity, into the suffering horror of the world, in empathy with that suffering, discovering its ghastly extent 'inwardly', and offering healing: the model is almost that of the psychotherapist. The emphasis that Smail misses in Fiddes is the clash of the holy God and unholy, rebellious humankind, the

---

[10] See Fiddes, *Creative Suffering*, p. 236.

[11] Fiddes, *Creative Suffering*, p. 243.

great act of judgement and justification at Calvary, once for all, finished, or again Barth's stress on evil as encountered and destroyed in the divine judgement undertaken at Calvary. Fiddes rejects this Christ event as a detached act done over our heads, a ticket we can pick up to salvation. Kierkegaard here found Hegel lacking in a radical doctrine of evil, and Barth likewise an unspeakable, unthinkable, 'surd' not produced by the Spirit in any way, but purely by creation gone unimaginably wrong. To cite Fiddes in the Hegelian family might help us tease out his distinctiveness on the doctrine of reconciliation.

Participatory Wisdom

A second area where I suggest comparison with Hegel might help our interpretation of Fiddes' corpus is in respect of his latest magnum opus *Seeing the World and Knowing God.*[12] Fiddes finds Wisdom suffusing all reality in all sorts of ways, and in particular finds the movements of the Spirit across the range of human experience and culture. This is perhaps a 'new style natural theology', but in dynamic mode not simply arising from personal existential experience, as for Macquarrie[13], but more widely. The book ends with a 'coda' on music and its patterns and rhythms, drawing us into the movements of the divine and its Wisdom. Wisdom in healthcare is discussed near the beginning of the book, linked to empathy and healing, inseparable from the divine. The human subject is never 'wise' when he or she enters a dominating mode of thought or behaviour; we need to be open to each other, to the other we have not experienced, and the divine Spirit at work in this great dance of mutuality and immersion in the other.

The striking feature of the work is the attempt to marry Hebrew Wisdom with French postmodernism and deconstructionism. Here I suggest Hegel again can help. He affirmed many different ways of perceiving, experiencing, reflecting, sketching, sharing in reality, both individual and corporate. He was very aware of our being participants in reality and history rather than simply detached minds observing events and phenomena. No question is off limits, no concept is closed: and so for the French postmodernist thinkers, all texts are there for cross examination, and there is always something else to be said, asked, or added. We inhabit a skein of ongoing meaning, a text, and that prompts us into new experiences and self-understandings. Wisdom runs through all life, as a whole, the divine Spirit immanent in its Trinitarian patterns of giving, receiving, offering, moving.

---

[12] Paul S. Fiddes, *Seeing the World and Knowing God: Hebrew Wisdom and Christian Doctrine in a Late-Modern Context* (Oxford: OUP, 2013).

[13] John Macquarrie, *Principles of Christian Theology* (London: SCM, 1977), p. 54.

The individual and the collection come together in true wisdom and freedom, annulling the threat of non-being.

Fiddes insists on looking at the world for wisdom using methods outside those of theology and its norms of revelation, just as Hegel found the same truth revealed but also gained through careful questioning and analysis of many conceptualities and human experiences. In his article 'Ecclesiology and Ethnography'[14] Fiddes argues that traditional ecclesiology of a 'top down' application of theological principles, seeking to articulate church through the revelation in the Scriptures and tradition, is not sufficient and that 'secular' methodologies, such as sociology and ethnography are needed, on theological grounds, to ensure that the cultural embodiedness of church communities are fully taken into account, in accord with the incarnational principle. We should find perichoretic movements in such 'secular' methods, the Trinity is real whether found through revelation or careful secular study – and for Fiddes, as for Hegel, these are different ways of approaching the same reality. Pannenberg has taken this kind of approach, again with a major cue taken from Hegel, but Pannenberg argues for the finality of the truth as found in Christianity while being committed to negotiate with secularity on an open field of knowledge. Fiddes is keen to find deep connections and interplay between church and communities outside the church, sacred and secular – in fact can we really speak of 'secular' in this view of truth as thoroughly interfused and part of the great whole? Like Hegel, Fiddes takes up different kinds of reasoning processes in approaching wisdom, truth, reality and revelation. He goes beyond Hegel in seeking to find commonality with fundamentalist Islam on its own terms and not allowing western critical questioning of its controlling holy text, an ethnographic move into the unknown, a journey of new experience and self-understanding.

Finally this dance of Wisdom in the world, the Body of Christ incarnating the divine, leads us to ponder a future life, the metaphorical eternal city in the divine Trinity[15], in these ever richer relationships, social personality or personal society, more corporate than individual, a form of society that transcended all conflicts between the individual and the collective, and was truly free while at the same time in no sense anarchic, Hegel's hope for the future, a dynamic synthesis, being as becoming, being annulling 'non-being'.

---

[14] Paul S. Fiddes, 'Ecclesiology and Ethnography' in Pete Ward (ed.), *Perspectives on Ecclesiology and Ethnography* (Grand Rapids, MI: Eerdmans, 2012), pp. 13-35.

[15] See Paul S. Fiddes, *The Promised End* (Oxford: Blackwell, 2000), pp. 282-88.

A Bibliography of Published Works
By Paul S. Fiddes

1980

Charismatic Renewal: A Baptist View (London: Baptist Publications, 1980)

1981

'The Signs of Hope' in *A Call to Mind: Baptist Essays Towards a Theology of Commitment* (London: Baptist Union of Great Britain, 1981) pp. 33-45

1983

'God and History', *Baptist Quarterly* 30 (1983) pp. 74-90

1984

'The Theology of the Charismatic Movement', in David Martin and Peter Mullen (eds), *Strange Gifts? A Guide to Charismatic Renewal* (Oxford: Blackwell, 1984) pp. 19-40

1985

'Covenant - Old and New' in Keith Clements, Paul Fiddes, Roger Hayden, Brian Haymes, and Richard Kidd, *Bound to Love: The Covenant Basis of Baptist Life and Mission* (London: Baptist Union, 1985) pp. 9-23

'Patrick White and the Vision of God' *Christian* 9/4 (1985), pp. 42-55

1986

A Leading Question: The Structure and Authority of Leadership in the Local Church (London: Baptist Publications, 1986)

'"Woman's Head is Man": A Doctrinal Reflection upon a Pauline Text', *Baptist Quarterly* 31 (1986), pp. 370-383

1987

A Call to Mind: Baptist Essays towards a Theology of Commitment, with Keith Clements, Roger Hayden, Brian Haymes, and Richard Kidd (London: Baptist Union, 1987)

1988
The Creative Suffering of God (Oxford: Clarendon Press, 1988)

1989
Past Event and Present Salvation: The Christian Idea of Atonement (London: DLT, 1989)

1990
'Mary in the Theology of Karl Barth' in Alberic Stacpoole (ed.), *Mary in Doctrine and Devotion* (Blackrock: Columba Press, 1990) pp. 111-126

'The Status of Women in the Thought of Karl Barth' in Janet Martin Soskice (ed.), *After Eve: Women, Theology and the Christian Tradition* (London: Marshall Pickering, 1990) pp. 138-55

1991
'C.S. Lewis the Myth-maker' in Andrew Walker and James Patrick (eds), *A Christian for All Christians: Essays in Honour of C.S. Lewis* (London: Hodder & Stoughton, 1991) pp. 132- 55.

Freedom and Limit: A Dialogue between Literature and Christian Doctrine (Basingstoke: Macmillan, 1991)

'Review of Hans Urs von Balthasar, *The Glory of the Lord*, vol. vii, *Theology: The New Covenant*', *The Expository Times* 102/11 (1991) pp. 349-350

'The Atonement and the Trinity' in Alasdair I. C. Heron (ed.), *The Forgotten Trinity 3: A Selection of Papers Presented to the BCC Study Commission on Trinitarian Doctrine Today* (London: British Council of Churches, 1991), pp. 103-122

The Trinity in Worship and Preaching (London: London Baptist Preachers' Association, 1991)

1993
'Process Theology' in A. E. McGrath (ed.), *The Blackwell Encyclopedia of Modern Christian Thought* (Oxford: Blackwell, 1993), pp. 471-6

'Suffering, Divine' in A. E. McGrath (ed.), *The Blackwell Encyclopedia of Modern Christian Thought* (Oxford: Blackwell, 1993), pp. 633-6

'The Cross of Hosea revisited: the Meaning of Suffering in the Book of Hosea', *Review and Expositor* 90 (1993), pp. 175-90

1994

'The Demand beyond the Commands' in Walter B. Shurden (ed.), *Proclaiming Baptist Vision: The Bible* (Macon, GA: Smyth and Helwys, 1994), pp. 51-62

'The Understanding of Salvation in the Baptist Tradition' in Rienk Lanooy (ed.), *For Us and for Our Salvation: Seven Perspectives on Christian Soteriology* (Utrecht: Interuniversitair Instituut voor Missiologie en Oecumenica, 1994), pp. 15-37

1996

'Baptism and Creation', in Paul S. Fiddes (ed.), *Reflections on the Water: Understanding God and the World through the Baptism of Believers* (Oxford: Regent's Park College / Macon, GA: Smyth & Helwys, 1996), pp. 47-47

'Church, Trinity and Covenant: An Ecclesiology of Participation', in Edwin Brandt, Paul S. Fiddes and Joachim Molthagen (eds), *Gemeinschaft am Evangelium: Festschrift für Wiard Popkes zum 60. Geburtstag* (Leipzig: Evangelische Verlagsanstalt, 1996), pp. 37-54

'Process Theology', in *Microsoft Encarta Electronic Encyclopedia* (Microsoft / Websters, 1996)

(ed.), *Reflections on the Water: Understanding God and the World through the Baptism of Believers* (Oxford: Regent's Park College / Macon, GA: Smyth & Helwys, 1996)

Something to Declare: A Study of the Declaration of Principle of the Baptist Union of Great Britain with Brian Haymes, Richard Kidd (ed.) and Michael Quicke (Oxford: Whitley, 1996)

'"Where Shall Wisdom be Found?" Job 28 as a Riddle for Ancient and Modern Readers' in John Barton and David Reimer (eds), *After the Exile, Essays in Honour of Rex Mason* (Macon, GA: Mercer University Press, 1996), pp. 171-190

1997

On the Way of Trust, with Brian Haymes, Richard Kidd, and Michael Quicke, (Oxford: Whitley, 1997)

1999

Pilgrim Pathways: Essays in Baptist History in Honour of B. R. White, Paul S. Fiddes, William H Brackney and John H. Y. Briggs (eds), (Macon, GA: Mercer University Press, 1999)

'Regent's Park College, Oxford' in *A Typology of Baptist Theological Education: American Baptist Quarterly* XVIII/2 (1999), pp. 106-117

'Towards a New Millennium: Doctrinal Themes of Strategic Significance for Baptists', in L. A. Cupit (ed.), *Baptist Faith and Witness: The Papers of the Study and Research Division of the Baptist World Alliance, 1995-2000* (Baptist World Alliance, 1999) pp. 13-22

'"Walking Together": the Place of Covenant Theology in Baptist Life Yesterday and Today', in Paul S. Fiddes, William H Brackney and John H. Y. Briggs (eds), *Pilgrim Pathways: Essays in Baptist History in Honour of B. R. White* (Macon, GA: Mercer University Press, 1999)

2000

Doing Theology in a Baptist Way, with Richard Kidd, Brian Haymes, and Michael Quicke (Oxford: Whitley, 2000)

'Facing the End: The Apocalyptic Experience in Some Modern Novels', in John Colwell (ed.), *Called to One Hope: Perspectives on the Life to Come* (Carlisle: Paternoster, 2000) pp. 191-209

Participating in God: A Pastoral Doctrine of the Trinity (London: DLT, 2000)

'Story and Possibility: Reflections on the Last Scenes of the Fourth Gospel and Shakespeare's *The Tempest*' in Gerhard Sauter and John Barton (eds), *Revelation and Story: Narrative Theology and the Centrality of Story* (Aldershot: Ashgate, 2000), pp. 29-52

(ed.), *The Novel, Spirituality and Modern Culture: Eight Novelists Write about Their Craft and Their Context* (Cardiff: University of Wales Press, 2000)

The Promised End: Eschatology in Theology and Literature (Oxford: Blackwell, 2000)

2001

'Creation Out of Love', in John Polkinghorne (ed.), *The Work of Love: Creation as Kenosis* (London: SPCK / Grand Rapids, MI and Cambridge: Eerdmans, 2001), pp. 167-91

(ed.), *Faith in the Centre: Christianity and Culture* (Oxford: Regent's Park College / Macon, GA: Smyth & Helwys, 2001)

'The Story and the Stories: Revelation and the Challenge of Postmodern Culture' in Paul S. Fiddes (ed.), *Faith in the Centre: Christianity and Culture* (Oxford: Regent's Park College / Macon, GA: Smyth & Helwys, 2001), pp. 75-96

2002

'Baptism and the Process of Christian Initiation', *The Ecumenical Review* 54 (2002) pp. 49-65

'Baptism and the Process of Christian Initiation', in Stanley E. Porter and Anthony R. Cross (eds), *Dimensions of Baptism: Biblical and Theological Studies* (London: Sheffield Academic Press, 2002), pp. 280-303

'Salvation and the Church: a Comparison of Baptist and Orthodox Thinking', in Anthony R. Cross (ed.), *Ecumenism and History: Studies in Honour of John H. Y. Briggs* (Carlisle: Paternoster Press, 2002), pp. 120-48

'The Quest for a Place Which Is "Not-a-place": The Hiddenness of God and the Presence of God', in Oliver Davies and Denys Turner (eds), *Silence and the Word: Negative Theology and Incarnation* (Cambridge: Cambridge University Press, 2002), pp. 35-60

2003

'Baptism and Membership in the Body of Christ: A Theological and Ecumenical Conundrum', in Lena Lybaek, Konrad Reiser, Stefanie Schardien (eds), *Gemeinschaft der Kirchen und gesellschaftliche Verantwortung. Die Würde des Anderen und das Recht anders zu denken. Festchrift für Professor Dr. Erich Geldbach*. Oekumenische Studien 30 (Münster: Lit. Verlag, 2004), pp. 83-93

'Receiving One Another: The History and Theology of the Church Covenant , 1780', in Rosie Chadwick (ed.), *A Protestant Catholic Church of Christ: Essays on the History and Life of New Road Baptist Church, Oxford* (Oxford: New Road Baptist Church, 2003), pp. 65-105

'The Canon as Space and Place', in Wolter, Michael (ed.), *Die Einheit der Schrift und die Vielfalt des Kanons (The Unity of Scripture and the Diversity of the Canon)*. Beihefte zur Zeitschrift für die neutestamentliche Wissenschaft und die Kunde der älteren Kirche, Bd. 118. (Berlin: W. de Gruyter, 2003), pp. 127-49

Tracks and Traces: Baptist Identity in Church and Theology (Carlisle: Paternoster, 2003)

2004

'Old Testament Principles of Wholeness,' in Sorin Sabou and Dorothy Ghitea *(eds), Iosif Ton - orizonturi noi in spiritualitate si slujire* (Oradea: Editura Cartea Crestina, 2004), pp. 35-48

'*The Promised End*: Response to a Review by Jennifer L. Geddes', *Conversations in Religion and Theology* 2/2 (November 2004), pp. 191-195

2005

'Atonement in the Life of the Church', in Otniel Bunaciu, Radu Gheorghiţa, Emil Bartoş (eds), "Care Împarte Drept Cuvântul Adevărului". Volum Omagial Ioan Bunaciu (Oradea: Editura Reformatio, 2005), pp. 195-208

'Baptism and Faith in the New Testament and Christian Doctrine', in Wilhelm Hüffmeier and Tony Peck (eds), *Dialog zwischen der Europäischen Baptistischen Föderation und der Gemeinschaft Evangelischer Kirchen in Europa zur Lehre und Praxis der Taufe* (Frankfürt am Main: Verlag Otto Lembech, 2005), pp. 134-145

'Baptist Ecclesiology: A Response to David Carter's Article Review of *Tracks and Traces*', *Ecclesiology* 1 (2005), pp. 87-100

'Baptists and the Leuenberg Documents on Baptism', in Wilhelm Hüffmeier and Tony Peck (eds), *Dialog zwischen der Europäischen Baptistischen Föderation und der Gemeinschaft Evangelischer Kirchen in Europa zur Lehre und Praxis der Taufe* (Frankfürt am Main: Verlag Otto Lembech, 2005), pp. 189-200

Conversations Around the World: 2000-2005: Report of the International Conversations between the Anglican Communion and the *Baptist World Alliance* (Co-Chair) (London: Anglican Communion Office, 2005)

(ed.) *Flickering Images: Theology and Film in Dialogue*, with Anthony J. Clarke (Oxford: Regent's Park College / Macon, GA: Smyth & Helwys, 2005)

Pushing at the Boundaries of Unity: Anglicans and Baptists in Conversation (Contributor; Council of Christian Unity / Baptist Union of Great Britain; London: Church House Publishing, 2005)

'When Text Becomes Voice: "You've Got Mail"', in Anthony J. Clarke and Paul S. Fiddes (eds), *Flickering Images: Theology and Film in Dialogue* (Oxford: Regent's Park College / Macon, GA: Smyth & Helwys, 2005), pp. 97-112

2006

'On God the Incomparable: Thinking about God with John Macquarrie', in Robert Morgan (ed.), *In Search of Humanity and Deity: A Celebration of John Macquarrie's Theology* (London: SCM, 2006), pp. 179-99

'Participating in the Trinity', *Perspectives in Religious Studies* 33 (2006), pp. 375-91

2007

'Salvation', in John Webster, Kathryn Tanner, and Iain Torrance (eds), *The Oxford Handbook of Systematic Theology* (Oxford: Oxford University Press, 2007), pp. 176-96

'The Passion Story in Literature', in Andrew Hass, David Jasper, and Elizabeth Jay (eds), *The Oxford Handbook of English Literature and Theology* (Oxford: Oxford University Press, 2007), pp. 742-759

'The Place of Christian Theology in the Modern University', *Baptist Quarterly* 42 (2007), pp. 71-88

2008

'Christianity, Culture and Education: A Baptist Perspective', in Roger Ward and David P Gushee (eds), *The Scholarly Vocation and the Baptist Academy: essays on the Future of Baptist Higher Education* (Macon, GA: Mercer, 2008), pp. 1-25

'*Ex Opere Operato*: Rethinking a Historic Baptist Rejection' in Anthony R. Cross and Philip E. Thompson (eds), *Baptist Sacramentalism 2* (Milton Keynes: Paternoster, 2008), pp. 219-238

'Learning from Others: Baptists and Receptive Ecumenism', *Louvain Studies* 33 (2008), pp. 54-73

'The Baptism of Believers', in Thomas F. Best (ed.), *Baptism Today: Understanding, Practice, Ecumenical Implications.* World Council of Churches, Faith and Order Paper 207 (Collegeville: Liturgical Press, 2008), pp. 73-80

'Spirituality as Attentiveness: Stillness and Journey', in Paul S Fiddes (ed.), *Under the Rule of Christ: Dimensions of Baptist Spirituality* (Oxford: Regent's Park College / Macon, GA: Smyth & Helwys, 2008), pp. 25-58

(ed.) *Under the Rule of Christ: Dimensions of Baptist Spirituality* (Macon, GA: Smith & Helwys, 2008)

2009

'Concept, Image and Story in Systematic Theology', *International Journal of Systematic Theology* 11 (January, 2009), pp. 3-23

'Daniel Turner and a Theology of the Church Universal', in John H. Y. Briggs (ed.), *Pulpit and People: Studies in Eighteenth-Century Baptist Life and Thought*. Studies in Baptist History and Thought, 28 (Carlisle: Paternoster, 2009), pp. 112-27

'G. M. Hopkins' in Rebecca Lemon, Emma Mason, Jonathan Roberts and Christopher Rowland (eds.), *The Blackwell Companion to the Bible in English Literature* (Oxford: Blackwell, 2009) pp. 563-76

'Something Will Come of Nothing: On *A Theology of the Dark Side*', in Pieter J. Lalleman (ed.), *Challenging to Change: Dialogues with a Radical Baptist Theologian: Essays Presented to Dr Nigel G. Wright on His Sixtieth Birthday* (London: Spurgeon's College, 2009), pp. 87-104

'Theology of Covenant', in J. H. Y. Briggs (ed.), *Dictionary of European Baptist Life and Thought*, vol. 33, SBHT (Carlisle: Paternoster, 2009), pp. 124-126

2010

'Ambiguities of the Future: Theological Hints in the Novels of Patrick White', *Pacifica* 23 (2010), pp. 281-98

'Baptist Theology', in David Fergusson, Karen Kilby, Ian A. McFarland and Iain Torrance (eds), *The Cambridge Dictionary of Christian Theology* (Cambridge: Cambridge University Press, 2010), pp. 54-56

'Church and Sect: Cross-currents in Early Baptist Life', in Anthony R. Cross and Nicholas J. Wood (eds), Ex*ploring Baptist Origins* (Oxford: Regent's Park College, 2010), pp. 33-60

'Glaube und Taufe im Neuen Testament und in christlicher Lebe', in Uwe Swarat (ed.), *Wer Glaubt und Getauft Wird* (Kassel: Oncken, 2010), pp. 139-148

'On Theology', in Robert MacSwain and Michael Ward (eds.), *The Cambridge Companion to C. S. Lewis* (Cambridge: Cambridge University Press, 2010), pp. 89-104

'The Body as Site of Continuity and Change' in Pamela Anderson (ed.), *New Topics in Feminist Philosophy of Religion: Contestations and Transcendence Incarnate* (Dordrecht: Springer, 2010) pp. 261-78

2011

'Christian Doctrine and Free Church Ecclesiology: Recent Developments among Baptists in the Southern United States', *Ecclesiology* 7 (2011), pp. 195-219

'Dual Citizenship in Athens and Jerusalem: The Place of the Christian Scholar in the Life of the Church', in Anthony R. Cross and Ruth M. B. Gouldbourne (eds), *Questions of Identity: Essays in Honour of Brian Haymes* (Oxford: Regent's Park College, 2011), pp. 119-140

'Not Anarchy but Covenant: a Nonconformist Response to Matthew Arnold's View of Religion and Culture' in Mike Higton, Jeremy Law and Christopher Rowland (eds.), *Theology and Human Flourishing: Essays in Honor of Timothy J. Gorringe* (Eugene, OR: Cascade, 2011) pp. 141-56

'Prophecy, Corporate Personality and Suffering: Some Themes and Methods in Baptist Old Testament Scholarship', in Helen Dare and Simon Woodman (eds), *The Plainly Revealed Word of God? Baptist Hermeneutics in Theory and Practice* (Macon, GA: Mercer University Press, 2011), pp. 72-94

'The Sublime and the Beautiful: Intersections between Theology and Literature', in Heather Walton (ed.), *Literature and Theology - New Interdisciplinary Spaces* (Aldershot: Ashgate Publishing, 2011), pp. 127-52

2012

'Ancient and Modern Wisdom: The Intersection of Clinical and Theological Understanding of Health', in Stephen Finamore and John Weaver (eds), *Wisdom, Science and the Scriptures: Essays in Honour of Ernest Lucas* (Oxford: Regent's Park College / Bristol: Bristol Baptist College, 2012), pp. 75-98

'Ethnography and Ecclesiology: Two Disciplines, Two Worlds?', in Peter Ward (ed.), *Perspectives on Ecclesiology and Ethnography*. Studies in Ecclesiology and Ethnography, vol. 1 (Grand Rapids, MI: Eerdmans, 2012), pp. 13-35

'Murdoch, Derrida and *The Black Prince*', in Anne Rowe and Avril Horner (eds), *Iris Murdoch: Texts and Contexts* (Basingstoke: Palgrave Macmillan, 2012), pp. 91-109

'Patterns of Hope and Images of Eternity: Listening to Shakespeare, Blake and T.S. Eliot', in Trevor Hart, Gavin Hopps, Jeremy Begbie (eds), *Art, Imagination and Christian Hope: Patterns of Promise* (Aldershot: Ashgate Publishing, 2012), pp. 31-50

'The Root of Religious Freedom: Interpreting Some Muslim and Christian Sacred Texts', *Oxford Journal of Law and Religion* 1/1 (Spring 2012), pp. 169-84

2013

'Attending to the Sublime and the Beautiful: Theological Reflection on Iris Murdoch and Emmanuel Levinas', in Alexei Bodrov and Michael Tolstoluzhenko (eds), *Theology of Beauty* (Moscow: St Andrew's Press, 2013), pp. 70-89 (in Russian)

'Baptists and 1662: The Effect of the Act of Uniformity on Baptists and its Ecumenical Significance for Baptists Today', *Ecclesiology* 9/2 (2013), pp. 183-204

'"For the Dance All Things Were Made": The Great Dance in C.S. Lewis's *Perelandra*', in Judith Wolfe and Brendan Wolfe (eds), *C.S. Lewis's*

Perelandra*: Re-Shaping the Image of the Cosmos* (Kent, OH: Kent State University Press, 2013), pp. 33-49

Seeing the World and Knowing God: Hebrew Wisdom and Christian Doctrine in a Late-Modern Context (Oxford: Oxford University Press, 2013)

'Suffering', in Nicholas Adams, George Pattison and Graham Ward (eds), *The Oxford Handbook of Theology and Modern European Thought* (Oxford: Oxford University Press, 2013), pp. 169-92

'The Late-Modern Reversal of Spirit and Letter: Derrida, Augustine and Film', in Paul S. Fiddes and Günter Bader (eds), *The Spirit and Letter: a Tradition and a Reversal* (London: Continuum, 2013), pp. 105-130

(ed.) *The Spirit and Letter: a Tradition and a Reversal*, with Günter Bader (London: Continuum, 2013)

'The Sublime, the Conflicted Self and Attention to the Other: Towards a Theopoetics with Iris Murdoch and Julia Kristeva', in Roland Faber (ed.), *Theopoetic Folds: Philosophizing Multifariousness* (New York: Fordham University Press, 2013), pp. 159-78

'Tragedy as Rhetoric of Evil', in Paul S. Fiddes and Jochen Schmidt (eds), *Vom Bösen Reden* (*The Rhetoric of Evil*) (Würzburg: Ergon Verlag, 2013), pp. 165-92

(ed.), *Vom Bösen Reden* (*The Rhetoric of Evil*), with Jochen Schmidt (Würzburg: Ergon Verlag, 2013)

'Whatever Happened to a Pauline Text? 2 Corinthians 3:6 and its Afterlife', in Paul S. Fiddes and Günter Bader (eds), *The Spirit and Letter: a Tradition and a Reversal* (London: Continuum, 2013), pp. 3-30